THE APOSTOLIC TRADITION
OF ST HIPPOLYTUS

ΑΠΟCΤΟΛΙΚΗ ΠΑΡΑΔΟCΙC

THE TREATISE ON
THE APOSTOLIC TRADITION
OF ST HIPPOLYTUS OF ROME
Bishop and Martyr

Edited by

THE REV. GREGORY DIX
MONK OF NASHDOM ABBEY

Reissued
with corrections preface
and bibliography
by

HENRY CHADWICK

*Master of Peterhouse College
in the University of Cambridge*

Routledge
Taylor & Francis Group

LONDON AND NEW YORK

First published 1937
Second revised edition 1968
Reissued with additional corrections 1992

Transferred to Digital Printing 2006

Published in UK & USA by Routledge
2 Park Square, Milton Park, Abingdon, Oxon, OX14 4RN
270 Madison Ave, New York NY 10016
ISBN 0 7007 0232 6

Library of Congress Cataloging-in-Publication Data

Hippolytus, Antipope, ca. 170—235 or 6.
[Traditio apostolica. English]
The treatise on the apostolic tradition of St. Hippolytus of Rome,
bishop and martyr = Apostolikē paradosis] / edited by Gregory Dix,
reissued with corrections, preface, and bibliography by Henry
Chadwick.
p. cm.
Parallel title romanized.
Translation of: Traditio apostolica, the Latin text of the lost
Greek treatise Apostolikē paradosis (title romanized).
Reprint with additional corr. Originally published: 2nd rev. ed.
London: S. P. C. K., 1968.
Includes index.
1. Christian life—Early church, ca. 30-600—Sources. 2. Church
history—Early church. ca. 30-600—Sources. I. Dix. Gregory.
II. Chadwick, Henry, 1920- . III. Title. IV. Title: Apostolikē
paradosis. V. Title: Apostolic tradition.
BR65.H84T7313 1991
270.1—dc20   91-7205
                                                                        CIP

Publisher's Note
The publisher has gone to great lengths to ensure the quality of this
reprint but points out that some imperfections in the original may be
apparent

REVERENDISSIMO DOMINO

DOMINO

GUALTERO HOWARD FRERE,

C.R., S.T.P.,

PRAESULI, PATRI, MAGISTRO

CONTENTS

I have to acknowledge my deep obligation to the Managers of the Hort Memorial Fund of the University of Cambridge and to various friends, without whose generous financial help the publication of this volume would have been impossible. I wish also to express my cordial thanks to the staff of the Cambridge University Press, whose patience, care and skill in this somewhat complicated piece of book-making have been beyond all praise. Above all, I owe a great debt of gratitude to Dr W. K. Lowther Clarke of the S.P.C.K., without whose frequent and resourceful counsel these pages would almost certainly have had to remain in manuscript.

Gr. D.

PREFACE TO THE SECOND EDITION AND SELECT BIBLIOGRAPHY

This book first appeared in 1937, and was a pioneer critical edition of a document with a transmission of extraordinary complexity. For technical scholars its text has now been replaced by the fine edition produced by Dom Bernard Botte in 1963.[1] Nevertheless, there remains a considerable demand for the earlier book, partly because of Dom Gregory Dix's brilliantly acute introduction, partly because his judgement on the textual problems retains high value in its own right, and partly because he provided an English version for the convenience of students. In many respects Dix's edition is still a very necessary complement to Botte's.

Dix's English translation was not the first. He was anticipated by the well-known American scholar B. S. Easton (1877–1950) in 1934. An unrevised reprint of this translation was issued in 1962 by Archon Books, U.S.A. Easton's volume is handy for the beginner and easy to use: but it has to be admitted that the student pays a high price for the convenience, since the truth about the complexities of the textual evidence is largely hidden from his sight. Moreover, Easton not only left out a few well-attested passages but took risks in his translation which the reader cannot check or correct without recourse to other books. In one respect Easton prescribed a pattern for Dix: he divided the work into chapter divisions and sub-divisions which Dix (against his own better judgement) decided to keep for the convenience of a uniform system of reference. The same numbering was preserved in the little edition of the Latin and Greek fragments together with a French translation produced by Dom Botte in 1946.[2] In his large critical edition, however, Dom Botte has felt free to adopt new chapter divisions. At one important point he has rearranged the order (see p. j below), and the present editor is convinced that he is right to have done so. But there have been strong practical deterrents to making any far-reaching changes in the printing of this second edition. Accordingly, I give here a concordance table of the relation between the two editions.

---

[1] *La Tradition Apostolique de Saint Hippolyte: essai de reconstitution* par Bernard Botte, Liturgiewissenschaftliche Quellen und Forschungen 39 (Münster, 1963).
[2] Sources Chrétiennes 11 (Paris, 1946).

Concordance of the chapter numbering in Dix and Botte

DIX	BOTTE	DIX	BOTTE	DIX	BOTTE
1	1	16.9–25	16	26.15 32	25
2	2	17	17	27	30
3	3	18	18	28.1 5	31
4	4	19	19	28.6 8	32
5	5	20	20	29	33
6	6	21	21	30	34
7	omit	22	21	31	35
8	7	23	21	32.1	36
9	8	24	22	32.2	37
10	9	25	23	32.3 4	38
11	10	26.1	23	33	39
12	11	26.2-4	26	34	40
13	12	26.5-6	27	35	41
14	13	26.7-12	28	36	41
15	14	26.13	29	37	42
16.1 8	15	26.14 17	24	38	43

The Progress of Work on the Text

It is only fair to add that, for all its excellences, Dom Botte's edition of 1963 will not be the last word on this controversial and difficult text. His volume appeared in the same year as an important diplomatic edition of the Latin version contained in the palimpsest in the Verona Cathedral library. This was the work of the Swedish philologist Erik Tidner.[3] Tidner's readings diverge in a number of details from those printed in Botte. There can be no doubt that more critical work is needed on the Oriental evidence. A new edition of the Arabic *Canons of Hippolytus* appeared in 1966. edited by René-Georges Coquin (*Patrologia Orientalis* XXXI. 2). In 1946 a good edition of the Ethiopic version. based on more manuscripts than were available to Horner, was produced by H. Duensing.[4] Duensing's disagreements with Horner are not very considerable. The Coptic version was re-edited with a German translation in 1954 by Walter Till and J. Leipoldt.[5] The late Dr Till himself was known

---

[3] *Didascaliae Apostolorum canonum ecclesiasticorum traditionis apostolicae versiones latinae.* Texte und Untersuchungen 75 (Berlin, 1963).

[4] *Der aethiopische Text der Kirchenordnung des Hippolyt.* Abhandlungen der Akademie der Wissenschaften in Göttingen. phil. hist. Kl., III Folge. 32. The Ethiopic has many more variants than Dix was able to record.

[5] Texte und Untersuchungen 58 (Berlin, 1954).

to be dissatisfied with this book, and some of the reviewers were severe to it[6]—not always justly so. The volume is primarily an edition of the Sahidic version, with notes on the variants of the Bohairic version. There is probably more to be said about the Bohairic translation. Dom Botte is perhaps over-inclined to dismiss it as being too recent and too likely to be contaminated by the Arabic tradition. The colophon in the Berlin manuscript[7] (or. quart. 519 (9488), now at Tübingen University Library) explains that the version was made in A.D. 1804, and that the translation has been made from the southern into the northern dialect, that is from Sahidic, not from Arabic. Admittedly the translator's native tongue must have been Arabic, but his version may still be a valuable witness to the Sahidic tradition, like the Arabic canon-collection (also made from the Sahidic).

One important witness, the *Testament of our Lord*, written in Greek in the fourth century but preserved in Syriac, has not lately received any special critical study. Rahmani's original edition of 1899 has been reprinted (1966). The English translation by J. Cooper and Bishop A. J. Maclean (1902), giving a revised translation and valuable notes, remains a rare book.

Two new Greek fragments have to be reported here. The first is preserved in a dogmatic florilegium of patristic quotations contained in two manuscripts, cod. Ochrid.86 (saec. XIII) f.192 and Paris.gr.900 (saec. XV) f.112. The discoverer, Professor Marcel Richard, printed the excerpt from the *Apostolic Tradition* in *Symbolae Osloenses* 38 (1963), page 79, and communicated it to Dom Botte in time for its inclusion in his edition of 1963. This new fragment preserves the original Greek of chapter xxxii.1 (= Botte 36):

Ἐκ τῶν διατάξεων τῶν ἁγίων ἀποστόλων·

πᾶς δὲ πιστὸς πειράσθω, πρὸ τοῦ τινος γεύσασθαι, εὐχαριστίας μεταλαμβάνειν· εἰ γὰρ πίστει μεταλάβοι, οὐδ' ἂν θανάσιμόν τις δώῃ αὐτῷ μετὰ τοῦτο, οὐ κατισχύσει αὐτοῦ (cf. Mark xvi.18),

The second Greek fragment comes from a ritual for the unction of the sick contained in an eleventh or twelfth-century manuscript at the monastery of St Catherine on Mount Sinai. It was found by the Russian scholar A. Dmitrievski and printed also by A. Trebelas, Μικρὸν εὐχολόγιον (Athens 1950–5), i, p. 180. In

[6] Lefort in *Muséon* 67 (1954), pp. 403–5; Botte in *Bull. Théol. Anc. Méd.* 7 (1954), pp. 26 f.

[7] In Botte's edition of 1963, p. xxii, this manuscript is said to be in the British Museum, but this must be a slip.

1964 Dr E. Segelberg[8] drew attention to the fact that it is an evident adaptation of the prayer for the consecration of oil contained in *Ap. Trad.* v. It reads:

Ἔκπεμψον, κύριε, τὴν πιότητα τοῦ ἐλέους σου ἐπὶ τὸν καρπὸν τῆς ἐλαίας τοῦτον, δι᾽ οὗ ἔχρισας ἱερεῖς, προφήτας, βασιλεῖς τε καὶ μάρτυρας καὶ ἐνέδυσας τῇ χρηστότητί σου δικαιοσύνης ἔνδυμα, ἵνα γένηται παντὶ τῷ ἀλειφομένῳ καὶ γενομένῳ εἰς ὄνησιν καὶ ὠφέλειαν ψυχῆς καὶ σώματος (καὶ) πνεύματος, εἰς ἀποτροπὴν παντὸς κακοῦ, εἰς ὑγείαν τῷ χριομένῳ διὰ τοῦ κυρίου ἡμῶν Ἰησοῦ [Χριστοῦ].

Segelberg draws attention to other descendants of Hippolytus' prayer scattered in strangely diverse places, such as the Coptic Euchologion of the White Monastery (edited by E. Lanne in *Patrologia Orientalis* XXVIII, 2, 393ff) and the "Gelasian" sacramentary (p. 70 Wilson, no. 381 Mohlberg).

Tidner's edition of the Latin text in the Verona palimpsest has been mentioned above. In the present reprint I have tried to take account of his revised readings, but have not consistently altered Dix's Latin text to make it conform with Tidner's printed text except where Tidner explicitly corrects Hauler. Hauler's work of 1900 was masterly, and left relatively little for later study to glean. There are a few places where Tidner diverges from Hauler without noting the fact (lxxiii.15; lxxv. 20; lxxx. 20), but as Tidner was not always impeccably served by his printer these divergences may be simply misprints.

The Debate about the Authorship

R. H. Connolly in 1916 first made it a matter of argument (rather than inspired conjecture) that an early third-century church order must be the foundation document underlying the Latin of the Verona manuscript, the Oriental canon collections in Coptic, Arabic, and Ethiopic, the eighth book of the *Apostolic Constitutions*, and *The Testament of our Lord*. Connolly's monograph[9] remains an education to read, and contains much illuminating commentary on the content of the work. His basic conclusion has

[8] E. Segelberg, "The Benedictio Olei in the Apostolic Tradition of Hippolytus", in *Oriens Christianus* 48 (1964), pp. 268–81. As Segelberg notes, its text supports the Latin *sanitatem* against Dix's emendation (accepted by Botte) *sanctitatem*.
[9] *The so-called Egyptian Church Order and derived documents*, Texts and Studies VIII, 4 (1916).

remained secure. But not everyone has accepted his identification of this recovered church order with the work entitled *Apostolic Tradition* known to have been written by Hippolytus of Rome.

The principal arguments for identifying the recovered church order with *Ap. Tr.* may be tersely summarized as follows:

(a) Hippolytus' name appears as author in two of the derived documents, namely the so-called *Epitome* of the *Apostolic Constitutions* and the Arabic *Canons of Hippolytus* (his name appears in Arabic as Aboulides). The *Epitome* introduces his name at precisely the place where the compiler first begins to incorporate matter directly from the recovered church order.

(b) The statue of Hippolytus found in Rome in 1551, now in the Vatican Library,[10] gives a list of his writings, and names a work *On charismatic gifts* immediately before the *Apostolic Tradition*. The initial chapter of the recovered church order, as attested by Latin, Greek, and Ethiopic, explains that the author, having said everything necessary concerning charismatic gifts, is now going to deal with "the tradition that befits the churches".

It has been argued,[11] with some reason, that these considerations taken by themselves are not sufficient to prove what they are claimed to show. The first point is especially weak, since the ascription of an apostolic church order to Hippolytus might be compared with the claim of the *Apostolic Constitutions* to be mediated by Clement of Rome, disciple of St Peter. In the *Lausiac History* of Palladius (c. 420), Hippolytus is said to have been "known to the apostles" (*H.L.* 65). Accordingly, the argument runs, the occurrence of Hippolytus' name in the *Epitome* and in the Arabic *Canons of Hippolytus* can be explained on the hypothesis that Hippolytus, with the reputation of being a disciple of the apostles, was the kind of person to whom church orders were easily ascribed. This argument, however, can be

---

[10] The statue stood in the Vatican until the time of Pius IX, was then moved to the Lateran Museum, and was placed in the Vatican Library by John XXIII. The best pictures and information about the discovery may be found in the inexpensive little book by G. Bovini, *Sant'Ippolito dottore e martire del III secolo* (Rome 1943).

[11] The Dutch thesis of R. Lorentz, *De Egyptische Kerkordening en Hippolyts van Rome* (Haarlem 1929) was answered in a very good monograph by H. Elfers, *Die Kirchenordnung Hippolyts von Rome* (Paderborn 1938). A strong sceptical attack came from Dom H. Engberding, "Das angebliche Dokument römischer Liturgie aus dem Begiun des dritten Jahrhunderts", in *Miscellanea liturgica in honorem L. C. Mohlberg* i (Rome 1948), pp. 47–71. Botte answered him in *Rech. de Théol. Anc. Méd.* 16 (1949), pp. 177–85.

quickly reversed; that is, the existence of a church order current under the name of Hippolytus entitled *Apostolic Tradition* would make it natural for a fifth-century writer to imagine that Hippolytus must have been directly known to the apostles.

A much more formidable argument against ascribing the recovered church order to Hippolytus is the extreme paucity of contacts and parallels between the church order and the later liturgical practice of the Roman community.[12] The principal descendants and imitators of the recovered church order lay in the East. The *Testament of our Lord* and the *Apostolic Constitutions* point to currency in Syria. The Coptic archetype, from which the extant Coptic, Arabic, and Ethiopic versions are all ultimately derived, proves that the work was influential in Egypt. The only strange figure is the Latin version of the Verona palimpsest. This Latin version, indeed, bears so little relation to other early Latin liturgies that there is at least some *a priori* attractiveness about the conjecture that the Latin version was produced for one of the Arian communities in North Italy about 350–400[13] (Milan itself had an Arian bishop, Auxentius from 355 to 373, and there were other Western Arian centres). The Arians tended strongly towards a liturgical conservatism. It was one of their better theological arguments that the pre-controversial, pre-Constantinian eucharistic formulas assumed the subordination of the Son in mediating to the Father the Church's prayers and thanksgivings.[14] An Arian group might have been specially interested in a pre-Nicene liturgical work with so august a title. Nevertheless, it is not easy to discover in the Verona Latin text any clear traces of Arianisms, that is, phrases which look like modifications in a specifically Arian direction. So the conjecture cannot be more than an interesting guess.

---

[12] This has been best argued in a long paper by A. Salles in *Revue de l'histoire des religions* (1955). Salles has also published a useful study of the baptismal prayers, not from Hippolytus but certainly early, interpolated in the Ethiopic version after ch. xxvii. See his provisional discussion in *Trois antiques rituels du baptême*, Sources Chrétiennes 59 (Paris, 1958).

[13] The suggestion that the translation originated in an Arian milieu was first made, I believe, by F. C. Burkitt in *J.T.S.* xxxi (1930), p. 261. The hypothesis is looked on with favour e.g. by A. F. Walls in *Studia Patristica*, iii, Texte und Untersuchungen, 78 (Berlin 1961), p. 161, and by J. H. Crehan in *J.T.S.* n.s. x (1959), p. 421.

[14] A striking example of the Arian argument from *lex orandi lex credendi* may be found in the fifth-century Arian fragments discovered by Cardinal Mai, *Script. Vet. Nova coll.* III (1827), ii, pp. 208ff; they are discussed by G. Mercati in *Studi e Testi* 7 (1902).

The fact that the recovered church order had so large a posterity in Egypt led Professor Hanssens in 1959 to propose a series of conjectural hypotheses.[15] He suggested that Hippolytus was originally an Alexandrian who moved to Rome to become a presbyter there, and that in the *Apostolic Tradition* he was describing his liturgical ideals with his memories of Alexandria as a model. This hypothesis would account for the Egyptian affinities of his church order. Professor Hanssens' book is a mine of learned information, but his principal thesis is highly speculative, and its plausibility might even appear weakened if all his arguments were here to be rehearsed.

The crux of the entire debate must be the internal evidence of the work itself. On any showing the recovered church order is unquestionably a product of the first half of the third century. The Church is liable to persecution and needs a ruling about the status of "confessors" who have been imprisoned for their faith (x.1–2, cf. xix.2). The church building is a private house (xvi.1). The liturgical practices fit well with other early third-century evidence, for example in Tertullian and Cyprian. There is nothing that requires or even suggests a later date: the rules for the admission of widows, virgins, subdeacons, and readers; the organization of the catechumenate; the admission of infants to baptism; the offerings of cheese,[16] olives, and fruit (but not vegetables; see p. m below); the segregation of the sexes in church services; the pattern of eucharistic rite with its basic structure of thanksgiving, recitation of the Institution, the Anamnesis, Invocation, and final doxology. Some curious features actually point towards rather than away from Rome. The Sanctus is absent from the Anaphora (if the transmitted text of the Latin and Ethiopic is what Hippolytus wrote; see below, p. l). It is not certain that the Sanctus had a place in the

---

[15] J. M. Hanssens, *La Liturgie d'Hippolyte*, Orientalia Christiana Analecta 155 (Rome 1959). A reprint appeared in 1965 with a substantial appendix of additional notes. Although the principal thesis of the book is precarious, and the argument sometimes extravagant, the book contains much learning and valuable comment.

[16] The blessing of cheese in ch. vi (the prayer seems to echo Job x.10) is preserved only in the Latin. It helps to explain why St Perpetua had a vision of a heavenly shepherd feeding her with cheese in paradise. Hippolytus' blessing of cheese goes with a blessing of olive oil: the oil from the tree of life was the elixir of immortality according to many ancient texts, e.g. *Life of Adam and Eve* 36; II Enoch viii.3–5; *Apocalypse of Moses* ix.3; *Acts of Pilate* 3 (19); *Acts of Thomas* 157. For gnostic sources see my note on Origen, *c.Cels.* vi.27. So both cheese and olive oil are associated with paradise.

Roman liturgy before the fifth century.[17] The baptismal inter-
rogations are closely akin to later Roman forms, for example in
the so-called "Gelasianum" (p. 86 Wilson = 449 Mohlberg). The
Latin pontifical (*Gelas*. p. 144 Wilson = 740 Mohlberg) has a
precise parallel to the direction that the deacon is ordained *non
in sacerdotio sed in ministerio* (ix.2). Moreover, in the "Gelasian"
prayers for Maundy Thursday (p. 70 Wilson = Mohlberg 381)
there is the parallel, already noted above (p. d), to Hippolytus'
prayer for consecrating oil for the sick.

The atmosphere of the Eucharist in this church order stands
much nearer to the second century than to the fourth. The
dominant idea is that it is a thank-offering sacrifice. There is no
language suggesting a propitiatory re-enactment of the death of
Christ. There is no memento of the living and dead. The absence
of any commemoration of the saints points to a date before the
middle of the third century.

The objection that all the affinities of the church order lie in
Egypt and Syria is a real one; but it can be answered by a number
of cumulative considerations. First, there is one obvious analogy.
The letter of Clement of Rome to the Corinthians came to have
a very similar history. The closing pages of the letter contain a
long prayer with manifest echoes of the contemporary liturgical
intercessions at Rome in the last decade of the first century. The
future influence of this unquestionably Roman document lay in
the Greek East. A papyrus leaf of the latter part of the third
century, now at Würzburg,[18] contains liturgical intercessions,
some of which are nearly related to the language of 1 Clement.
The papyrus is the earliest scrap of Egyptian liturgy hitherto
found. It would be hard to find any discernible influence of the
letter of Clement on later Roman liturgy. As the language spoken
by the Christians of Rome gradually changed from Greek to
Latin (a process going on during the century from 230 to 330), the
Roman community did not remember very much about its Greek
past. The writings of the greatest theologian to live at Rome

---

[17] A very interesting sermon transmitted under the name of St Ambrose and
probably of about A.D. 400 says that the Sanctus, though universal in the Greek
East, was not so in the West: *de Spiritu sancto* iv.2 (Migne, *P.L.* 17.1005–12) re-edited
by L. Chavoutier in *Sacris Erudiri* xi (1960), pp. 136–92. The author is dependent on
Ambrose and is to be placed probably in Northern Italy; but whether he is Niceta
of Remesiana (as K. Gamber proposes in *Ostkirchl. Studien* xi (1962), pp. 204–6) must
remain guesswork.
[18] Würzburg papyrus 3, saec. III, ed. U. Wilcken in *Abhandl. Berl. Akad.* (1933),
no. 6, pp. 31–6.

during the second century, Justin Martyr, did not achieve translation into Latin until the sixteenth century; and Justin did not
even gain entry to the Latin Kalender of saints until the ninth
century.[19] It is impossible to know what degree of continuity
was maintained when the liturgy at Rome was first put into
Latin, probably in the time of Pope Damasus (366–84).[20] In any
event, in the third century liturgical forms were still extremely
fluid. The author of the recovered church order was apparently
trying to resist rapid changes, but he makes it explicit that his
prayers are only models, designed to show the kind of thing that
is desirable. He never supposed that he was taking an important
step towards the establishment of fixed forms.

The Order and Integrity of the Text

Liturgies in the ancient Church were never thought of as immu-
table documents. Each bishop (as Justin puts it) "prayed to the
best of his ability".[21] Some were long. Justin says that the Greek
anaphora at Rome c. 150 was of considerable length.[22] But
whereas Greek liturgies tended to be long, as in the immense
prayers in the eighth book of the *Apostolic Constitutions*, the
Latin genius was for brevity. Cyprian believed that high-flown
prose and grandiloquent periods were out of place in public
worship, and thought that the prayers of the Eucharist should be
restrained and quiet (*orat. dom.* 4). So each bishop would in some
degree make his own liturgy. Hippolytus' work probably contri-
buted much to making for more stable usages. But all liturgies
before 600 were subject to a continual process of alteration and
adaptation as they were brought up to date by subsequent users.[23]
A text such as the *Apostolic Tradition* had a long snowball

---

[19] I have collected evidence in my *Early Christian Thought and the Classical
Tradition* (1966), p. 127.

[20] T. Klauser, "Der Uebergang der römischen Kirche von der griechischen zur
lateinischen Sprache" in *Miscellanea G. Mercati* I, Studi e Testi 121 (Rome 1946),
pp. 467–82. The two principal pieces of evidence are Marius Victorinus, *adv. Arium*
ii.8, written about 360, who cites parts of the contemporary Roman liturgy in Greek,
and Ambrosiaster, *Quaestiones Veteris et Novi Testamenti* 109.21 (ed. Souter, *C.S.E.L.*
50.268), written between 374 and 382, who cites the Roman liturgy in Latin.

[21] Justin, *Apol.* i.67.5.

[22] *Apol.* i.65.3.

[23] There is much food for thought in the programmatic remarks of F. L. Cross,
"Early Western Liturgical Manuscripts", in *J.T.S.* n.s. xvi (1965), pp. 61–7. Cf. R.P.C.
Hanson, "The Liberty of the Bishop to improvise prayer in the eucharist", in
Vigiliae Christianae xv (1961), pp. 173–76.

history in which it suffered additions and modifications with each successive recension. This process is most obviously seen in the actual differences of order among the various witnesses.

The order of the chapters is virtually consistent in three of the witnesses, namely the Latin, Coptic, and Arabic; and the deviation of the *Testament of our Lord* from this norm is not great. In the *Canons of Hippolytus*, however, chapters xxiv-xxviii (= 22–32 in Botte) appear after xxix–xxxvii (= 33–42 Botte). The Ethiopic has been less drastically arranged, but has two important transpositions. The opening chapter as it stands in the Latin appears in the Ethiopic just before the section about offering the first-fruits (xxviii = 31 Botte). The Ethiopic, moreover, disagrees with all other witnesses in its placing of the sections on the deacon's duties in taking the bread round to the sick and poor, and on the prayers at the bringing in of the lamps at the evening Agapē (xxvi.14–32).[24] For most of these sections the Ethiopic (E) is the sole witness. Nevertheless parts of the material occur in *Test. Dom.* and the *Canons of Hippolytus* (K), where they are placed before xxvi.2. Since in E the words of xxvi.2 are repeated as a doublet after xxvi.32, it is easy to see that E bears witness against its own arrangement. In 1937 Dix accepted E's order as original, and was therefore faced with the difficulty that the Latin goes straight on from xxvi to xxvii.1, and apparently omits the section in a way that must raise the gravest doubts about the authenticity of the block if E's order is right. Everything falls into place if E's material is indeed accepted as authentic Hippolytus but if the true order is that given by *Test. Dom.* and K. The entire block then falls at a point where, owing to a lacuna in the Verona MS., the Latin is deficient. No objection to the authenticity of the block can then be grounded on its "omission" by the Latin version.

A very minor additional reason can be given for regarding xxvi.14–32 as being at least no invention of the Ethiopic tradition, namely that the transmitted text of E in xxvi.14–17 is obscure and corrupt and bears all the marks of a poor rendering by an uncomprehending translator.

[24] The hymn φῶς ἱλαρόν, "O gladsome light", long traditional in the time of Basil the Great and still sung at Greek Vespers, was probably a third-century hymn sung at this point. The moment when lights were brought in at a feast in antiquity was marked by an acclamation and was the signal for the party to become excited. This is the background of the vulgar slanders about the Christian agape and the enormities that followed the bringing in and extinction of the lights. In fact the Christians saluted the entry of the light with praise and prayer.

For the prayers in chapter vii, E again stands quite alone, without a morsel of support from any other version. These prayers were rightly marked by Dix as a much later addition, and the chapter is entirely left out by Botte.

The Anaphora

The most controversial place where modification of the original text has been suspected is in the Anaphora (chapter iv). Its external attestation by LET (three completely independent witnesses), with some partial support from *Ap. Const.*, is extremely powerful in its favour. The language of the first part of it fits Hippolytus perfectly. It is sufficient to refer here to the magistral commentary on the Anaphora in the article by R. H. Connolly in *J.T.S.* xxxix (1938), pp. 350–69. Controversy has concentrated on the epiclesis. At this point the witnesses divide, LE being abandoned by T and *Ap. Const.* This is not in itself surprising. The epiclesis underwent considerable modification towards the end of the fourth century, and became much more prominent in Greek liturgies. Here is the point at which modernization would be natural and predictable. In the *Ap. Const.* it has become an unambiguous invocation of the Spirit upon "this sacrifice" to "make this bread the body of thy Christ and this cup the blood of thy Christ". In LE, on the other hand, the purpose of the invocation is not to change the bread and wine but to bless the Church in making that offering that it may be a bond of unity and a means of grace.

In T almost all of Hippolytus' anaphora is incorporated within a much longer and more elaborate prayer. The compiler took Hippolytus' text and filled it out with expansions and some minor omissions. But T has no equivalent of the words found in LE "And we pray thee that thou wouldest send thy Holy Spirit upon the oblation of thy holy Church". Instead, at the critical point, T passes into a long invocation of the Trinity, with intercessions, finally coming back to the text of Hippolytus with the prayer "Grant that all those who partake of thy holy things be made one with thee, that they may be filled with the Holy Spirit for the confirmation of the faith in truth". The elaborate prayer to the Trinity does not include an unambiguous epiclesis of the Spirit. But the shape of this long prayer is so individual, without a parallel in other ancient anaphoras, that it is extremely hazardous to deduce that the author of T had a text of the Apostolic Tradition which had no invocation of the Spirit.

In a widely noticed paper in the first volume of the *Journal of Ecclesiastical History*, Professor E. C. Ratcliff suggested that the epiclesis as given by LE was a fourth-century development replacing the final paragraph of the original prayer which ended with the Sanctus. The theory has attractions and is well argued, but it has difficulties to circumvent which are probably fatal to its acceptance. First of these is the absence of any certain evidence that the Sanctus actually formed a normal part of the earliest Roman liturgy. The well-known text of 1 Clement 34 is sometimes taken as evidence of the liturgical use of the Sanctus in Rome before the end of the first century. It may be so. But there is nothing in Clement's words to make this conclusion necessary. All that he says is that the divided Corinthian community ought to try to imitate the harmony of the angelic choir who, though numbering ten thousand times ten thousand (and therefore liable to find it hard to keep together), nevertheless chant their hymn in absolute unison. Secondly, there is the real possibility that the author of the Testament may well have had personal reasons for passing over Hippolytus' epiclesis. In fact, Professor Ratcliff himself thinks that the epiclesis of LE, which he believes to be post-Hippolytean, already had a place in the form of text lying before the compiler of the Testament. The concession, wrung from him perhaps by the absence of any evidence that the compiler had a Sanctus before him at this point, is surely very damaging to the conjecture.

There is nothing in the transmitted text of LE that Hippolytus of Rome could not have written. It is worth quoting the decisive judgement of R. H. Connolly (*J.T.S.* xxxix, p. 367): "Reading the Epiclesis of our prayer in the light of contemporary ideas, I am unable to find in it a petition for any action of the Holy Spirit on the oblation itself. The only action of the Holy Spirit which it speaks of, or implies, has for its object the minds and hearts of the faithful communicants, while the constituent elements of the oblation, as already unified, suggest what that action should be . . . to bring God's people together 'into one'." If this is correctly stated, then it is quite within the bounds of possibility that Hippolytus' epiclesis owed something to models of the Greek synagogue.

Dix liked to lay great stress on the presence of Jewish liturgical tradition in the background of the *Apostolic Tradition*. He was surely right to do so. For example, Hippolytus' rule, at first sight curious, forbidding the offering of pumpkins, melons, cucumbers, (leeks), onions, and garlic (xxviii.6) must simply reflect the text of Numbers xi.5 as interpreted in contemporary synagogue tradition. His direction that at baptism female candidates must loose their hair and lay aside all jewellery, has been convincingly explained by Frank Gavin and by W. C. Van Unnik as a custom directly drawn from Jewish lustrations attested in the contemporary Mishnah (*Shabbath* vi.1, translated by Danby, p. 104) and elsewhere. Nevertheless most of the anaphora is not marked by any features strongly suggesting the use of Jewish liturgical models. There is no long commemoration of the creation, and the principal stress lies on the redemptive event of the incarnation and atonement: on the triumph over evil powers at the Descent to Hades, the "limit" of which (in time or space) was "fixed"[25] and on the narrative of the institution of the Eucharist. This anaphora is Hippolytus' personal creation. It is only in the institution narrative and probably in the epiclesis that he is likely to be using traditional formulas, and that for the epiclesis could have been taken from some hellenistic Jewish prayer. Its motif is not far from the prayer in the Didache praying that God would unite his people scattered upon the mountains.

Note on xvi.22

A small detail in the text deserves brief mention. In xvi.22 the list of occupations to be renounced at baptism includes various kinds of dealer in magic and spells—a charmer, an astrologer, an interpreter of dreams, a mountebank who gathers crowds in the market place to watch his tricks, a cutter of the fringes of clothing (*psalistes*), and a maker of amulets. *Psalistes* would mean a snipper with scissors. It is given only in the Coptic text, and could be a gloss by the Coptic translator. The Sahidic text actually reads *psellistes*, stammerer, but the Coptic spelling of Greek words may take unusual forms: *psalistes* was restored as the correct reading here by W. E. Crum in 1934 in a note buried

[25] There is an analogous idea in the long fragment on Hades ascribed (probably rightly) to Hippolytus, *de universo*, and cited in the *Sacra Parallela*; printed in K. Holl, *Fragmente vornicänischer Kirchenväter aus den Sacra Parallela* (1899), p. 139, line 48. For this lost work of Hippolytus see W. J. Malley, "Four unedited fragments of the *De Universo* . . .", in *J.T.S.* n.s. xvi (1965), pp. 13-25.

in his *Coptic Dictionary*, p. 422. Botte, however, takes the word *psalistes* as the clue to the sense, and interprets it to mean "one who pares off the gold from the edge of coins while leaving the circular form (*schema*) untouched".[26] This form of sharp practice was not common till late antiquity, but is condemned in the *Theodosian Code* (ix.22) and is mentioned in these terms by the historian of Justinian's wars, Procopius (*Gothic War* iii.1.30).

The three available witnesses to Hippolytus' text at this point disagree in details, but all agree in saying that what was snipped was clothing, not coins. Botte most ingeniously answers this difficulty by pointing out that the Greek word *schema*, which Procopius uses of the shape of coins, may also mean clothing. There remains, however, a considerable obstacle to accepting Botte's clever argument. namely that the forbidden occupation occurs in a catalogue of magicians or purveyors of *materia magica* such as amulets. One would therefore expect the occupation, whatever it was, to be concerned with some superstitious purpose rather than with dishonest dealing with imperial coinage. Moreover, there is evidence that fringes attached to clothing were regarded in antiquity as a means of protecting the wearer against evil. In Judaism fringes (zizit), like phylacteries, were a prescribed observance to remind the wearer of his duty to the Law. There is therefore no reason to doubt that our Coptic, Arabic, and Ethiopic witnesses are correct in understanding the occupation to be concerned with cutting fringes or tassels on clothing. which the wearers regarded as protective against evil spirits.

H. CHADWICK.

Select Bibliography

For a very full bibliography to 1952 see J. Quasten, *Patrology* ii (1953). pp. 180-94. The following special studies are noteworthy:

J. B. Bauer. "Die Früchtesegnung in Hippolyts Kirchenordnung". *Zeitschrift für katholische Theologie* 74 (1952). pp. 71-5.

J. Blanc. "Lexique comparé des versions de la Tradition apostolique de S. Hippolyte". *Recherches de théologie ancienne et médiévale* 22 (1955), pp. 173-92

---

[26] *Revue des études byzantines* 16 (1958), pp. 162-5.

B. Botte, "L'epiclèse de l'anaphore d'Hippolyte", *Rech. théol. anc. med.* 14 (1947), pp. 241–51.

—— "L'authenticité de la Tradition apostolique de S. Hippolyte", ibid. 16 (1949), pp. 177–85.

—— "Note sur la symbole baptismal de S. Hippolyte", *Mélanges J. de Ghellinck* I (Gembloux, 1951), pp. 189–200.

—— "Le texte de la Tradition apostolique", *Rech. théol. anc. méd.* 22 (1955), pp. 161–72.

—— "Psellistes-Psalistes", *Revue des études byzantines* 16 (1958), pp. 162-5.

—— "Un passage difficile de la Tradition apostolique sur le signe de croix", *Rech. théol. anc. méd.* 27 (1960), pp. 5–19 [on ch. 37 Dix = 42 Botte].

—— *La Tradition Apostolique de Saint Hippolyte, Essai de Reconstitution.* (Aschendorff, Münster, 1963).

C. Callewaert, "Histoire positive de canon romain: une epiclèse à Rome?", *Sacris Erudiri* 2 (1948), pp. 95-110 (speculative attempt to find evidence for an epiclesis in the early Latin mass on evidence of Gelasius, fr. 7 p. 486 Thiel = P.L. 59.143 A and *Sacr. Leon.* 576 Mohlberg = p. 74, 14 Feltoe).

B. Capelle, "L'introduction du catéchuménat à Rome", *Rech. théol. anc. méd.* 5 (1933), pp. 129–54.

O. Casel, review of Elfers' book in *Archiv für Liturgiewissenschaft* 2 (1952), pp. 115–130 (accepting Hippolytus' authorship).

R. H. Connolly, "An ancient prayer in the mediaeval euchologia", *J.T.S.* 19 (1918), pp. 132-44.

—— "The prologue of the Apostolic Tradition", *J.T.S.* 22 (1921), pp. 356-61.

—— "On the text of the baptismal creed of Hippolytus", *J.T.S.* 25 (1924), pp. 131-9.

—— "The eucharistic prayer of Hippolytus", *J.T.S.* 39 (1938), pp. 350-69.

J. H. Crehan, *Early Christian Baptism and the Creed* (London, 1950), pp. 159 75.

H. Elfers, *Die Kirchenordnung Hippolyts von Rom* (Paderborn, 1938) (defence of Hippolytus' authorship).

—— "Neue Untersuchungen über die Kirchenordnung Hippolyts", *Festschrift K. Adam* (Düsseldorf, 1952), pp. 169 211.

H. Engberding, "Das angebliche Dokument romischer Liturgie aus dem Beginn des dritten Jahrhunderts", *Miscellanea Liturgica in honorem L. C. Mohlberg* I (Rome, 1948), pp. 47 -71 (attack on attribution to Hippolytus).

F. Gavin, "Rabbinic Parallels in early church orders", *Hebrew Union College Annual* 6 (1929), pp. 57–67.

J. M. Hanssens, *La Liturgie d'Hippolyte* (2nd edn, Rome, 1965).

J. A. Jungmann, "Beobachtungen zum Fortleben von Hippolyts Apostolischer Ueberlieferung", *Zeitschrift für katholische Theologie* 53 (1929), pp. 579–85.

—— "Die Doxologien in der Kirchenordnung Hippolyts", ibid. 86 (1964), pp. 321 -6.

J. Lécuyer, "Episcopat et presbytérat dans les écrits d'Hippolyte de Rome", *Recherches de science religieuse* 41 (1953), pp. 30-50.

A. G. Martimort, "La Tradition apostolique d'Hippolyte et le rituel baptismal antique", *Bulletin de littérature ecclésiastique* 60 (Toulouse, 1959), pp. 57–62 (criticism of Salles).

P. Nautin, *Je crois à l'Esprit-Saint dans la sainte église pour la résurrection de la chair* (Paris, 1947).

E. C. Ratcliff, "The Sanctus and the Pattern of the early Anaphora", *Journal of Ecclesiastical History* 1 (1950), pp. 29–36, 125–34.

C. C. Richardson, "The so-called Epiclesis in Hippolytus", *Harvard Theological Review* 40 (1947), pp. 101–8.

—— "A note on the epicleses in Hippolytus and the Testamentum Domini", *Rech. théol. anc. méd.* 15 (1948), pp. 357–9.

A. Salles, "La Tradition apostolique est-elle un témoin de la liturgie romaine", *Revue de l'histoire des religions* 148 (1955), pp. 181–213 (contrast of baptismal procedure in *Ap. Tr.* with Roman practice after A.D. 500).

E. Segelberg, "The Benedictio Olei in the Apostolic Tradition of Hippolytus", *Oriens Christianus* 48 (1964), pp. 268–81.

W. C. Van Unnik, "Les Chevaux défaits des femmes baptisés: un rite de baptême dans l'Ordre ecclésiastique d'Hippolyte", *Vigiliae Christianae* i (1947), pp. 77–100.

A. F. Walls, "A Note on the apostolic claim in the church order literature", *Studia Patristica* 2 = Texte und Untersuchungen 64 (Berlin, 1957), pp. 83–92.

R. J. Z. Werblowsky, "On the baptismal rite according to St. Hippolytus", ibid. pp. 93–105.

PREFACE TO THE FIRST EDITION

It is now generally recognised that the *Apostolic Tradition* of St Hippolytus is the most illuminating single source of evidence extant on the inner life and religious polity of the early Christian Church. Its study is likely to bring about considerable changes in many currently accepted conceptions of primitive Church Order, changes which would already be taking place were it not for the difficulty of studying the treatise itself. It is an unfortunate fact that its text has reached us in a more deplorably battered condition than that of any other important early Christian document.

For some four and a half years I have had in preparation an edition which should bring out the value of this treatise for the study of early Christian institutions and the *spirit* of the primitive Church. The text here presented had been constructed for some two years before Prof. Easton's recent translation (Camb. Univ. Press, 1934) was available, and though this has afforded me the opportunity of reviewing my own conclusions by the judgement of a distinguished textual scholar, I may say that only in two cases have I found something to alter in the readings I had already adopted.

The Introduction and Commentary I had planned have now taken on a much more elaborate form than was originally intended, largely because Hippolytus casts light on much which is found only in scattered allusions in other writers of the pre-Nicene period. Certain obstacles have arisen to their immediate publication which will allow of an opportunity for further revision.

But in the meantime it has seemed worth while to place at the disposal of others a much fuller reproduction of the materials available for the reconstitution of the authentic text of the treatise than is yet available. The texts of Jungklaus and Easton, useful as they are, consist only of a German and an English version with little in the way of *apparatus criticus* or variant readings, and it is very difficult to justify some of the renderings which they adopt. Hippolytus' own evidence, which is crucial on many disputed questions of early Christian history and practice, is still very hard to come at. The interpolated and adapted versions in which alone much of it is now preserved are available only in separate editions for some time out of print. I had for a short time thought of essaying from these materials a reconstitution of the lost Greek original text, of the kind attempted by Lagarde in Bunsen's *Analecta Antenicaena*, vol. ii (1854) on the basis of the Sahidic text alone. While I do not think that this would be impossible to do for some parts of the *Apostolic Tradition* with relative certainty, it soon became clear that for the text as a whole it involved begging too many questions to serve any useful purpose. I have therefore presented a bald English version, through which the probable form of the Greek can often be inferred. The divisions of the text are those of Easton. They are not invariably quite those I would myself have chosen, but the disadvantages of diversity are obvious. I have added an historical Introduction for those who have no previous acquaintance with the work, a discussion of the textual materials and a few notes on readings adopted. The detailed Introduction and all consideration of the book's contents and setting are reserved for another volume.

The time has not, perhaps, yet come for a definitive text of the *Apostolic Tradition*, though I hope that this edition can claim to have brought that pressing need of patristic and liturgical studies a long step nearer. If it will lighten for others that labour of consulting and reconsulting the complicated array of works by Hauler, Horner, Funk, Rahmani, Riedel and others, which is at present necessary to be sure of the authentic form of almost every sentence of the text, it will have served a useful purpose.

GREGORY DIX.

NASHDOM ABBEY
BURNHAM, BUCKS.

GENERAL INTRODUCTION

i. The *Apostolic Tradition*

The little Greek treatise whose title is Ἀποστολικὴ Παράδοσις, the *Apostolic Tradition*, was put out at Rome by the anti-Pope and martyr St Hippolytus in the second decade of the third century.* It is the sort of document of which Martène and the Maurists must sometimes have dreamed. Here from the pen of a disciple of St Irenaeus is what claims to be an accurate and authoritative account of the rites and organisation of the Church as the men of the later second century had received them from the subapostolic age.

Nevertheless it must be said at the outset that the respect accorded it to-day is vastly greater than anything it received in antiquity. This is not one of those documents that have made history. There are indeed grounds for suspecting that it was already on the way to being obsolete as a manual of Christian practice on the day it was first published. Its author was a scholar and an exegete rather than a man of creative mind, an avowed reactionary who in his own generation stood for the past rather than the future. His treatise settled no great problem for his contemporaries and inaugurated no great developments. Nor did it profess to do so. It claims explicitly to be recording only the forms and models of rites *already* traditional and customs *already* long-established, and to be written in deliberate protest against innovations. Its contents fall easily into three main parts. The first deals with the inauguration of the various ranks of the Christian hierarchy, and adds some brief details of their functions. The second deals with the initiation

* The grounds for this attribution are presented in *The So-called Egyptian Church Order and Derived Documents* (Cambridge Texts and Studies, viii. 4), 1916, by Dom R. H. Connolly, and, more summarily, by E. Schwartz, *Ueber die pseudo-apostolischen Kirchenordnungen* (Schriften der wissenschaftlichen Gesellschaft in Strassburg, vi), 1910. The only criticism of their conclusions is by R. Lorentz, *De egyptische Kerkenordening en Hippolytus van Rome*, Haarlem, 1929, which has not won any following. (See Preface to the Second Edition.)

of the laity. The third might almost be headed "The Devout Life for Normal Christians". On the face of it, if its claims be justified, such a document could effect no revolutions.

But though it is thus cast in the form of a manual of liturgy and piety, the *Apostolic Tradition* is in fact a document of controversy. "Where you find the Christian life so ordered and so lived, there—and only there—you may be sure you have the original authentic Apostolic Church and doctrine"; this is a fair summary of the book's Prologue and Epilogue. And the Prologue, with its contemptuous allusion to "the recent apostasy or error and ignorant men", makes almost open reference to the pamphlet's main address. In writing the *Apostolic Tradition* Hippolytus the schismatic has in view chiefly the adherents of the contemporary legitimate Pope.

ii. St Hippolytus

We are not abundantly informed concerning this author's life. Since he was already publishing controversial works *c.* A.D. 195 we must suppose that he was born before A.D. 170, perhaps some ten or fifteen years before. He himself tells us that his birth took place "at about the same time" as that of Callistus,* the man with whom he afterwards disputed the throne of the Roman Church. The latter is traditionally described as *Romanus* "born in Rome", in Trastevere. He was a Christian slave born in the household (οἰκέτης) of Carpophorus,† a wealthy Christian freedman of the Emperor Marcus Aurelius. Hippolytus shows himself well acquainted with his rival's history in his early years. It has been suggested (by Döllinger) that he owed this knowledge to personal accounts from Carpophorus, but the story sheds so unpleasant a light on the character of Carpophorus himself that this seems on the whole improbable. Hippolytus may even mean to imply that he is writing from his own knowledge of the story he records.‡ We are entitled to infer from all we know that Hippolytus himself was also born in the City. It has been

---

* *Philosophumena*, ix. 11. 4.
† This man's epitaph is still extant. C.I.L. 13,040.
‡ "It seems good to us to recount the lovable life of this fellow, since he was born about the same time as ourselves", *Phil.* ix. 11. 4.

suggested also, though for this there is no evidence, that he too had originally some connection with that vast "Caesar's Household" which from the first furnished so many Christians to the Roman Church.*

The pupil—according to Photius†—of St Irenaeus, and his life-long admirer, Hippolytus rose to a position of some prominence as a theologian and controversialist at Rome in the time of Pope St Victor I (c. A.D. 189–197) by whom, almost certainly, he was ordained to the presbyterate. In the meanwhile Callistus was experiencing a very different fortune. A disastrous business speculation with funds provided by his master Carpophorus and a number of other Christians, followed by an attempted flight, brought upon him the terrible punishment of the treadmill from his infuriated master. When the protests of the Church at this unchristian harshness finally secured his release, Callistus tried to recover for Carpophorus some of the money lost in the unlucky venture. Some Jewish debtors with whom he was foolish enough to fall out in their own synagogue raised a disturbance, and covering him with blows haled him before Fuscianus the Prefect of the City, denouncing him as a Christian.‡ Carpophorus, fearing to lose his slave, went so far as to deny in evidence that Callistus was a Christian. But the prisoner himself must have admitted it, since Fuscianus ordered him to be scourged and sentenced him to penal servitude in the deadly Sardinian mines, which was at that time the usual sentence at Rome for those pleading guilty to a charge of Christianity. Hippolytus' account of the whole matter is evidently biased by malice, but even he does not deny that Callistus' sentence was incurred on the specific charge of Christianity, though he tries to burke the issue. It is clear that Callistus was in the strict sense a "Confessor for the faith".

---

* We find him towards later life in learned correspondence with princesses of the Imperial house. This might suggest some connection with the household, though as a writer of some eminence he might well have attracted the notice of the versatile and cultured Empress-Mother Mamaea (who with her daughters showed strong leanings towards Christianity) without any such connection.

† *Bibliotheca*, 121. The last known visit of Irenaeus to Rome was in A.D. 177. Hippolytus frequently quotes him.

‡ This fixes the date. Fuscianus was Prefect A.D. 188–193.

Some time later the Emperor Commodus* at the intercession of one of his concubines, the Christian Marcia, ordered a general release of all the Confessors detained in Sardinia. Hippolytus declares that Callistus' name was not included in the list of these which had been furnished by Pope Victor, but that he owed his freedom to the mistaken sympathy of the presbyter† bearing the rescript of release, who persuaded the commandant to include Callistus on his own authority. In view of the strictness of Roman prison administration and the fact that the officer might have to answer with his own life for the unauthorised release of a prisoner, this is, to say the least, a dubious story.‡ On Callistus' return to the City, Victor accorded him the usual small allowance with which the Church then honoured those Confessors who were in need, though Hippolytus declares that Victor "was much annoyed, but said nothing, being a compassionate man",§ and paid the pension to get Callistus out of the way. The latter retired to Antium, according to Hippolytus in order to steer clear of his old master Carpophorus. But again this seems the invention of malice. A sentence of penal servitude was a legal emancipation of a slave from his private owner, and upon his release by the state Callistus would have nothing to fear from Carpophorus. On the other hand the facts will well bear a very different interpretation. A prisoner from the Sardinian *metalla* was likely to return with his health completely shattered, and the payment of the pension indicates that Callistus was unfit to earn his own living. Antium, thirty-five miles South of Rome, was a health-resort in repute in this period,‖ and in sending him to live there and supporting him while doing so Victor would only be testifying to the esteem

---

* Died Dec. 31, A.D. 193.

† Dom Leclercq has suggested that this presbyter was Hippolytus himself, but Hippolytus gives his name as "Hyacinthus", *Phil.* ix. 12. 11.

‡ Had there been anything irregular about his release Callistus could not have ventured to return to Rome either then or later; nor could Zephyrinus afterwards have made him the legal property-holder of "the cemetery" for the Roman Church, as it would have been liable to confiscation if he could be proved a runaway convict.

§ This is not the usual estimate of Pope Victor, whose firmness with the Asiatic Churches in the Paschal controversy has generally brought upon him very different epithets. Either, as is very possible, Hippolytus is adding verisimilitude to his explanation of Victor's acceptance of Callistus, or Victor has been much misunderstood by historians.   ‖ Cf. Strabo, *Geography*, v. 3. 5, etc.

in which he held Callistus as a genuine Confessor. There Callistus remained until after the death of Victor (c. A.D. 197).

In the next pontificate, that of St Zephyrinus (A.D. 197–217), Callistus played a notable part. The new Pope brought him back from Antium and made him the Papal archdeacon.* He speedily became the most influential of Zephyrinus' advisers. As the deacons were, like the Pope, elected by the whole body of the Church, and the large majority of the laity later emphasised their approval of Callistus by electing him to succeed Zephyrinus, we may take this as the final vindication of his character by his Christian contemporaries against the posthumous scurrilities of Hippolytus' *Philosophumena*. Hippolytus, indeed, as he watched his own influence being eclipsed by that of the archdeacon, seems to have developed a consuming hatred of the man. The clash of temperaments as well as of doctrines and policies is plainly discernible beneath Hippolytus' rancorous account of the differences which ended in his schism.

Hippolytus' character is written in his own works. A wide rather than a deep or accurate scholar, an exegete and commentator rather than an original thinker, with a mind awake to theological difficulties but not sufficiently balanced or profound to contribute adequate solutions, proud of his own learning and bitterly resentful that his real gifts were not generally appreciated at his own valuation,† passionately sincere and high-minded in his own personal life, he was clearly narrow, obstinate and quite unsympathetic in his dealings with others. He seems to have alienated even his own supporters in his quarrel with the hierarchy by his rigour,‡ and no man with any sweetness in his nature could have written the odious account of Callistus'

* Callistus is never so described in so many words. But Hippolytus tells us that Zephyrinus "had him as his assistant in the management of the clergy...and set him over the cemetery" (*Phil.* ix. 12. 14). These are functions of the archdeacon of Rome.

† Cf. his complaint in his *Commentary on Daniel* iii. 16: "And so it is down to our own days that often when some man becomes worthy to receive a special grace from God and to be found more learned than his fellows, forthwith they all eye him askance and hate him, they persecute, insult, dishonour, calumniate him, drive him out—that thus they may themselves seem to be something, being naught." This work is generally ascribed to the period before the author's schism, but this is not the only passage suggesting a date after A.D. 215.

‡ *Phil.* ix. 12. 21.

sufferings as a slave, even if every word were true, which there is good reason to doubt.*

Of Callistus we have little information which does not come from the pen of his malignant enemy. But he seems to have been an ecclesiastic of a type not uncommon in the later history of the Curia. Of humble birth, with little learning himself and probably apt to be impatient of the speculations of minds with a greater intellectual curiosity than his own, he was content for his own part to abide unquestioningly by the traditional formulations of dogma. Yet in practical affairs he was clearly shrewd† and capable of originality in facing the needs of the time. His enemy makes it a fault in him that he was able and diplomatic with a gift for influencing and leading men. Above all he was—what Hippolytus certainly was not—most generously alive to the practical religious needs and difficulties of the plain man and the poor. He is chiefly associated in Church history with the "decree on Penance" which laid down that those who after baptism fell into sins of the flesh might hope after due penance and absolution to be restored to the Communion of the Church. It roused the vociferous wrath of two highly individualistic publicists of exceptionally austere personal character—Hippolytus and Tertullian—and his reputation has suffered something from their denunciations. Possibly it was an innovation in some ways; more probably it systematised a somewhat sporadic earlier practice. At the very least the idea was not unprecedented, as Hippolytus and others tried to make out.‡ If the Church was to be a leaven for the lump of the pagan

* The offence is worse if, as F. Legge has argued in the Introduction to his translation of the *Philosophumena*, that work as we have it is a republication of old material put together years after Callistus had died a martyr's death.

† Even the unfortunate business venture proves that. Carpophorus and the others would hardly have trusted him with a large sum of money had he not already shown some talent for affairs.

‡ It could claim Apostolic precedent from St Paul's treatment of the incestuous Corinthian. Apart from Hermas' teaching on penance, which stands somewhat apart, St Irenaeus, *Adv. Haer.* i. 13. 5 *sq.*, takes it for granted that a Christian married woman who had committed adultery could be restored to Communion after penance. Hippolytus' own prayer for the consecration of a bishop (*Ap. Trad.* iii. 6) recognises the bishop's power of absolution without restriction. The Montanists who objected to the episcopal absolution of carnal sins explicitly affirmed the Church's power to do so, but held it inexpedient, or else transferred the episcopal power in the matter to their own "prophets". At the same time there *was* another

Empire she could not adopt the outlook of a puritanical sect, nor had her Master's practice been such as to suggest that she should. Callistus' decree has been acted upon ever since not only by the lax and the sinful but by the Christian wisdom of the Saints in all ages. Christian history since the Apostolic age tends to show that it is to good men that the distance between penitence and untarnished human virtue is most plainly apparent. Saints, on the contrary, have tended to make less of such distinctions, being too blinded by the holiness of God not to see all men, themselves included, as almost equally in need of penance. Honour is due to the Pope who in the face of certain opposition from the zealots first formulated gentleness with sinners into the Church's rule.

Connected with the question of penance is the charge which Hippolytus brings against Callistus of conniving at irregular unions between free women and men of servile birth. Roman law refused to accord the status of *matrimonium* (full marriage) to any union a slave might form, whether the partner were free or servile. An exceedingly difficult position was created for the Church by the fact that thus a slave could not legally enter on an indissoluble marriage at all. However stable it might be in fact, it was always legally a *contubernium* (a recognised concubinage), terminable at the will of the owner. This degradation which society imposed upon the slave was a perpetual encouragement to moral laxity, and, so long as the social canker of slavery with its denial of the human dignity of the slave endured, the Church was perpetually harassed by the problem.

Callistus the ex-slave was well aware of the peculiar difficulties which surrounded the Christian slave, and in one direction at least he seems to have tried to vindicate in the eyes of the Church the full moral personality and responsibility of the slave, and his religious equality with the free man. Hippolytus tells us that "Callistus allowed women if they were unmarried and in the

tradition, represented by *e.g.* the Epistle to the Hebrews, which did refuse hope of absolution to post-baptismal mortal sin, and it was increasing in strength in certain circles. It crops up again in Novatianism, and doubtless derives from the same rigourist tendency that was producing Encratites, Montanists, etc. in such numbers everywhere in the Church at this time.

ı rime of life and desired someone unworthy of their own station...to take any bedfellow they pleased, slave or freedman, and reckon this rascal in the place of a husband, though not legally married to him".* From this hostile account it seems that all Callistus did was to extend to slave *men* the rule which Hippolytus himself sets down for slave *women*.† The law held that a slave girl was bound to serve her master's passions at his will, but denied her any status but that of concubine. The Church, on the contrary, unable to prevent the exercise of the master's legal rights, insisted on treating the slave-girl's concubinage (in which she was not a free agent), as full Christian marriage, provided that she herself treated it as such.‡ Callistus appears similarly to have allowed to unions between Christian women and their Christian slaves the full status of Christian marriage, with all its responsibilities and duties, though the civil law refused to recognise such unions as full legal marriages. That seems to be the whole extent of his innovation. Hippolytus preposterously accuses the Pope of "thus teaching adultery and murder at one stroke", because some of the women concerned— he implies all—made attempts at abortion. Probably he is thinking of some particular scandal, but even if such occurred, Callistus had not preached abortion, nor *ex hypothesi* were such unions adulterous. The experiment may not have been altogether successful. Such unions must always have tended to be unsatisfactorily lax and clandestine so far as society at large was concerned, however openly they were acknowledged to the Church. But Callistus' regulation had at least the merit of being conceived in the true Christian spirit of equality and of insisting on the slave's human and religious dignity and freedom. Hippolytus' account of the matter, on the contrary, breathes that contempt for slaves as a class which is one of the most painful characteristics of paganism.

Between two such men co-operation could not be easy. But though it is clear that personal antipathies had much to do

* *Phil.* ix. 12. 24. There is some textual uncertainty in this passage. The above follows Roeper's emendations.
† *Ap. Trad.* xvi. 23.
‡ Cf. *Ap. Trad.* xvi. 23.

with the quarrel, it is also certain that the theological differences alleged were not mere pretexts.

The great Christian crisis of the previous generation had been the confused series of Gnostic controversies, in which Christianity itself had very nearly foundered by disintegration. At the basis of every Gnostic system was the doctrine of a remote transcendent Godhead, more or less impersonal, from which proceeded a whole genealogy of Divine Emanations each somewhat less Divine than its immediate predecessor, until at length the God who created this world was reached, a God who was incompetent if not definitely evil. The orthodox reaction from these long trails of "Aeons", as they were called, took the form of a renewed insistence on the perfection and the *uniqueness* of God. All that is Divine is contained within the plenitude of the One perfect Divine Nature. Whatever is outside this is not God. This is the doctrine of the Divine "Monarchia"—so far as it goes good Christian teaching springing directly from the healthy root of Apostolic and Old Testament monotheism. But it is obvious that such teaching raises considerable problems around the Incarnation. It was common ground to all the orthodox that Jesus is God. What, then, is the relationship of the Incarnate to Transcendent Deity, and how was the relationship to be expressed?

One answer commonly returned at this time was that they were without qualification one and the same. This was taught with slight variations by a whole group of Roman theologians at this time, many of whom like Epigonus, Cleomenes and Praxeas seem to have come from Asia Minor.* On this view, within the single Divine "Monarchia" there can be no real distinctions of any kind. It was one and the same undifferentiated Godhead which created as "Father" in heaven, redeemed as "Son" on earth and indwelt the Church as "Spirit". Basing themselves on such texts as "I and the Father are one" and

---

* One reason for the popularity of this doctrine with orthodox Asiates in this period may have been the tendency to a wrong emphasis on the *separateness* of the Divine Persons visible in the Asiatic Montanist heresy with its doctrine of the Paraclete. There are actions and reactions of this sort between heresy and orthodoxy everywhere at this time.

"He that hath seen Me hath seen the Father", these Monarchians, as they are termed, insisted that words like "Father" and "Son" denoted only different assumed and external relations of the one undifferentiated Godhead *with men*, not real and eternal relationships *within the Divine Nature*, and as such had no ultimate truth or meaning. On this view it was possible to say not only that God had suffered on Calvary, but that the eternal Father of heaven Himself had been born and crucified and had died.

This was an impossibly sweeping reaction. Hippolytus was the chief contemporary teacher of another view which had been elaborated at Rome some fifty years before by St Justin Martyr, and which could claim wide acceptance in the Church ever since by men like St Theophilus of Antioch and Clement of Alexandria, and even (with reservations) by his own master St Irenaeus. This view made use of the Platonic philosophical doctrine of the *Logos*, which had long ago found a home in Hellenistic Judaism, and for which a scriptural basis could be found in the Prologue to the fourth Gospel. As taught by Hippolytus this theory admitted that the unique Divine Nature was capable of real distinctions within Itself. God had ever possessed within Himself His *Logos*, His Divine innate Wisdom or Word, as it were *latent* from all eternity. At a point in time determined by Himself* God "manifested" the Word to Himself and by the Word created all things. Thus the Word was truly God, within and of the One Divine Nature, but "Another" over against the Father, by Whom and from Whom He was manifested. But Hippolytus refused to apply to the Creative Word thus manifested the term "Son" in any proper sense, maintaining that to the "Word" the term "Son" was only applied allegorically or prophetically by God, and that the Word only strictly and really became "Son" by the Incarnation.†

* So Hippolytus, *Contra Noetum*, x. He did not necessarily mean exactly what he says here or realise all its consequences. As he puts it his doctrine is half way to Arianism on this point.

† *Contra Noetum*, iv, xv, etc. The same view appears in *Ap. Trad.* iv. 6. Cf. *Contra Noet.* xi: τὸ δὲ πᾶν Πατήρ, ἐξ οὖ δύναμις Λόγος. οὖτος δὲ νοῦς, ὃς προβὰς ἐν κόσμῳ ἐδείκνυτο παῖς θεοῦ.

This theology did a great deal more justice to both traditional Christianity and the evangelical facts than was attempted by the thoroughgoing Monarchians, but it suffered from several grave defects. It left no adequate place or justification for the Person of the Holy Ghost, and Hippolytus' working theology is patently "Binitarian", despite his frequent references to the Spirit.* The Word Itself in his teaching has something of the air of a mere Divine device for creating. It is hard to see in his Logos viewed *sub specie aeternitatis* anything more than an impersonal Divine attribute, for the completion of whose Personality the Incarnation was a radical necessity. When the later exponents of this theology set about remedying this indistinctness as to the Second and Third Persons, the only mode open to them of emphasising their Personal distinction from the Father was by insisting on their subordination and inferiority to Him, and the theory was thus fatally compromised. Along this line Hippolytus' theology led straight to extreme Arianism and Macedonianism, doctrines which actually denied the real Deity of the Son and Spirit altogether. At the best it could develop only into that theory of two or three *coordinate* Gods only nominally and abstractly united in a single Godhead which, in Egypt at least, was for a time adopted as orthodox by some of the opponents of Arius. It is a sufficient justification of Zephyrinus' and Callistus' attitude towards the teaching of Hippolytus that, though a clause summarising the Logos-theology was actually proposed for insertion into the oecumenical Creed at Nicea, the Council ultimately refused even to use the word Logos, scriptural though it is, as leading straight to Arianism and Ditheism.

The doctrine of Hippolytus was thus really as unsuccessful in

* Thus in the long explanation of *credenda* which closes the *Philosophumena* he never once mentions the Holy Ghost, though he goes into all sorts of minor topics like the sex of angels, until he suddenly introduces "in the Holy Spirit" in the doxology with which it closes. So, *Contra Noetum*, xiv, he deliberately refuses to apply the word "Person" to the Holy Ghost. In God there are "Two Persons and the third Distribution, the grace of the Holy Spirit". He constantly attributes to the Logos operations which later theology attributes to the Third Person. It is possible that he regarded the Holy Ghost as an *impersonal* effluence of Godhead. Cf. his doxologies in *Ap. Trad.*

its attempt to provide an intellectual reconciliation of the Incarnation with strict Monotheism as was, in a different way, the Monarchian theory to which it was opposed. Both ended by destroying the very Monotheism they sought to protect, the Logos-theory by impairing the unity of the Divine Nature Itself, the Monarchians with their passible Godhead by sacrificing the real Divinity of the Divine Nature to its Unity. But it was these two inadequate theologies, each by intention sincerely orthodox, but each in fact less than evangelically Christian, which were at grips in Rome during the Pontificate of Zephyrinus.

We have from Hippolytus a brief, biased and vivid account of the controversy.* Cleomenes and Sabellius† were the Monarchian leaders, Hippolytus himself the protagonist of the Logos-theology. He declares, however, that Callistus was the real leader of the Monarchians,‡ though cunningly professing himself in agreement now with one side now with the other, in order to retain the support and friendship of both. Hippolytus tops this with the statement that Zephyrinus was led to do the same only because he was bribed to do so by his own archdeacon, and that Sabellius himself was disposed to adopt the Logos-theory, from which he was prevented only by the machinations of the same evil genius. These are obviously the senseless imaginings of personal hatred. It is plain from Hippolytus' own statements that neither the Pope nor the archdeacon was a partisan. They were concerned only to preserve the traditional breadth of the faith to which neither of the rival schools was doing full justice. Both sides retained important (but not the same) essentials of the tradition, and with these wherever they were found Zephyrinus and Callistus could whole-heartedly agree.

* *Phil.* ix. 11. 1.
† This name, of ill-omen in later days, was still that of an accepted "teacher" of the Roman Church in the days of Zephyrinus, though he was excommunicated a few years later by his successor Callistus. Hippolytus speaks first of Cleomenes as the Monarchian leader, and then without explanation replaces him by Sabellius, Cleomenes disappearing thenceforward from his excited and disconnected narrative.
‡ He also accuses him of the exactly contradictory heresy of Adoptionism. *Phil.* ix. 12. 19.

Zephyrinus' final ruling, for which Hippolytus makes Callistus really responsible, was impartial enough. "Now Callistus bringing forward Zephyrinus persuaded him to say in plenary assembly (δημοσίᾳ), 'I know one God, Christ Jesus, and beside Him I know no other who was begotten and passible.' And again he said, 'The Father did not die but the Son.'" From these isolated fragments of what was evidently a balanced statement it is possible to recognise the effort of the Pope to safeguard on the one hand the wholehearted Monotheism of the primitive Church which the Logos-theology seriously endangered, and on the other to insist against the Monarchians that God, as God, cannot abdicate His Divinity. It was simply a restatement of scriptural *data* left without explanation because they were incapable of explanation by either of the currently proposed solutions. The Papal pronouncement settled nothing but the full scope of the problem to be solved.

It was a very Roman utterance. Now, as before and after, the Roman watchword was always *Quod traditum est*—the whole tradition and nothing else. The genius of the Roman Church was *religious*, not speculative. It sought always to confine its requirements simply to *credenda*, to the facts for belief, and so far as possible to leave the *explanations* of these, the theology, a very wide latitude. Its method was always to set complementary truths side by side with hardly a pretence of reconciliation, to declare that this *and* this is the faith, and that all metaphysical systematisation which cannot find full room for each of these facts is thereby ruled out as defective, and then to leave the matter at that. If the doctrines so established appear contradictory, that is the affair not of the hierarchy but of the theologians. But the latter must willy-nilly begin with the state of the question as the hierarchy propounds it, and must diminish nothing in the process of rationalising and explaining the Church's findings. It is the method not only of Zephyrinus with Hippolytus, but of Pope St Denys with his namesake of Alexandria, of Pope St Leo at Chalcedon, of Pope Agatho with Constantine V. It is a method which over and over again has rendered great service to Christendom by insisting on the correct posing of questions which Christian doctrines raise for the intelligence, and by preventing the final adoption of facile solutions which must afterwards have proved disastrous just because they missed the real point of the question at issue. But it is not a method which has ever been or is ever likely to be satisfying to metaphysicians in dispute.

Hippolytus informs us that on this occasion the Papal decision "maintained without ceasing the faction among the laity". But since he adds in the next sentence that "every one concurred—but we did not", it seems that Zephyrinus' pronouncement might well have secured peace in the Church but for the disastrous obstinacy of Hippolytus himself. There is in fact no evidence that the jangling of Doctors excited more sympathy among the laity then than it does now. Contemporary scholars like Tertullian and Clement, who were beginning to address themselves to the theological problems presented by the vague traditional Trinitarianism, are loud in their complaints of the lack of interest and even of the suspicious opposition of the great bulk of the laity.* The inevitable accident that so much of the flotsam and jetsam which is all that survives of early Christian writing is of *literary* origin—the product of the rival Christian "lecturers" of Rome—lends an adventitious importance to the endless disputes of διδάσκαλοι pictured in the writings of Justin and Rhodon and the rest. The humble Hermas probably speaks the mind of the average Roman layman when he grumbles at those "who praise themselves as having understanding and desire to be self-appointed 'teachers' (ἐθελοδιδάσκαλοι), senseless though they be. Owing then to this pride of heart many while they exalted themselves have been made empty."† Liturgy and rites and prayer, issuing in conduct—these are always the layman's religion. These things and the standards they imply are admittedly and necessarily intimately dependent on doctrine. But the plain man who believes and practises any given religion, who is indeed the strength and

---

* Tertullian, *Prax.* 3; Clement Al. *Strom.* i. 1. 18. 2; i. 9. 43. 1, etc.

† Hermas, *Sim.* ix. 22. The διδάσκαλοι of Rome were not officials of the Church, though recognised to some extent by the hierarchy.

raison d'être of all religion, is invariably blind to this dependence, and is usually much inclined to resent what little he hears of the activities of theologians. It is so now and it was so then. As Harnack puts it: "Hippolytus does not conceal the fact that the bishops had on their side the great bulk of the Roman community, but he rages about the hypocrisy, rancour and flattery of all concerned. Yet to-day we can see that the bishops were only desirous of protecting the unity and peace of their flock from the *rabies theologorum*. In this they were simply fulfilling the duty of their office."[*]

The Monarchians appear to have accepted the Papal decision, at least for the moment. Hippolytus alone, in his own phrase, "did not give way to him but refuted and withstood him for the truth's sake"—in other words, made a vigorous public attack before the whole Church on his own bishop's solemn dogmatic pronouncement. And then the archdeacon Callistus—unforgivably—put his finger on the fatal weakness of Hippolytus' theology with the cry "Ye are ditheists."[†] One can feel the public insult rankling years afterwards in the repeated quotations of the words in the *Philosophumena*.

After a public scene of this kind there could be no more place for the contumacious presbyter in Zephyrinus' council without some explicit acceptance of the Papal definition, and this such a man as Hippolytus was not likely to give in the circumstances. We have no exact evidence as to the date when this breach took place. But since St Jerome tells us[‡] that Hippolytus once preached in the presence of Origen when the latter came "desirous" as he himself put it "of visiting the most ancient Church of the Romans",[§] and as this visit can scarcely be placed earlier than A.D. 210, we may take it that Hippolytus was then still a presbyter in good standing, and that Zephyrinus' doctrinal pronouncement was made in the last years of his

[*] *Dogmengeschichte*, i. 740, n. 2.
[†] St Justin (*Dial.* 56) had incautiously said that the Logos is "another God". Hippolytus, *Contra Noetum*, xi, carefully guards himself against the charge: "And so there is set over against the Father 'Another' (ἕτερος). When I say 'Another' I do not say two Gods, but as light from light or water from a spring or a ray from the sun." He may well have been less cautious in his furious protests at the council.
[‡] *De Viris Illustr.* 61.   [§] *Ap.* Eusebius, *E.H.* vi. 14.

reign. From the contemptuous dislike with which Hippolytus everywhere speaks of this Pope it is clear that his real breach with the Church took place under that Pontificate. But he nowhere suggests that Zephyrinus had excommunicated him, nor does he ever directly question his right to be considered the lawful bishop. (It would indeed have been hard for him to do so.) In Hippolytus' eyes it was Callistus who first "set up a school against the Church" and Callistus' accession which inaugurated a schism. Though Hippolytus lays claim in the *Philosophumena* to be himself the lawful bishop of Rome, he is always entirely silent as to the occasion and circumstances of his own election and consecration, which in such a situation argues some considerable irregularity. It looks as though after refusing to accept Zephyrinus' dogmatic decision Hippolytus simply withdrew from the Church and sulked in isolation, without himself claiming to be head of the true Church or seeking episcopal consecration. Zephyrinus, who seems to have been far from an imperious character, may for his part have held his hand, trusting to time and the man's substantial orthodoxy to bring the obstinate presbyter to a better mind. Only at Zephyrinus' death, when he was faced with the virtual certainty that the detested archdeacon would succeed to the episcopal throne, does Hippolytus seem to have seized the occasion to have himself recognised as bishop by some faction of sympathisers. Doubtless he obtained consecration in some hole-and-corner way like Novatian thirty years later. If such clandestine proceedings actually anticipated the official electoral assembly of the Roman Church, a pedant like Hippolytus would feel amply justified in styling those who did not accept him "schismatics".

He himself speaks of the "multitudes" of Callistus' adherents and of his "teaching" being "spread throughout the whole world". Some of his own small following soon abandoned him for the "school of Callistus", dismayed by his fierce temper. It is clear that Hippolytus' claim to the Papacy was rejected both by the great majority of the Roman Church and by the Catholic world at large. So gifted a man could not fail to find some whom he could influence, but it is likely that they were only a handful of personal disciples and that his petty schism was negligible from the point of view of numbers by the successors of Zephyrinus. At least the memory of it furnished no precedents to either side in the great Roman schism a generation later. Every excommunicated διδάσκαλος at Rome carried out with him a group large or small which had frequented his lectures, and which continued to find its religious centre in his διδασκαλεῖον or lecture-hall, very much as it had done before its breach with the Church.* Such *ecclesiolae* generally lasted out the lifetime of their founders and often for longer. Some of them even had bishops of their own, like that group of excommunicated Adoptionists who for a while bribed the confessor Natalius with a small salary to act as their bishop, until he repented and flung himself at the feet of Zephyrinus imploring pardon.† The incident is significant. Hippolytus was not the first or only anti-Pope in Rome in his own lifetime, nor necessarily the most important in the eyes of contemporaries. It is doubtful whether there is a single mention outside his own works of the body he founded, and it is certain that it did not long survive him, if indeed he had any successors. In the next cen-

---

* The Roman system was very tolerant. Apparently any Christian arriving from any Church, even one already under censures in another Church, like Marcion, was allowed to open a lecture-room and there to teach with the authorisation of the Church the version of Christian doctrine he had received or elaborated for himself to such hearers as he could attract. These "lecture-rooms" were private ventures, hired and carried on by the lecturers themselves, who lived by the proceeds. Some of the teachers were clerics, others not. The hierarchy appears to have exercised very little in the way of censorship, and when one reflects on the number of early heresiarchs who were for years accepted "teachers" of the Roman Church, and on the fact that apparently most catechumens received almost all their preparation for baptism in these establishments, the drawbacks of the system become apparent. Only when a teacher had demonstrated beyond a doubt that his creed really did differ in essentials from that of the Roman Church did "the presbyters" expel him from Communion. This of course did not close his lecture-room and his disciples generally remained faithful to him for a time. It is possible that Hippolytus' sneer at Callistus as having opened a "διδασκαλεῖον against the Church" is a hit at the establishment of an official episcopal "catechetical school" at Rome in his time on the model of that which had flourished for more than a generation at Alexandria. Certainly the later third-century bishops appear to have exercised more control over the "teachers" than their predecessors. *Acta Justini*, 3 gives a curious glimpse of the way in which the rooms even of a "teacher" in full communion with the Church could become the focus of a little congregation almost in isolation from the main body of the faithful. We have to remember the immense difference which the lack of Church *buildings* made to the cohesion of the Church.

† Eusebius, *E.H.* v. 28.

tury the historian Eusebius (born within fifty years of his death) and scholars like St Jerome and Rufinus were very vague as to who Hippolytus was, and professed themselves quite unable to discover the name of his see, though they deduced from his writings that he had been a bishop.* His general orthodoxy secured the survival of a fair amount of his writings, and his interest for the history of theology has probably led modern scholars to attribute an exaggerated importance to the schism he formed.

How long this schism endured is not certainly known, but it is generally assumed that it lasted throughout the Pontificates of Callistus (A.D. 217–222), Urban I (222–230) and Pontian (230–235). Outside Hippolytus' own writings we have only three references to him which are of importance on this question.

(1) The first is a brief statement in the *Liberian Catalogue* of the Popes which Lightfoot has convincingly assigned† to an anonymous compiler writing in or very soon after A.D. 255. It is thus virtually the evidence of a contemporary. "At that time Pontian the Bishop and Hippolytus the Presbyter were banished and deported to the unhealthy island of Sardinia in the Consulship of Severus and Quintian [A.D. 235]. In that same island Pontian resigned on the 28th of September and in his place Antheros was ordained on the 21st of November‡ in the aforesaid Consulship." The anonymous author of this notice had made free use in his *Catalogue* of the *Chronica* of Hippolytus, and it is doubtless this which had prompted him to insert this little note of the author's fate.

(2) The second is an inscription erected by Pope St Damasus§ (A.D. 366–384) at the tomb of Hippolytus, by then greatly reverenced as a martyr by the Catholic Church in Rome. This records that "Hippolytus the *presbyter*" is said (*fertur*) to have been an adherent of the schism of Novatian, but when being led

* All the same, later Eastern writers like the editor of the *Canons of Hippolytus* style him "bishop of Rome".
† *Apostolic Fathers, Clement of Rome*, i. 262 (1890).
‡ The real date seems to have been Sunday, Nov. 22. Cf. Turner, *J.T.S.* xvii. 345.
§ Its text is conveniently accessible in Lightfoot's *Apostolic Fathers, Clement of Rome*, ii. 328, or in *D.A.C.L. s.v.* Hippolyte (Leclercq).

away to die in a season of persecution he exhorted his followers to return to the Catholic Church. He thus deserved to be reckoned a Catholic martyr. Damasus adds that he is only repeating the story as it had reached him and seems justifiably dubious of its truth. (*Haec audita refert Damasus, probat omnia Christus.*)

(3) Thirdly, there is a brief entry in the *Depositio Martyrum*, a sort of calendar of the Roman martyrs, compiled not later than A.D. 335 and probably going back to third-century sources. "On August 13th: (Commemoration) of Hippolytus in (the cemetery on the *Via*) *Tiburtina* and of Pontianus in (that) of Callistus."* A later authority, the *Liber Pontificalis*† (which, however, makes use of third- and fourth-century documents) records that Pope St Fabian (A.D. 236–250) accompanied by his clergy brought back the body of St Pontian in a ship from Sardinia and buried it in the cemetery of Callistus. This makes no reference to Hippolytus. Nevertheless the celebration of the *Depositio* of both Saints on the same day within a century of their deaths points to their simultaneous translation. The Emperor Maximin I, in whose persecution they suffered, was a fanatical anti-Christian; and since an Imperial rescript was necessary before the bodies of condemned criminals could be moved, the translation could scarcely have taken place in his reign. He died in A.D. 238, and the next five years saw six Emperors in Rome and continuous tumults and confusion. It is possible that it was only after the accession of Philip (A.D. 244), who if not—as Eusebius affirms—himself a Christian was at least very well disposed to the Church, that the bodies of Pontianus and Hippolytus were laid to rest at Rome.

The different places of burial accorded to the two Saints are in themselves significant. Pontian lay in the famous "Crypt of the Popes" in the cemetery that went by the name of Callistus, where already rested the bodies of his predecessors Zephyrinus and Urban and his successor the martyred Anteros. Their brief sepulchral inscriptions were discovered by de Rossi. (Callistus

---

* *Id. Aug. Ypolite in Tiburtina et Pontiani in Calisti.*
† Ed. Duchesne, i. 146.

himself, though the whole cemetery bore his name and he had
been its organiser and first administrator,* by force of circumstances had been buried elsewhere. Having been martyred,
apparently, in a popular tumult in Trastevere and not by process
of law, his body had perforce been hurriedly taken to the
nearest Christian burial-ground, the cemetery of Calepodius on
the other side of Rome, the Christians not daring to carry it
through the City to lay it beside that of Zephyrinus.) We
possess the customary epitaph which the Church set over its
martyred bishop, "Pontianus, Bishop, Martyr", and even in
this brief inscription the monogram for "Martyr" seems to be
a later addition. Upon the doorway of the Papal crypt some
third-century hand has scratched the prayer, ∈N Θ∈ω Μ∈ΤΑ
ΠΑΝΤω(ν ἐπισκόπων?) ΠΟΝΤΙΑΝ∈ ΖΗϹΗϹ, "Pontian, dwell in God with
all the (Bishops?)."

Hippolytus was buried away from the Papal cemetery in the
Ager Veranus, a piece of ground beside the road to Tibur which
may well once have been his own property. The presence of his
relics here later gave rise to a sanctuary which was the centre
of a considerable cultus. Here in the sixteenth century was
found the headless statue which depicts him as throned and
teaching (*i.e.* as a *bishop*). On the chair in which he is seated is
inscribed a list of some of his works, including the *Apostolic*

---

* *Philos.* ix. 12. 14. The earlier Christian burial-grounds of Rome had been the
private property of prominent Christian families who permitted other Christians to
use them. "*The* cemetery" (a new term, κοιμητήριον) was the property of the Church
as a corporate body, which appears to have come into the Church's possession early
in the reign of Zephyrinus. It involved the registration of the Church (under some
harmless designation like the *Cultores Verbi*, which was used in similar cases elsewhere) as a "burial club" in the registers of the Prefecture of the City; its property
would have to be entered there in the names of a *gerens* and an *actor syndicus* who
would be legally responsible for its proper administration. The former could only be
the bishop, Zephyrinus; the archdeacon, as the officer customarily charged with the
Church's common funds, was naturally the latter. There are indications that it was
sometimes called "the cemetery of Zephyrinus" (he is said in the *Lib. Pont.* to have
been buried first *in coemeterio suo*). The earlier burial-grounds, known as *praedia*,
were named after their original Christian owners, like those of Domitilla, Priscilla,
etc. This custom evidently nearly carried the day here also. The later third-century
cemeteries were named after the first prominent martyr buried there, like the
cemeteries of Calepodius or Hippolytus. But in popular speech what was for some
years evidently called "*the* cemetery" remained associated with the name of Callistus,
though he was neither its legal owner nor was buried there. Probably the energy
and care with which he had organised and administered it as archdeacon had
unconsciously impressed the mind of the Church.

Tradition, together with a sort of perpetual calendar which he had compiled for calculating the correct date of the annual Paschal feasts, beginning with the year A.D. 222. But the computation is seriously faulty and its practical use would have had to be abandoned before many years were past. The list of his works also does not appear to have contained some of his later writings like the *Philosophumena*. We may therefore safely take it that it was made in his own lifetime and before the Paschal *computus* had been proved defective. It may once have adorned Hippolytus' own lecture-hall.* It seems virtually certain that the crypt in the cemetery of Hippolytus was first arranged by the remnants of his supporters and not by the Catholics. The burial apart from the common cemetery in ground not previously used for Christian burials is significant in itself. And the statue with its implied claim that he was a bishop and its boast of works like the *Apostolic Tradition* which attacked the Catholic bishop would hardly have been tolerated by the Catholics. We have, too, to remember the unparalleled nature of the reverence this statue implies. So far as we know no other early Roman Christian however eminent was ever so honoured. One has only to compare it with the little marble slabs set over the martyred Pontianus and Anteros for the difference to leap to the mind. This is the veneration of a sect for its founder, not the charity of the Church for a rebel who made a tardy repentance.

Yet there is the indubitable fact that as early as A.D. 255 the Liberian editor reckons him a Catholic martyr, and he was obviously in a position to know the truth. The deliberate qualification of him as "presbyter" marks a denial of his claim to the episcopate.† One or two dubious instances can be quoted in

---

* In the fourth century a house in the *Vicus Patricius* was already traditionally connected with Hippolytus in some way. This may have been the site of his διδασκαλεῖον.

† Dr Easton concludes (*Ap. Trad.* p. 24) that "the reunited factions completed the reconciliation by pronouncing both bishops to be Saints and Martyrs". *No* Roman writer ever calls Hippolytus anything but "*presbyter*", down to Gelasius (492–496) who calls him Bishop of Bostra in Arabia, through a misunderstanding of Eusebius *E.H.* vi. 20. The first document to connect him with the bishopric of Portus at the mouth of the Tiber is the seventh-century (Eastern) *Chronicon Paschale*. The long train of hagiological confusions upon which the alleged connection with

which martyrs who died outside the communion of the Church were subsequently honoured as martyrs by the Catholics,* but none, I think, where the facts can have been so notorious as they must have been in this case to the Liberian chronographer. As a rule the Church was fierce in her refusal to acknowledge them, as on that pathetic occasion at Apamea in this period when the Catholic martyrs turned their backs on their Montanist fellows at the supreme moment of their own passion, that they might not seem even in death to consent with their witness.†

The particular form in which St Damasus reports Hippolytus' reconciliation is historically impossible. Though he was indeed of the *farouche* stuff of which Novatians were made, Hippolytus must have been dead for more than ten years before that unpitying sect was founded. Nevertheless it is likely that the popular tradition which Damasus records does give us a substantial hint of the true facts. Evidently the fact of Hippolytus' schism still lingered in tradition, even though no separate memory remained of the body he had founded (another indication that it was unimportant and short-lived). It had already been confused with the much more imposing and tenacious schism of Novatian nearly a generation later. Possibly he remnants of the Hippolytean Church lingered on at Rome until they were absorbed by the very similar rigourists of Novatianism. After all, the original grounds of the quarrel were

Portus rests was partly cleared up by Lightfoot (*Apostolic Fathers, Clement of Rome,* ii. 370 *sq.*), though he unfortunately continued to subscribe to their erroneous result that Hippolytus did not claim to be bishop of Rome itself, but was really a sort of missionary bishop of Portus. The muddles of the hagiographers have been finally dissipated by the Bollandist H. Delehaye S.J. (*Analecta Bollandiana,* li. 58 *sq.*). It is to be hoped that the legend of Hippolytus' bishopric of Portus, where the modern cathedral has been dedicated to him, will now disappear. Those deplorable documents the seventh- and eighth-century Roman *Passionals* have further complicated matters by making Hippolytus into a soldier, the converted warder of St Lawrence the deacon, who was not martyred till some fifteen years after Hippolytus' own death. In this curious disguise Hippolytus still appears in the lesson of the Secular Breviary for his ancient feast on August 13th. The old commemoration of Pontian on the same day has disappeared, the anti-Pope thus very strangely surviving the Pope in the Roman liturgy!

* *E.g.* the African martyrs of Madaura supposed to have been second-century Catholics have been reasonably suspected of being in reality fourth-century Donatists. Cf. J. H. Baxter, *J.T.S.* xxvi. 21.

† Eusebius, *E.H.* v. 16. 22.

very largely personal, and Callistus had already been dead some
thirteen years when Hippolytus was hurried off to his sentence
of hard labour. This was certain to prove quickly fatal to an old
man, if his end was not hastened by deliberate brutalities, as
his fellow-exile Pontian is said to have died in Sardinia after
being "beaten with clubs".* In the absence of any possible
means of ensuring an episcopal succession for his little flock,
Hippolytus might well have advised a return to the Catholic
Church in the hour of imminent persecution. Or it may be that
in the loneliness of exile the old quarrels and their bitter sequel
stood revealed in all their futility to the dying anti-Pope. His
earlier works abound in references to the unity and uniqueness
of the Catholic Church. "In one house must the Paschal Lamb
be eaten and thou shalt not bear its flesh without the house.
For one is the assembly ($\sigma\upsilon\nu\alpha\gamma\omega\gamma\acute{\eta}$), one the household; that is
the one Church in which the holy Body of Christ is eaten. And
therefore that Flesh shall not be borne outside the one house of
the Church. He that eateth of it outside shall be chastised as
impious and a thief."† How could he alone with his handful of
followers, rejected as well by the City as by the world, con-
stitute the one household of the whole Church of Christ? If the
exiled Pontianus could resign his claims that the Roman Church
might be free at once to choose a new pastor who might lead
her through the storm already raging, Hippolytus too could
resign his doubtful throne that the old sore might be healed.
He nowhere implies that he himself was ever excommunicated,
but rather that he had plunged off into separation of his own
accord and excommunicated Callistus. With his own abdication
the road to unity was open. And with a wise charity the Roman
Church chose to remember him only as he was before his fall—
as "Hippolytus the Presbyter" who in the end died a martyr
for the faith.

---

* In the *Liber Pontificalis*. Possibly this was simply the action of the warders
driving the old convict to work a little harder.

† Hippolytus, Περὶ τοῦ Πάσχα, vi. 4. This important work by Hippolytus, supposed lost, has actually been in print for centuries among the *Spuria* of St Chrysostom (ed. Paris, 1836, vii. 933 *sqq.*). [Crit. ed. P. Nautin, *Homélies Pascales* i, 1950,
p. 163: he thinks the sermon dependent on, not by, Hippolytus.]

That there was some sort of reconciliation seems certain from the entry in the *Liberian Catalogue*. But it does not follow that his adherents fully accepted his rehabilitation in the Church, accompanied as it was by the virtual denial of his status as a bishop. At least when his body was returned to his legal heirs by order of the government they buried him as a bishop and apart from the Catholic dead.

There is just one scrap of later evidence which might suggest the continued existence of his sect. Eusebius reports among the letters of St Denys of Alexandria "a *diaconic* epistle" of his "to those in Rome through Hippolytus. To the same people he composed another On Peace, and likewise On Repentance, and yet another to the Confessors there while they still agreed with the opinion of Novatus."* Scholars have spent their conjectures in vain to suggest what manner of document a "diaconic epistle" might be.† If for ἐπιστολὴ διακονικὴ διὰ Ἱππολύτου we might read ἐπιστολὴ δικανικὴ διὰ Ἱππόλυτον, "an epistle giving his judgment on account of Hippolytus" we might find here a trace of the continuance of the schism. Those "to the same people 'On Peace' and 'On Repentance'" would be appropriate enough to a body whose founder had organised a sect out of a personal quarrel and attacked Callistus' decree on Penance. These evidently formed part of a collection written by St Denys in the hope of reuniting the Roman Church torn by the schism of Novatian after A.D. 251. If this emendation be thought gratuitous we have no evidence whatever that Hippolytus' schism continued beyond his own lifetime, or even that he had not already been reconciled to the Church when he was exiled in A.D. 235.

That he soon died a victim of his sufferings in the Sardinian

---

* Eusebius, *E.H.* vi. 46. 5: καὶ ἑτέρα τις ἐπιστολὴ τοῖς ἐν Ῥώμῃ τοῦ Διονυσίου φέρεται διακονικὴ διὰ Ἱππολύτου. τοῖς αὐτοῖς δὲ ἄλλην περὶ εἰρήνης διατυποῦται καὶ ὡσαύτως περὶ μετανοίας, καὶ αὖ πάλιν ἄλλην τοῖς ἐκεῖσε ὁμολογηταῖς ἔτι τῇ τοῦ Νοουάτου συμφερομένοις γνώμῃ.

† Benson's rendering, "a serviceable letter", is not open to objection; but this would tell us nothing about the contents of the letter, whereas all these brief notes of Eusebius are meant to do so. "Through Hippolytus" is generally taken to mean that some otherwise unknown Hippolytus was the bearer. It seems an odd way of putting it. I cannot help suspecting that this "Hippolytus" introduced without explanation has some connection with the anti-Pope previously mentioned.

convict-station, where the youthful Callistus had been a Confessor nearly fifty years before, may be taken as certain. Whether he is rightly to be reckoned a Roman bishop or a Roman presbyter, Hippolytus was unquestionably a Roman martyr.

iii. Date of the *Apostolic Tradition*

It seems now to be generally assumed that the *Apostolic Tradition* is a manifesto against Callistus published soon after his accession in A.D. 217. But there are a number of indications that it really belongs to the closing years of Zephyrinus.

(1) Hippolytus explicitly charges Zephyrinus with being "an ignorant man and unlettered and *unversed in the ecclesiastical ordinances*".* He brings no such charge against Callistus, much as he disliked his theology, but grudgingly admits that the "school" of Callistus did "keep the customs and the tradition"† (*i.e.* much as he kept them himself). The *Apostolic Tradition* is written because "the Holy Ghost bestows on those who believe correctly the fulness of grace that they may know how those who are at the head of the Church should teach and maintain the tradition in all things" (i. 5). Hippolytus in this work nowhere claims (as he very grandiloquently does claim in the *Philosophumena* written in or after the reign of Callistus) himself to exercise the responsibilities of the episcopate. On the contrary, this passage of the *Apostolic Tradition* suggests that he is *not* himself "at the head of the Church", but is proposing to correct *someone else who is* by the light of the superior knowledge and inspiration which are the reward of his own superior orthodoxy. Such a claim accords remarkably well with the position he took up under Zephyrinus, but not at all with that which he took up under Callistus.

(2) *Apostolic Tradition*, ix. 2 *sq.* contains what may fairly be called an attack on deacons under cover of an outline of their duties, and a corresponding exaltation of presbyters. It is hard

---

* ἄνδρα ἰδιώτην καὶ ἀγράμματον καὶ ἄπειρον τῶν ἐκκλησιαστικῶν ὅρων, *Phil.* ix. 11. 1.
† φύλασσον τὰ ἔθη καὶ τὴν παράδοσιν, *Phil.* ix. 12. 26.

to resist the conclusion that the activities of Callistus the arch-deacon were in the mind of Hippolytus the presbyter when he wrote that "the deacon is *not* the counsellor of the whole clergy ...and is not appointed to receive the spirit of greatness in which the presbyters share".

(3) *Apostolic Tradition*, xxxiv contains a hint that the ad-ministration of "*the* cemetery" leaves something to be desired. The possession of a common burial-ground by the Christians for the use of "all the poor" was a novelty in this period and Callistus was its first administrator. As late as the writing of the *Philosophumena* "*the* cemetery" needs no further identifica-tion. It is the one of which Callistus the archdeacon was once in charge and, it seems likely, was still in charge when this was written.

(4) Had Callistus' decree on penance already appeared, it is hard to believe that the prayer specifying the bishop's "au-thority to forgive sins according to Thy command" (iii. 5) would have been left just as it is. There is indeed a singular absence throughout the work of reference to the innovations with which the *Philosophumena* charges Callistus. The *Liber Pontificalis* assigns to Callistus the institution of the fasts of the Saturday Ember days,* and Tertullian (*De Jejuniis*, xiv) also glances at it as an innovation of the Catholics in this period. In his *Com-mentary on Daniel* (iv. 20) Hippolytus violently attacks "the ignorant and light-minded men" who "following human traditions" have begun to observe Saturday fast-days "which Christ never commanded, that they may show their contempt for the Gospel". Yet in the *Apostolic Tradition* (xxv) he simply sets down the old Roman rule of fasting as we find it in operation in Hermas† and as Tertullian‡ also testifies that it stood in his day, with no suggestion that attempts were now being made to elaborate on it.

The only indication one can see that Callistus may be the bishop for whose improvement the *Apostolic Tradition* was designed is the regulation (xvi. 24b) forbidding free *women* as

---

* In this period three, not four, Ember Seasons.
† *Sim.* v.   ‡ *De Jejuniis*, ii, xiii.

well as free men to take slave-concubines, which might have reference to Callistus' innovation already discussed. But (1) the genuineness of this regulation is at the best doubtful, being found only in one version against six which omit it. (2) Callistus' practice is said to have been contrary to that of previous Popes. If xvi. 24b be genuine it may be simply representative of the normal discipline of Zephyrinus' time, with no idea of reprobating a breach of it which had not yet occurred.

On these grounds a date towards the end of the reign of Zephyrinus rather than early in that of Callistus seems probable. It was written within a year or two either way of A.D. 215, in any case. The only importance of the point is this: If Hippolytus was not yet at the head of a sect whose practices he might regulate at his own pleasure, his evidence is all the more likely to represent faithfully the practice of the contemporary Catholic Church in Rome, or even that of a period twenty or thirty years earlier under Eleutherus and Victor. This is a question which needs further consideration.

iv. The Representative Value of the Evidence of the *Apostolic Tradition*

The history of its author must needs raise serious questions about the contents of his treatise. How far can we be certain that the usages it describes represent more than the preferences, perhaps exceptional and perverse, of a schismatic individualist? How far back does the "Tradition" go, and to what extent does it represent what was normal in the Great Church in the second century?

A complete answer to these doubts can only be given by minute comparison of Hippolytus' regulations with the whole *corpus* of scattered and allusive information given us by other, and particularly by earlier, Christian writers. Such a comparison I hope to attempt in another volume. It can, I think, be now said with certainty that the result of such a comparison will be to justify a high degree of confidence in the evidence of Hippolytus.

The usages he describes have a surprising number of contacts with those referred to by other early writers. But there are also certain general considerations which reinforce Hippolytus' credit.

(1) Besides what I will venture to call the probability that when the book was written Hippolytus was still formally a presbyter of the Roman Church—albeit an exceedingly loosely attached one—we must bear in mind the circumstances of the book's publication. He is openly attacking what he considers the innovating tendencies of those with whom he is at logger-heads on other grounds by making a public appeal to the past. In the circumstances it is of the very essence of his case that he should, for the most part at least, be really doing what he says he is doing, setting down genuine old Roman customs and rules of which the memory of Roman Christians then "went not back to the contrary".

(2) Hippolytus' other writings reveal him as a writer careless and inaccurate to a degree in his use of evidence, but not, I think, given to deliberate invention. Even in the deplorable account of Zephyrinus and Callistus, in which his own passions were engaged to the utmost, it is doubtful if the statements of *fact* which he makes can be convicted of sheer falsity. What he has done there is to imagine *motives* for which there seems to be little if any justification. But he has not falsified facts. On the contrary he has set them down, even when they go far to dis-prove the motives to which he attributes them. He is entirely capable of exaggeration and one-sided statements whenever the spur of controversy pricks him to vehemence. Few ancient authors were not. But it is psychologically untrue that such a man as Hippolytus reveals himself to have been would have been capable of writing what he knew to be entirely without foundation.

(3) We can trace in later Roman liturgy and in later Roman writers the gradual modification of much which Hippolytus reports. The later Roman rite *e.g.* of baptism was clearly originally based on something in outline and content very like *Ap. Trad.* xx–xxiii. Either the Roman rites were at some point

deliberately adapted to the *Apostolic Tradition*,* which is highly improbable; or else they and Hippolytus are independent witnesses to early Roman usage. It is noticeable that the out-lines of the same baptismal rite are clearly represented also in the Valentinian Gnostic writers excerpted by Clement of Alexandria.† This evidence is older by a generation, at least, than the *Apostolic Tradition*. If there has been borrowing at all it is on the side of Hippolytus. No one who has read the trouncing which Hippolytus accords the Valentinians in the *Philosophumena*, including the statement that Valentinus was a Pythagorean and not a Christian at all,‡ will suspect Hippolytus himself of being the borrower; and before him we are actually back in the very generation of Popes and presbyters at Rome who had witnessed the excommunication of Valentinus. We have to remember that Valentinus had been for years a venerated "teacher" of the Roman Church, and is even said to have been the narrowly defeated second candidate at a Papal election.§ It is far more likely that Valentinus carefully retained in use for his own followers the rites already ancient at which he had so often assisted as a loyal son of the Roman Church than that there was once a direct borrowing of Gnostic rites by the most conservative and traditionalist Church in Christendom. Hip-polytus, as we have noted, grudgingly admits that the "Callis-tians" faithfully preserved "the customs and the tradition" (*i.e.* as he himself practised them). We may safely take it that in outline and essentials the rites and customs to which the

---

* The Blessing of Chrism on Maundy Thursday in the Gelasian Sacramentary (of which that in the current Pontifical is only a verbal modification) contains reminiscences of phrases found in *Ap. Trad.* v and vi. They may be directly imitated from Hippolytus, or they may be independent survivals of a *traditional* prayer incorporated by Hippolytus (not literary borrowings from that document). The blessing of milk and honey and water at the Baptismal Mass of the Vigil of Pentecost in the Leonine Sacramentary also contains reminiscences of *Ap. Trad.* xxiii. Here Hippolytus does not give a model prayer, but makes certain comments on the rite. And it is noticeable that it is just what is most obviously his own in the comments, the identification of the milk and honey with the "*Flesh of Christ*" and of the water with "the laver" which does *not* reappear in the later prayer. In both cases my own feeling is that the Sacramentaries have not *borrowed* from Hippolytus, but that he and they independently reproduce the same enduring liturgical tradition.

† *Excerpta ex Theodoto*, 77 *sqq.* They require some piecing together with other information.

‡ *Phil.* vi. 21 *sq.*   § Tertullian, *Adv. Valent.* 4.

Apostolic Tradition bears witness were those practised in the Roman Church in his own day, and in his own youth *c.* A.D. 180. And it is also safe to say that this Roman tradition was, *mutatis mutandis*, typical of the practice of the Great Church everywhere in the second century.*

(4) In estimating the age of the tradition here represented we have to weigh not only Hippolytus' explicit claim that this *was* the unquestioned way of doing things at Rome time out of mind but the occasional confirmations of writers like St Justin, and the character and form of the rites themselves. His whole initiation rite is recognisably derived from the initiation of *Jewish* proselytes. His baptismal rite is derived directly from the baptismal rite for Jewish proselytes. His confirmation rite, "the sealing",† plays in Christian initiation precisely that part which *Circumcision* "the seal of the covenant" played in the initiation of a Jewish proselyte.‡ Lastly the Jewish proselyte was strictly obliged forthwith to provide his first sacrifice. So Hippolytus requires that every Christian neophyte shall bring with him to baptism his own personal προσφορά (oblation of bread and wine) to be offered forthwith at the Baptismal Mass.§ The parallel is even closer than this would imply. It extends down to rubrical details of the two initiation rites.

Similarly Hippolytus' Canon is, so far as form goes, modelled strictly on those old Jewish "eucharistic" prayers of which many examples are to be found in the Old Testament, *e.g.* those ascribed to Solomon (ii Chron. vi. 4), Ezra (Neh. ix. 5 *sq.*‖), Judas the Maccabee (i Macc. iv. 30) and others. The outline of such prayers is always the same—a series of thanksgivings, often in the form of blessings of God, for outstanding mercies in the

* Variations in practice were beginning to cause trouble in the later second century, chiefly the day of the observance of the *Pascha*. But the variations which we can trace are all variants of the *same* practices, not entirely different traditions, so far as the Great Church is concerned.
† Cf. *Theology Occasional Papers*, No. 5. "Confirmation or Laying on of Hands?"
‡ There was a difference between Palestinian and Hellenistic Judaism on this. In Palestinian Judaism, Circumcision was first administered and then the Baptism; in the Diaspora the Baptism sometimes preceded Circumcision. In exactly the same way the *Syrian* Church down to *c.* A.D. 650 administered "the seal" of Confirmation *before* Baptism (cf. Connolly, *Homilies of Narsai*, p. xlii *sq.*), other Churches *after*.
§ *Ap. Trad.* xx. 10.　　　　　‖ Cf. esp. the LXX.

past which bear upon and *justify* certain petitions appended, generally with the formula "Now, therefore".* In Hippolytus the items of this thanksgiving are four, for the action of the Word of God in Creation, in the Incarnation, in the Passion, at the Last Supper—in that order. It is important to note that of over sixty early liturgies, *one* only, that of Sarapion, has not this arrangement.† The others all arrange the thanksgiving under these four heads, and all in that order, with the Last Supper out of its historical place, *after* the Passion.‡ Even the Edessan rite of "Addai and Mari", which does not contain the actual Words of Institution, refers at the correct point to "having received the example which is from Thee delivered unto us".§ "Addai and Mari" and certain other rites like the Ethiopic so-called "Anaphora of St Gregory of Armenia" (which is Egyptian in origin) are indisputably free from all influence of Hippolytus' rite. Nor, indeed, was he the inventor of this outline of the thanksgiving. The same four items are noted half a century before him by St Justin Martyr as the theme of the bishop's Eucharist.‖ It was not, then, that the influence of Hippolytus upon the subsequent practice of Christendom was all-embracing. Personally I believe it to have been very small, though writers who merit the greatest deference have thought otherwise.¶ It is simply that he is the first writer to present us with the complete type of the universal primitive rite of Christendom as it remained at the end of the second century. And this primitive rite is *Jewish* through and through, Jewish in form and feeling, saturated in Paschal conceptions, transcended and Christianised, but recognisably Jewish all the same.

The remainder of Hippolytus' outline of worship is equally

---

* This is the μεμνημένοι τοίνυν of Hippolytus, the *Te Igitur* of the Roman Canon, etc.

† The Roman Canon, of course, has not, but that is known to have undergone "dislocation". It retains traces only of the primitive arrangement.

‡ The reason is that the Last Supper and the Institution is the supreme *Justification* for the communion petitions about to follow. In this sense, and only in this sense, it is the primitive "moment of consecration".

§ To recover the ancient form of "Addai and Mari" the intercessions and secret prayers within the anaphora must be removed. What is left is a "eucharistia" of normal type but addressed *to the Son*.

‖ *Dialogue*, 41.

¶ Lietzmann, Easton, Frere, Cagin, to name but a few.

Judaic. The blessings of objects still take the form of a blessing *of God* over the object (*e.g.* the prayer for blessing first-fruits, xxviii) and not of the thing itself. The regulations for the Agape, xxvi, are very Jewish. Even down to the direction to wash the hands before prayer after sleep (for which rite the Rabbis provided a special ejaculatory "benediction"), there is scarcely one element in the cultus as described by Hippolytus for which clear Jewish parallels cannot be found.

Yet it appears from other writers that the Jewish origin of much in second-century Church Order had been practically lost sight of by the time the *Apostolic Tradition* came to be written. Hippolytus himself had nothing but contempt for "the People" and their dumb observances. Nor are these Judaic elements obviously developed from Old Testament scripture. They compare for the most part better with the later Jewish pieties of the home, the Synagogue and the *Beth-ha-midrash* than with the earlier Judaism of the Old Testament. Once the temper represented by the *Epistle of Barnabas* and parts of Aristides' *Apology* had got the upper hand in the Church, the direct borrowing of these things from the Synagogue is very difficult to contemplate. They have, too, as they stand in Hippolytus, in many things been radically Christianised, even though their derivation is still plain, which speaks of long Christian usage. They must be legacies from the period when most of the Christian leaders were still Jews by birth and upbringing and habit of mind, who unquestioningly carried over into their new faith all which did not seem directly superseded in the Church Order and practice of piety of the old Israel of God. This period was virtually ended by about A.D. 100.

After this the breach with the Synagogue and the pressure of the Hellenistic atmosphere made of Christianity more and more a religion for Gentile converts, not for Jews. The *thought* of Christians like Ignatius or Aristides or Justin or Athenagoras is cast in a Gentile, Hellenistic mould. Yet the real Hellenisers, men like Marcion and the Gnostics, eventually found the Church uninhabitable because even the strongly Gentile Christianity of the Great Church did steadily retain an incurably Judaic side to its soul, as Marcion quite truly asserted. The Church was founded not only on the Hellenist Paul of Tarsus, who in some things was a rebel against his own Jewish past, but on him whom Paul called by his Aramaic name of Cephas and on all the Apostles—men of whom it was foretold that they should be "*put* out of the Synagogues", and who through their very reluctance to depart formed the strong link between the old and new Peoples of God. The fact that this Judaic element persisted so much more strongly in the Church's liturgy and devotional practice than in its literature and quasi-philosophical theology is only a proof of its potency. From the point of view of the historian it cannot be too vigorously insisted on that it is liturgy and devotion which are the really formative element in the religion and "culture" (in the sense of the whole system of accepted ethics and unquestioned assumptions and instinctive mental attitudes) of the immense dumb but praying multitudes which form the strength of Christendom in every age.

Hippolytus reveals clearly for the first time how firmly the Jewish liturgical basis persisted in the Catholic cultus after a century and a half of Gentile Christianity. That is a fact—not yet adequately appreciated—which must have great weight in such questions as the alleged influence of Hellenistic Mysteries on primitive Christianity. And it reveals, too, something of the immense importance of παράδοσις, "tradition", in the formation of the Christian *spirit*. "Tradition" for the early Church, as Hippolytus' title indicates, meant much more than the mere process of instruction or "handing on".* It stood for the whole Christian *via vitae*, belief, ethics, worship, "the Way", the established and received Christian *life*. In an age when the "Apostolic" documents of the New Testament were only slowly making good their position as an authoritative Canon beside the old Jewish scriptures,† the importance of the Christian "tradi-

---

* Originally (in the N.T.) it means any *Christian* teaching, as opposed to γραφή, scripture, which means *only* the *Jewish* scriptures of the O.T. The phrase "Scripture and Tradition" comes from the earliest age of the Church, and means "the *whole* of Revelation". It has no idea of "oral" as against "written".

† They were of course in circulation, but they really make good their position as an *exclusive* doctrinal fount and standard only with their canonisation, completed in essentials c. A.D. 175–200.

tion" was incalculable in preventing the distortion of authentic "Apostolic" Christianity into a mere theosophy by Hellenistic influences. The appearance of these Jewish features in the *Apostolic Tradition* is in itself some justification for styling its tradition "Apostolic". They do bring us at second hand into contact with the Church Order and devotional practice of the Apostolic age itself.

This is not to say that every phrase of Hippolytus can be taken at once as likely to be endorsed by the whole of the second-century Great Church. He writes as a controversialist and a vigorous one. Some passages have a clear polemical intention. The actual phrasing of the prayers, though not their purport and outline, is manifestly his own composition, and in the anaphora at least is designedly an expression of his own anti-Monarchian theology. It was still the recognised privilege of the celebrant to clothe with his own wording the fixed outlines of the rite already traditional. We can watch Hippolytus at work on his material, adapting and supplementing a little here and there with his own comments, perhaps in one or two cases misunderstanding the origin and intention of the practices already ancient which he describes. But making all due allowance for these cases, there remains a much larger part of the contents, some of it supported by allusions in other writers, of which we can safely say that his material comes to him rather than from him. It represents the mind and practice not of St Hippolytus only but of the whole Catholic Church of the second century. As such it is of outstanding importance.

v. The Influence of the *Apostolic Tradition*

The subsequent history of this little occasional pamphlet with its personal references and strictly contemporary and local allusions is curious in the extreme. There is no certain trace of its influence or indeed of its existence in the rest of the third century. Dom Connolly has suggested that one paragraph in the *Syriac Didascalia** written *c.* A.D. 250 may indicate that the

---

* Connolly, *Syriac Didascalia*, 1929, p. lxxxiii. I give the passage in the ancient and accurate Latin version made by the same translator who was responsible for

Apostolic Tradition was among the documents known to that surprisingly well-read author. This is possible, but the resemblances are hardly more than might be expected when two authors are independently treating of the same usage. Careful search fails to reveal any other passage in the *Didascalia* suggesting a knowledge of the *Apostolic Tradition*, and it is clear that if the Syrian author did know Hippolytus' work, he has not allowed it to affect the contents of his own parallel but very dissimilar treatise.

In the next century it is again possible that we have a reminiscence of the *Apostolic Tradition* in the writings of Aphraates, a Syriac writer *c.* A.D. 340.* But here again the similarity is scarcely a demonstration of literary dependence, and search reveals no further traces of contact with the *Apostolic Tradition*.

It is, however, from Syria, but a generation later, that we get our first certain evidence of the pamphlet's circulation. The use made of it in the *Apostolic Constitutions*, Bk viii (*c.* A.D. 375), and —if this be Syrian—in the *Testament of our Lord* (*c.* A.D. 400 or later) is unmistakable. In the same period we find St Jerome at Bethlehem referring apparently to something now found in the *Apostolic Tradition* as the work of Hippolytus.† The

the Latin version of the *Ap. Trad.* (ap. Hauler, fol. lxii). *Et uir et mulier legibus ad nuptias conuenientes et ab alterutrum exurgentes sine obseruatione et non loti orent et mundi sunt.* With this compare *Ap. Trad.* xxxvi. 10. I do not myself see that the two passages are sufficiently close to show an actual knowledge of *Ap. Trad.* by the author of *Syr. Did.* (The latter is unquestionably the later work.)

* *Demonstration*, 23. 3: "The light of the understanding has shone forth and the glistening olives have borne fruit wherein is the seal of the sacrament of life, whereby Christians are made and priests and kings and prophets; it enlightens the darkness, anoints the sick and by its secret mystery brings home the penitent." Cf. *Ap. Trad.* v and vi, but note "priests and kings and prophets" not "kings, priests and prophets" as in *Ap. Trad.* This trio occurs fairly commonly in references to anointing and is obviously derived from the O.T., a fact which must be taken account of in weighing the evidence for a direct dependence of the Blessing of Chrism in the Gelasian Sacramentary on Hippolytus.

† *Ep.* lxxi. 6: "What you ask about Saturday, whether one ought to fast on that day, and about the eucharist, whether one ought to receive it daily, observances which the Roman Church and Spain recommend, has been treated of by Hippolytus, a man of great learning." The references appear to be to Hippolytus, *in Dan.* iv. 20, and to what now appears as *Ap. Trad.* xxxii. The question whether this is an authentic part of *Ap. Trad.* is discussed on p. 84. The style seems in any case to show that it is from the pen of Hippolytus, though it may have been transferred to its present position from another work, or from elsewhere in *Ap. Trad.* It is unfortunate that St Jerome does not say what works of Hippolytus he means.

Tradition was later incorporated bodily into the Egyptian canonical collection known as the *Sahidic Heptateuch*, which cannot as a collection be older than the fifth century. To the fifth century or the sixth must be assigned also the *Epitome of Ap. Const.* viii and the *Canons of Hippolytus*, both of which made considerable use of the *Apostolic Tradition*. It is remarkable that both these late authors must have had MSS. which still retained the statement that Hippolytus was the author of the *Apostolic Tradition*, since they headed their adaptations, the one *Constitutions of the Apostles through Hippolytus on Ordinations* and the other *Canons of the Church and the Commandments which Hippolytus the Chief Bishop of Rome wrote according to the Commands of the Apostles by the Holy Ghost.* It is important to note that all these documents are of Syrian or Egyptian origin.

The Latin version made about or after A.D. 400 is evidence of a circulation in the West, but there are very strong grounds for attributing a *Syrian* origin to the codex from which it was made, if not to the translator himself. There seems to be a clear use of *Ap. Trad.* ix in the *Statuta Ecclesiae Antiquae*, a document which in its present form comes from the Church of Arles, *c.* A.D. 525.* Apart from this and the possible slight traces in the Gelasian and Leonine Sacramentaries there is no vestige of any influence of the treatise in the West.

Its direct influence in the Greek Churches is confined to a single prayer transcribed bodily into the Barberini *Euchologion* (written *c.* A.D. 800).

So far as the extant evidence carries us, therefore, the circulation of the *Apostolic Tradition* was virtually restricted to the Churches of Syria and Egypt. The reason is simple. It was in this region that the literature now generically styled "the Church Orders" was invented; there alone that literature took firm root, and there alone it continued to be valued long after the rest of Christendom had forgotten it. These "Church Orders" are a closely inter-related group of pseudo-Apostolic documents, all professing to give direct "Apostolic" prescriptions on matters

* *S.E.A.* iv: *Diaconus cum ordinatur solus episcopus qui eum benedicit manum super caput illius ponat, quia non ad sacerdotium sed ad ministerium consecratur.*

of liturgy and Church Order. Their earliest extant members, the *Didache* and the sources underlying the fourth-century *Apostolic Church Order*, were originally written at a date comparable with that of the *Apostolic Tradition*.* The succession of these documents covers the third and fourth centuries, each of them to some extent adapting and revising the contents of earlier members of the series. Except, perhaps, for the *Testament of our Lord*, one of the latest, which may come from Asia Minor, all these documents are certainly either of Syrian or Egyptian origin. Its title and contents caused the *Apostolic Tradition* to be included in this pseudo-Apostolic literature. But it is important to note that it only enters the group towards the very end of the series when the "Church Orders" have already taken on the character of compilations from all sorts of sources rather than original productions. The use made of it in the latest Church Orders has caused modern scholars to class it with the group without further ado. But its inclusion seems originally largely accidental. It was due to the general search for older matter of this kind going on in Syria in the later fourth century in order to strengthen the appeal and hold of a dying type of literature. When the *Apostolic Tradition* makes its appearance in the Church Orders their day is already nearly over. The growth of a *Statute* canon law in the East† by the activities of the fourth-century councils and the immense expansion of Christian liturgical texts due to the changed circumstances of Christian public worship after Constantine combined to deprive the Church Orders of their usefulness. In the fourth century we meet the first Syrian Canonical collection, that

---

* The case of the *Didache* is peculiar and complicated. Robinson, Connolly and now J. Muilenburg (especially the last two) have demonstrated beyond any reasonable question the direct dependence of the *Didache* on Christian documents of the first half of the second century. It must itself therefore be later than that, and is reasonably to be assigned to the period when "Apostolic" prescription was first being sought on questions of Church Order. I do not think that anyone attentively studying the references to "Apostolicity" *as such* in second-century Christian literature will be inclined to place the beginning of that period before A.D. 170. Development was rapid, but the *Didache* exhibits the conception in a fully developed form, and a date c. A.D. 190 would best suit all the circumstances.

† The West had had the conception for two centuries, in Africa at all events. This may partly explain the lack of Western interest in the *customary* codes of the Church Orders.

Antiochene compilation which has bestowed an unnecessary immortality on the decrees of local synods like that of Gangra. From the same period comes the first known purely liturgical codex, the Sacramentary of Sarapion. It is no accident that the *Apostolic Constitutions*, the climax of the Church Orders, and the *Testament of our Lord*, the last (as I think) of the Church Orders proper, have expanded the proportion of directly liturgical matter in their contents out of all comparison with their predecessors; or that *Apostolic Constitutions* ends with a code of Canons largely based on actual fourth-century Syrian enactments. These things were necessary by then if the works were to retain a circulation. But the material which the Church Orders had formerly combined was expanding beyond their possible scope. As a matter of convenience in use fixed liturgical texts (now becoming general) needed to be copied separately. The future lay with more scientific and specialised documents which eventually grow into the vast separate literatures of the canon law and the liturgy.

The contents of the *Apostolic Tradition* naturally allied it with this "Church Order" literature, but its inclusion in it both in ancient times and modern study has done something to obscure its true character as a controversial pamphlet for a particular place and occasion. We need not regret this inclusion, for it is this alone which has accidentally brought about its survival with all the invaluable information it contains. The complete dearth of reference to it in other writers and the extreme scantiness of traceable quotations from it outside the Church Orders clearly indicate what would have been its fate had it not become involved in that group of documents. Both in the Statue-catalogue of its author's works and by the opening of its own Prologue the *Apostolic Tradition* is closely connected with another treatise by Hippolytus, *On Charismata*. From this twin-work not one identifiable quotation has descended from antiquity and it is not certain that a single sentence of it survives to-day.* Had it not happened to be useful to the

---

* Since the time of Lightfoot it has been customary to assume that Hippolytus' Περὶ Χαρισμάτων underlies *Ap. Const.* viii. 1 and 2 as the *Apostolic Tradition* underlies later portions of the book. Careful comparison with parts of *Ap. Const.* i–vii which

collectors of "Church Order" material the *Apostolic Tradition* would have perished utterly.

In the fifth century the Church Orders—except for *Apostolic Constitutions* which is in many ways their summary—practically disappear from Greek ecclesiastical literature. The Latin West had never valued them. Only the vernacular-speaking "native" Churches with their much poorer literatures and their ossified conservatism continued to copy them. And so it comes about that though the Church Orders were all originally composed in Greek* they are now known only or chiefly in oriental vernacular versions, because the Greek text so early ceased to be copied and was lost. In this way the original Greek text of the *Apostolic Tradition* also has perished except for the few fragments recoverable from later adaptations. For the bulk of it we are indebted to the fragmentary Latin version (of *oriental* origin) supplemented by more complete but somewhat adapted texts in Ethiopic, Arabic and Coptic, and by Syriac and Arabic revisions.

Only in these distant and barbaric Churches to-day does that "tradition", which Hippolytus so proudly affirmed "befits the Churches" *urbi et orbi*, continue in some form in use at the Christian altars after seventeen centuries. In the Abyssinian Church the anaphora of Hippolytus is still in use in two adaptations. The first, the "Anaphora of the Apostles", is the normal ferial anaphora of the rite. It is an expansion of Hippolytus' anaphora itself as it is found in the Ethiopic version of the *Apostolic Tradition* (which now forms an integral part of the Ethiopic canon law book, the *Sinodos*).† The second, the

are the undoubted product of the compiler himself and not of his sources suggests that so much of viii. 1 and 2 is from the pen of the compiler that little if anything of Hippolytus' work is recoverable from it. One might even go so far as to doubt whether Περὶ Χαρισμάτων has been used at all. There is nothing to indicate that it has, beyond the fact that passages treating of *charismata* precede the passages which draw on the *Apostolic Tradition*, but the composition of these might be suggested to the author of *Ap. Const.* by *Ap. Trad.* i. 1.

* Except the Edessene *Canons of the Apostles*, which stand somewhat apart.

† The *Sinodos* is largely composed of an Ethiopic translation of the *Sahidic Heptateuch* (cf. p. lvii *sq.*). There is reason to suppose that this Ethiopic version was made (from an Arabic version) about the thirteenth or fourteenth century A.D.; and the "Anaphora of the Apostles" is clearly derived from the text of Hippolytus found in the *Sinodos*, so that it must be later still. Probably the "Liturgy of St Mark" had previously been in use. Cf. *Rev. de l'Or. Chrétien*, xxix. 187.

"Anaphora of our Lord", is used only on feasts of our Lord, and consists of the farced and expanded version of Hippolytus' prayer found in the *Testament of our Lord* (which in its Ethiopic version is generally bound up with the *Sinodos*). Among the Egyptian monophysites Hippolytus' prayer for the consecration of a bishop is still in use (also in the expanded form found in the *Testament*) for the consecration of the Coptic Patriarch of Alexandria.* The inclusion of Hippolytus' prayer for the blessing of first-fruits in the eighth-century Greek *Euchologion* of the Barberini collection and the traces of his blessings of oil and olives in the current Roman Pontifical have already been spoken of. These are the only vestiges still to be found of any direct influence on the subsequent practice of Christendom of this its most ancient extant manual of liturgy and canon law.†

But it is not for its direct influence on the future that the *Apostolic Tradition* is now valuable. Had it had any overwhelming influence of its own,‡ its recovery might only have made the study of Christian liturgical origins even more difficult than it is. It is because it looks backwards and illuminates the half-Judaic past already vanishing when it was written, because it was from the first an old-fashioned exposition of Christian practice, because it affords us a glimpse of the upper reaches of the great stream of the Christian liturgical tradition but is *not* one of its main sources, that the *Apostolic Tradition* is really important to-day.

There have been many Canutes in Christian history who have imagined that "the Tradition which befits the Churches" must cease to advance when it reached them and petrify for ever in their formulation of it. They have all been disabused, and few more rudely than Hippolytus. In a fury he cast himself out of the great Roman Church that would not narrow her teaching to his own. The Roman Church passed serenely on her way

---

* Renaudot, *Liturgiarum Orientalium Collectio*, ed. Frankfurt, 1847, i. 448. (Latin version only.)

† The *Didache* may perhaps be a little older in actual date of writing, but it represents in some things a more developed state of affairs, *e.g.* in its arrangements about fast-days; nor has it the representative value of *Ap. Trad.*

‡ Of the kind attributed to it, *e.g.* by Prof. Easton, *Ap. Trad.* 1934, p. 73 *sq.*

without him, and proved quite great enough in the end to remember nothing of him in malice, honouring all that was good and her own in Hippolytus "the Presbyter" who died a martyr in the Sardinian mines. Had he not boasted of his own unhappy schism in his own works, the memory of it would have been quite irrecoverable from the records of the Roman Church.

By the irony of history the occasional pamphlet which he wrote on the *Apostolic Tradition* to envenom a purely Roman quarrel and to stultify the living progress of the local Roman tradition has been conspicuously devoid of influence in the Roman Church itself. There tradition has progressed independently of his work and against the dearest principles of its author. Only in the remotest borderlands of Christendom it still serves as it has for centuries to bring down the Bread of Heaven upon those Abyssinian hills that when he wrote were still an unknown and pagan wilderness. Perhaps the perfected Saint would say that this reward is greater than the intention of his tract deserved. The couplet which Prudentius set upon his lips is more apt than its author ever knew:

Quae docui docuisse piget: venerabile Martyr
Cerno quod a cultu rebar abesse Dei.*

* *Peristephanon*, 11. 33. Prudentius accepted Damasus' report that Hippolytus was a Novatian presbyter who recanted on the road to martyrdom at Porto, and this forms part of the recantation in Prudentius' hymn.

THE TEXTUAL MATERIALS

As has been said the original Greek text of the *Apostolic Tradition* in its entirety is no longer extant. We depend for our knowledge of the work for the most part on later versions and adaptations in other languages, supplemented by a few small portions and reminiscences of the Greek identifiable in later Greek documents. Taken alone any one of these sources would be decidedly inadequate for the reconstitution of the original. In combination they are sufficiently numerous and independent to furnish us with the sense of the entire document and in good part with a clear enough perception of its actual wording. The authenticity of three or four sentences remains doubtful, and the exact form of three or four more seems impossible to recover, though their purport is clear. But at least nineteen-twentieths of the treatise may be said to be known with certainty and accuracy. Where the branches of the textual tradition cover so wide a variety of languages as is here the case, their joint witness establishes the original with certainty. Where they differ they have undergone independent alteration, and careful consideration will as a rule establish with certainty which of the conflicting texts is original when the general characteristics of each document are borne in mind.

The materials available are as follows:

L. = A fragmentary Latin version, late fourth or early fifth century.

Ar.S.Boh. = Arabic, Sahidic and Bohairic versions of the whole treatise, omitting certain prayers.

E. = An Ethiopic version of the whole treatise, including the prayers omitted by Ar.S.Boh. It is possible to show that E. together with Ar.S.Boh. all descend from the same slightly adapted version of the *Apostolic Tradition*, and that this adaptation can scarcely be earlier than the fifth century. They therefore all rest ultimately on a *single* MS. of the *Ap. Trad.* and that unfortunately not of the best. Ar.E.S.Boh. are therefore ultimately *one* witness to the text of the *Ap. Trad.*, not four.

T. = The *Testament of our Lord*, a seventh-century Syriac translation of a lost fourth- or early fifth-century Greek expansion and adaptation of Hippolytus' treatise.

A. = The reminiscences of the original Greek text of the *Ap. Trad.* now discoverable in a fourth-century Greek work, the *Apostolic Constitutions,* Bk viii.

Ep. = Independent quotations from the original Greek text of the *Ap. Trad.* introduced by a later writer into his *Epitome of Ap. Const.* viii.

K. = The *Canons of Hippolytus,* an Arabic version of a lost Greek adaptation of the *Ap. Trad.* made in Egypt, probably in the sixth century. Though clearly based on Hippolytus, this has been so much altered as to be only of minor service in reconstituting the original.

Gk. = Isolated fragments of the Greek text of the *Ap. Trad.* found in *Vienna MS. Hist. Gr.* vii and the Barberini *Euchologion.*

It will be useful here to give the main facts about each of these documents.

i. The Latin Version (L.)

Any reconstruction of the *Apostolic Tradition* must be largely based on this wherever it is available, but it is unfortunately very incomplete. It is found in a single parchment MS. of the Library of the Cathedral Chapter of Verona (lv. 53) now containing a copy of the "Sentences" of St Isidore in a N. Italian hand of about the eighth century. Forty-one leaves of this MS. are, however, palimpsest,* and once formed part of a MS. of the late fifth century. This older MS. contained in a Latin version a small collection of those Greek codes of embryonic canon law and liturgy already described which are now known as the Church Orders. Fragments still remain in this MS. of three members of the group, the *Apostolic Didascalia,* the *Apostolic Church Order,* and the *Apostolic Tradition.* It may be added that the style of one and the same translator is easily detectable in the Latin version of each of the three.

The first leaf of the original MS. bore a list in an uncial hand of the consuls from A.D. 439 to 486 which has been carried on to A.D. 494 by another (semi-uncial) hand very similar to the writing of the rest of the leaves. This sufficiently marks the date of our

---

* *I.e.* Parchment leaves once part of an older MS. which have been made use of for a second time after being scraped and/or washed to prepare them to receive a second writing. Parchment is a "thirsty" material and absorbs ink deeply into its pores, with the result that even washing and scraping as a rule only fades the first writing to a greater or lesser extent without entirely removing it, particularly if the pigment contains any great proportion of acid.

copy of L., which is a copy, not the translator's autograph. The philological peculiarities of the Latin have suggested to most experts in patristic Latinity that the translation from the Greek was made about a century before this, about the time of St Ambrose, though I have been given to understand that the late C. H. Turner was led to suspect that its date was somewhat later than this, perhaps about A.D. 420–430.

The credit for first observing the character and importance of this under-writing is due to the palaeographer W. Studemund, but it was first read in full and published by the young Viennese scholar Edmund Hauler, whose edition is a model of palaeographical publication.* Unfortunately he died before he could complete his projected volume of *Epilegomena*. The fragments of the *Apostolic Tradition* contained in this MS. begin on f. lxvii. 31 *sq.* (Hauler, p. 101) and are reproduced here in full.

The work does not appear to have aroused much interest in the West and nothing is known of the translator. His Latin is peculiar, being of the most popular kind and yet slavishly subservient to the exact form and construction of the fluent Greek of the sentences before him. He seems at times even to be *thinking* in Greek. Thus *e.g.* he writes *ex quibus* for ἐκ τούτων regardless of the fact that this is meaningless in Latin, and *spiritus...id quod*, apparently thinking of πνεῦμα. He invents words like *conquaglans* which do not exist and constructions which defy the whole spirit of Latin idiom. In places the style is like nothing so much as the "English" of Dutch Bulb Catalogues. Yet the translator was not merely an ignorant Italian rustic. He has a good grasp of Hippolytus' not always easy Greek. The question suggests itself (though I have not found it raised hitherto) whether this translator who seems more at home with Greek than with Latin was not himself from the *Pars Orientis*. The contents of the Greek codex which he thought it worth while so laboriously to translate are very "un-Western". The *Apostolic Didascalia* certainly, the *Apostolic Church Order*

---

* *Didascaliae Apostolorum Fragmenta Veronensia Latina. Accedunt Canonum qui dicuntur Apostolorum et Aegyptiorum Reliquiae. Fasc.* 1. Leipzig, 1900.

possibly,* are works of Syrian origin. The *Apostolic Tradition* is, of course, originally Roman, but all the other evidence of its circulation in the fourth century comes from Syria. The taste for the pseudo-Apostolic "Church Orders" was, as we have said, very largely confined to this South-East corner of the Mediterranean, and its title had caused the *Apostolic Tradition*—rather unfairly—to be classed with this literature in Syria in the fourth century. That the Greek codex from which the Latin version was made came originally from Syria seems indubitable. Speculation settles nothing—but it is hard in thinking of the translator to prevent the mind from turning to those Syrian traders and ecclesiastics who were to be found everywhere in the West in the fourth and fifth centuries, and who have left as their permanent memorial in Italy the more than half Syrian architecture of Ravenna. The translator's nationality and the origin of his Greek codex have this much importance: any adaptations of Hippolytus' third-century prescriptions to fourth-century practice which may be found in L. are more likely to represent the practice of the *East* in the fourth century than of the West.

And it seems clear that despite its very high value for the reconstruction of the authentic form of the treatise L. does contain one or two such adaptations. One such, for example, seems to be found at xxi. 20 in the rubric which connects baptism with confirmation: ...*se iam induantur et postea in ecclesia* (sic) *ingrediantur*. In the Syriac of T. the last clause is represented by "Afterwards let them *be together* in the Church." At first sight this is only the difference between ϹΥΝΙѠϹΙ and ϹΥΝѠϹΙ in fourth-century codices. But there is probably a little more in it than that. By writing *in ecclesia* where we should expect *in ecclesiam*, L. itself suggests that its Greek original read ἐν ἐκκλησίᾳ not εἰς ἐκκλησίαν and that T.'s συνῶσι is right. What L. seems to have in mind is the imposing procession of the neophytes from the Baptistery to the Altar in the great fourth-century Basilicas. It is only when one recognises that everywhere in the *Apostolic Tradition* "the Church" means *the congregation, not the building*, that the magnitude of the

---

* It is either Syrian or Egyptian, and certainly circulated in Syria.

change imported here by L. becomes apparent. It is doubtful if
in Hippolytus' day there were as yet any public buildings set
aside in Rome for Christian worship. Probably the Christians
met still in large private houses, or in the "lecture-halls" of
the διδάσκαλοι which were hired or owned by them as private
individuals, just as the pagan lecturers hired or owned their
premises. In any case, the improbability of the State tolerating
a Christian building in Rome itself at this period large enough to
contain the Paschal Assembly of the whole Church is very great
indeed.* The original form of his baptismal rubric (xxi. 2), also
preserved by T., strongly suggests baptism beside a stream.†
What the original form of the rubric—"let them be together in
the assembly"—seems to intend is that the Catechumens who
have hitherto been forbidden to pray with the faithful (xxii. 5)
and who have had to stand *apart* from them during the lessons
(xviii. 1) are from this moment full members of the ἐκκλησία
and are to take their place in it accordingly. L., therefore, seems
here to be guilty of making a change in Hippolytus' text, minute
in itself but of far-reaching importance for the mental picture
of Church life which it calls up.

A similar instance in the same passage may be quoted. L.'s
confirmation rubric runs *Postea oleum sanctificatum infundens
de manu et inponens in capite.* So far as this goes it is the oil only
which is "placed on the head". T. on the contrary has "pouring
the oil, placing *a hand* on his head". Again the textual difference
represented is slight; L. = ἔλαιον ἐκχέων χειρὸς ἐπιτιθεὶς ἐπὶ τῇ
κεφαλῇ, but T. = ἔλαιον ἐκχέων χεῖρα κτλ. Yet in Tertullian, or such
early authorities as the *Didascalia*, or the ancient document
preserved in *Ap. Const.* vii. 44, confirmation is by affusion with
oil accompanied by the imposition of one hand. In the fourth

* There were of course Christian "meeting-places" (συνέλευσις), but Justin,
Acta, 3 formally denies the existence of a "Church" in the sense of a building set
apart for Christian worship. Hippolytus, *in Dan.* i. 20, speaks of "the house of
God (οἶκος τοῦ θεοῦ) where all are praying and hymning God" as being attacked
by pagans, but there is nothing to show that he does not mean a private house
where the ἐκκλησία was assembled. His avoidance here of the term ἐκκλησία for
the *building* is noticeable.
† The earliest baptismal "tanks" seem to date from about the middle of the
third century.

century the imposition of the hand was losing its significance in Syria. It has disappeared altogether in Cyril of Jerusalem (A.D. 348). It is T., not L., which has preserved the original form of Hippolytus' rubric.

A third such instance, perhaps of greater importance, is found in Hippolytus' eucharistic rite, where L. has a rudimentary form of epiclesis which is omitted by T. But the textual facts here are sufficiently complicated to warrant a special note.

Besides these small but tendencious changes we have to note that L. rests on a Greek MS. which had itself acquired some measure of textual corruption. Instances may be noted at i. 2, $\kappa\alpha\tau\dot{\eta}\chi\epsilon\iota$ for $\kappa\alpha\theta\dot{\eta}\kappa\epsilon\iota$; v. 2, $\chi\rho\eta\sigma\theta\epsilon\hat{\iota}\sigma\iota$ for $\chi\rho\iota\sigma\theta\epsilon\hat{\iota}\sigma\iota$ and perhaps $\dot{\alpha}\gamma\dot{\iota}\alpha\sigma\mu\alpha$ for $\dot{\upsilon}\gamma\dot{\iota}\alpha\sigma\mu\alpha$; xxvi. 9, $\pi\alpha\rho\rho\eta\sigma\dot{\iota}\alpha$ for $\dot{\upsilon}\pi\epsilon\rho\upsilon\sigma\dot{\iota}\alpha$. A number of others will be found in the *apparatus*.

But setting aside these and similar lapses, it must still be recognised that L. is quite invaluable wherever it is extant. Its readings supply a standard by which we may judge those of other versions; and though the comparison, especially with T., is not always in its favour, the difficulties of establishing the true text are always increased where L. is wanting.

ii. The Arabic, Ethiopic, Sahidic and Bohairic Versions (Ar.E.S.Boh.)

We owe our most complete texts of the *Apostolic Tradition* to the accident that it was incorporated bodily into an Egyptian compilation which modern scholars have christened the *Sahidic* or *Clementine Heptateuch*. All the documents now contained in this Sahidic collection were originally written in Greek, but it is impossible to say whether the collection as a collection ever circulated in Greek or was originally put together in Sahidic translations. It may be described as a less striking attempt by some Egyptian writer to do what the Syrian author of the *Apostolic Constitutions* had done with conspicuous skill, viz. to collect all that was most worthy of preservation in the older literature of the Church Orders (which in the later fourth century was evidently a declining *genre*), and by re-editing it and combining it to try to supplement its deficiencies and retain it in circulation.* The contents of the *Heptateuch* are as follows: (1) The *Apostolic Church Order*. (2) The *Apostolic Tradition*. (3) *Ap. Const*. viii. 1-2. (4) An adaptation of those parts of the *Apostolic Tradition* which had been used in *Ap. Const*. viii. 4 *sq.* in a form which shows clearly that Hippolytus' own work has been consulted afresh, though the much-edited version of it in *Ap. Const*. viii has largely dictated the character of what is here reproduced. It seems probable that this fourth section of the *Heptateuch* was once a separate document in independent circulation like the other items of the collection, and was unintelligently inserted by the compiler of the *Heptateuch* to increase its representative character, though it really reproduced matter he had already included in its original form in (2). To these four sections are usually appended other items which do not here concern us, and these alone may have constituted the original nucleus of the work.

That the *Heptateuch* was compiled in Egypt there seems no reason to doubt, since it is virtually certain that all the other extant versions are derived from a Sahidic text. The inclusion of matter from the *Apostolic Constitutions* indicates a date later than A.D. 400 for the compilation. How much later is not very easy to say. The heading of *Ap. Trad*. xxxii in the Sahidic version, "That it is proper to eat of the Eucharist early *at the time when it will be offered up* before tasting any food", suggests a date not earlier than the later fifth century. It appears that the words italicised are an interpolation. Hippolytus here has in mind communion *at home* from the reserved Sacrament, which this interpolation envisaging a public eucharist directly contradicts. It is certain from St Basil, *Ep.* 93, and other sources that such private communion was well known in Egypt at the end of the fourth century, but it seems to have died out there in the fifth or sixth century. The interpolation suggests a date when the custom had been forgotten. Canon 65, too, of the *Sah. Hept.*

* Such collections of Church Orders must have been fairly common in the fourth century, *e.g.* the Greek MS. from which L. was translated.

assumes the practice of eucharistic consecration by the epiclesis
of the Spirit. The older Egyptian tradition was to invoke the
Logos for this,* but consecration by the Spirit was already being
taught in Egypt c. A.D. 400,† so that again we get no definite
terminus ad quem. All things considered a date c. A.D. 500 is not
unreasonable for the compilation, and it seems to have enjoyed
a certain influence among the Egyptian Monophysites.

Monophysite influence subsequently caused the whole work
to be translated into Syriac‡ and Ethiopic, while local convenience in Egypt gave rise to Arabic and Bohairic versions.
But it is certain that ultimately a Sahidic text lies at the base of
all the extant versions.

For the Bohairic version this last remark is true in the most
direct sense. The colophon of the only Bohairic MS. published§
(now Berlin *Sachau* Or. 519) states that it was rendered from the
Sahidic as recently as A.D. 1804. Boh. follows minutely almost
every corruption in S., adding frequent further blunders through
the stupidity of its own translator. Boh. is entirely negligible
save for a single passage (xxi. 18 *sq.*) where it serves to fill a
lacuna of two folios in the only available MS. of S.

We are left therefore with Ar.E.S. to consider. That these
represent a single textual tradition and derive ultimately from
a single archetypal MS. of Hippolytus of a not over-reliable kind
will be clear from the following collation of Ar.E.S. in *Ap. Trad.*
xxi. 11–18 with the text of Hippolytus' baptismal creed as it
emerges with virtual certainty from a combination of all the
materials available.‖ Variants common to Ar.E.S. alone of all the
sources are italicised. Singularities of any one of them are spaced.

---

* So Sarapion and Athanasius (cited by Funk, *Did. et Const. Ap.* ii. 176 n.), and
several of the lesser Ethiopic anaphorae which are of Egyptian origin.

† Theophilus Al. *ap.* St Jerome, *Ep.* 98. 15; St Isidore Pelus, *Ep.* i. 109.

‡ In its Syriac form it is usually known as the *Syriac or Clementine Octateuch*, the
extra book being the *Testament of our Lord* in Syriac prefixed before the first book
of the *Heptateuch* (and so in some Ethiopic MSS. also). Otherwise there is no difference between the Syriac and the Sahidic. The only MS. of the Syriac appears to be
Paris *S. German* 38, which lacks Bks iv and v (= the *Ap. Trad.*), so that it can here
be entirely neglected.

§ By H. Tattam, *Apostolical Constitutions.* London, T. and T.S. 1848. A collation
of Boh. with S. is appended by Horner to his *Statutes of the Apostles.*

‖ Dom Connolly (*J.T.S.* xxv. 131 *sq.*), Dom Capelle (*Rev. Ben.* xxxix. 35 *sq.*) and
H. Lietzmann (*Symbolstudien.* xiv. 81) are agreed on this reconstruction with only
the slightest verbal differences.

	Hipp.	Ar.	E.	S.
1.	πιστεύεις εἰς θεὸν πατέρα παντοκράτορα;	om.	om.	om.
2.	πιστεύεις εἰς Χριστὸν Ἰησοῦν τὸν υἱὸν τοῦ θεοῦ	Dost thou believe in Jesus Xt. *our Lord the only* Son of God *the Father*	Dost thou believe in the name of Jesus Xt. *our Lord the only* Son of God *the Father*	Thou believest (*sic*) *our Lord* Jesus Xt., *the only* Son (μονογενής) of God *the Father*
3.	τὸν γεννηθέντα ἐκ πνεύματος ἁγίου καὶ Μαρίας τῆς παρθένου	that He became man *by an incomprehensible miracle* from the Holy Spirit and from Mary the Virgin *without seed of man*	that He became man *by an incomprehensible miracle* by the Holy Spirit and by Mary the Virgin *without seed of man*	and that He became man *by a miracle for our sake in an incomprehensible unity* in His Holy Spirit from Mary the holy Virgin *without seed of man*
4.	τὸν σταυρωθέντα ἐπὶ Ποντίου Πιλάτου καὶ ἀποθανόντα	*and* was crucified in the time of Pilate of Pontus and died *by His own will to save us withal*	*and* He was crucified in the time of Pontius Pilate and died *by His own will to save us*	*and that* He was crucified for us in the time of Pontius Pilate, He died *of His own will to save us withal*
5.	καὶ ἀναστάντα τῇ τρίτῃ ἡμέρᾳ	and rose up *from the dead* on the third day *and released the captives*	and rose *from the dead* on the third day *and released the captives*	He rose (om.) in the third day *He released the captives*
6.	ζῶντα	om.	om.	om.
7.	ἐκ τῶν νεκρῶν	(*sup.*)	(*sup.*)	om.

and ascended into the heavens	and ascended into the heavens	and ascended into the heavens	and ascended into the heavens	8. καὶ ἀναβάντα εἰς τοὺς οὐρανοὺς
He sat down at the right hand of His good (ἀγαθός) Father in the height	and sat down at the right hand of the Father	and sat down at the right hand of the Father	and sat down at the right hand of the Father	9. καὶ καθήμενον ἐν δεξιᾷ τοῦ πατρὸς
and He comes again to judge the living and the dead according to His appearing and His kingdom.	and He shall come to judge the living and the dead at His appearing and His kingdom.	and He shall come to judge the living and the dead at His appearing and His kingdom.	and He shall come to judge the living and the dead at His appearing and His kingdom.	10. ἐρχόμενον κρῖναι ζῶντας καὶ νέκρους;
And thou believest in the Holy good (ἀγ.) and life-giving Spirit purifying all things	And dost thou believe in the Holy Spirit the good and the sanctifier	And dost thou believe in the Holy Spirit and the sanctifier	Dost thou believe in the Spirit, the Holy, the good, the Sanctifier	11. πιστεύεις εἰς πνεῦμα ἅγιον
in the Holy Church [Here S. is interrupted by the loss of two folios]	and in the Holy Church	and in the Holy Church	in the Holy Church [Joined to the last clause]	12. καὶ ἁγίαν ἐκκλησίαν
[S. def., om. Boh.]	and dost thou believe in the resurrection of the body which shall happen to all men and the kingdom of the heavens and eternal judgement?	and dost thou believe in the resurrection of the body which shall happen to all men and the kingdom of the heavens and eternal judgement?	and dost thou believe in the resurrection of the body which shall happen to all men and the kingdom of the heavens and eternal judgement?	13. καὶ σαρκὸς ἀνάστασιν;

It is, I think, sufficiently obvious that all three versions represent with minor variations a single interpolated tradition, descending from a single MS. There cannot have been many texts of the creed in circulation which entirely neglected to state belief "in God the Father Almighty"! The agreement of Ar.E.S. among themselves here against all other authorities is as a matter of fact even more complete than this collation shows. These three texts all omit the rubrics which the other versions insert before 2 and 11 above. Hippolytus' creed took the form of a threefold question and answer which Ar.E.S. are at one in obscuring.

There can be little doubt as to where the archetypal inter-polations were made—in Egypt. Ar.E.S. are again alone in inserting at xxi. 11 a sort of preliminary creed also in the form of a threefold question and answer:

"Dost thou believe in one God the Father Almighty?

And in His only-begotten ($\mu o \nu o \gamma \epsilon \nu \eta \varsigma$) Son Jesus Christ our Lord and our Saviour?

And in His Holy Spirit, Giver of life to all creatures, the Trinity of One Substance ($\tau \rho \iota \grave{\alpha} \varsigma \; \delta \mu o o \upsilon \sigma \iota o \varsigma$), one Godhead, one Lordship, one Kingdom, one Faith, one Baptism in the Holy Catholic Apostolic Church?

And he who is baptised shall say ⟨each time⟩ thus: Verily, I believe."

Some of this phraseology is evidently later than the Council of Constantinople I (A.D. 381). But this type of three-clause creed is very ancient and actually preceded that developed Roman baptismal creed of which Hippolytus gives us the late-second-century text, and which we are accustomed to call the "Apostles' Creed".* This ancient type of creed lasted longer in Egypt than elsewhere as is proved by the baptismal creed of a papyrus from Deir Balizeh, which seems to be a seventh–eighth-century copy of a fourth-(?) century rite:

---

* Traces of the shorter form of creed are found in Irenaeus, *e.g. Epideixis*, iii, and also (among the Marcosians) *Adv. Haer.* i. 21. 3. So also the Creed of the *Epistula Apostolorum* (Asia Minor *c.* A.D. 175): "I believe in God the Father Almighty, and in Jesus Christ, and in the Holy Ghost, the Holy Church and the remission of sins."

"I believe in God the Father Almighty
And in His only-begotten Son (μονογ.) our Lord Jesus Christ
And in the Holy Ghost and in the resurrection of the flesh
and the Holy Catholic Church."

A very large number of concordances of Ar.E.S. against the other sources in what are obviously false readings will be found in the *apparatus*. This is a matter of some inconvenience wherever L. is wanting, because Ar.E.S. together present what is our only complete text of the *Apostolic Tradition*, and to judge by the text of the creed there is often reason to fear that they are not over-faithful to the original. Wherever, therefore, in the absence of L., two of the remaining texts which we know to be independent of each other agree against Ar.E.S. combined, there is good reason to suspect that the latter has undergone a certain amount of editing, and that the alternative reading is the more original. Ar.E.S. together represent only one MS. of the *Apostolic Tradition* and that not of the best. Where Ar.E.S. differ among themselves that one of them is likely to be most faithful to the original from which the whole group descends which agrees best with texts outside the group.

The texts of the creed collated above also offer an accurate idea of the individual characters of these three versions. S., as in 3, 9, 10 above, is given to frequent and futile little embroideries and omissions, which make it in its present form the least reliable of the three. Note also how Monophysite doctrine has affected the form of the elaboration of 3 in S., but not, apparently, in Ar.E. E. is on the whole very faithful though not free from interpolation. But being only a translation from the Arabic, which is itself a translation from the Sahidic, which is ultimately a translation from the Greek, E. is frequently so confused as to be meaningless if it stood alone. Against this, it has the inestimable advantage of going back to an older form of the joint Ar.E.S. tradition than that presented by the extant MSS. of Ar.S., and it contains certain important sections which Ar.S. omit. These were undoubtedly found in the archetype, and have been omitted in later recensions largely because they consisted of prayers not in use in Egypt which might well seem better omitted. We have also to remember that the *Sahidic Heptateuch* came to be regarded as a document of the canon law and not of the liturgy, and there was a steady tendency for canonical documents to omit strictly liturgical *texts* as outside their province.*

The present text of Ar. is based on an almost identical recension of the Sahidic with that found in the MS. of S. here used, though the variants are sufficient to show that that particular MS. is not the one actually used. Making allowance for a certain vagueness of phrasing and for the omissions it shares with S., Ar. is the best of the three versions by which to come at the original of the group because it is the least given to casual omissions and interpolations. I have therefore cited it first of the three though it is neither so ancient in tradition as E. or so close to the source as S. The earliest known MSS. of Ar. come from the thirteenth century. How much earlier than this the translation was made it is impossible to say, but there is no trace of any Christian Arabic literature in Egypt before the tenth century.

The present text of S. is known chiefly from B.M. Or. 1320, written in A.D. 1006. Its text was first printed by P. de Lagarde, and translations in German and English were published by Achelis and Horner,† all from this MS. A later MS. now in the Patriarchal Library at Cairo was published by U. Bouriant in 1884–5.‡ But collation shows that either the Cairene MS. was actually copied from the MS. now in the British Museum or else that both are exceptionally faithful copies of the same third MS.; I have therefore not given Bouriant's variants. There are also fragments of a third MS. of S. now divided between the British Museum and the Bibliothèque Nationale. Its extremely fragmentary state is to be regretted, as it clearly contained a better text than B.M. Or. 1320.

We are therefore reduced to this single eleventh-century MS.

* Thus an Ethiopic MS. which includes the *Testament of our Lord* in the canon law of the Ethiopic Church (B.M. Or. 794) omits all the prayers it contains, though the anaphora of that document actually is the chief festal anaphora of that Church.

† Achelis, H., *Die Aeltesten Quellen des Orientalischen Kirchenrechts* I (*T.U.* i. vi. 4), Leipzig, 1891; Horner, G. W., *The Canons of the Apostles*, London, 1904.

‡ *Recueil de travaux relatifs à la philologie égyptienne*, v.

for the original version of the group. In view of the excessive
reliance sometimes placed on it, it seems necessary to point out
that its text is a very degenerate one for all its antiquity, though
the MS. itself is exceptionally well and carefully written. Were
it not that S., in the fashion of all Coptic texts, transliterates
many Greek words, it would be of even less account than it
actually is. Even so, the occurrence of ἀγαθός in a purely private
embroidery in 9 in the creed above warns us that all its transliterated Greek words are not from Hippolytus.

The existence of E. in its present form makes it necessary to
postulate an older recension of Ar. than that now extant, certain
corruptions in E. being only explicable as mistranslations of
unpointed Arabic words. It is clear that Ar. itself derives from
a Sahidic version (having inherited a number of Sahidic constructions), but not quite like that found in S. (cf. *e.g.* xxvi. 13,
where both Ar. and S. omit the following sentences but Ar. has
a sentence less than S.). An earlier recension of S. less complete
than E. but less corrupt than the present S. text must underlie Ar.
The relations of the group are therefore as follows:

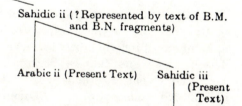

Sahidic i (Full Text. Lost)

Arabic i (Full Text. Lost)   Sahidic ii (? Represented by text of B.M.
                                              and B.N. fragments)

Ethiopic (Present Text)   Arabic ii (Present Text)   Sahidic iii
                                                               (Present
                                                                Text)

                                                             Bohairic

For the recovery of the original Ar.E.S. present each a
different advantage, E. its more ancient textual tradition, Ar.
its pedestrian faithfulness and S. its occasional retention of
Greek words and the fact that it is a translation direct from the
Greek, and not a version of a version. Between them the
authentic text of the *Heptateuch* is generally plain enough. What

is more difficult is to be sure that we have the readings of the
MS. of Hippolytus from which this was made. I believe that the
apparatus will show that the compiler made more changes than
has been supposed. Where L. is wanting the true text is sometimes preserved in the professed "adaptations", T. and K., while
the supposed "translations", Ar.E.S., represent in fact an
"adapted" text.

Oddly enough E., the latest of all the versions of Hippolytus now extant,
was the first to be made known to Western scholars—in an incomplete text
with a Latin version published by Job Ludolf in his *Commentarius ad suam
Historiam Aethiopicam* (Frankfort, 1691, pp. 314–328). The Bohairic text next
appeared edited by Tattam, and then the Sahidic edited by Lagarde. Finally
in 1904 G. W. Horner in his *Statutes of the Apostles* published the first text of
the Arabic and the first complete text of the Ethiopic, with English versions of
both, and an English version of Lagarde's Sahidic, collated with the Bohairic
and with the fragments in the B.M. and B.N. The versions are all of a most
scientific accuracy and literalness. Where Horner's version of S. appeared to
differ from Achelis and (in two points) from Lagarde's print, I have had occasion to refer to the B.M. MS., in every case to the vindication of Horner. The
work has long been out of print in its original form. It has since (1915) been
reissued by the Oxford Univ. Press without the oriental texts of the 1904 edition
and in this form is, I believe, still procurable as a publisher's remainder. It is
safe to say that without this laborious and thankless monument of Horner's
beautiful scholarship the *Apostolic Tradition* would not have been recovered
with its present completeness, if at all.

iii. The Testament of our Lord (T.)

The origin of this curious work is not yet finally settled. Esti-
mates of its date vary between *c.* A.D. 350 and the fifth century,
attributions of its origin between Asia Minor, Syria and Egypt,
descriptions of its author's ecclesiastical position between a
somewhat eccentric orthodoxy and the heresies of Apollinar-
ianism, Montanism and the Audians. A certain hectic and
strained tone in its piety, more easily felt than illustrated, certainly suggests the fervid sects of Asia Minor. If I may express
a personal opinion, a date early in the fifth century and an
origin in the conservative and relatively orthodox Novatian
bodies of Asia or Cappadocia would suit all the facts very well.
It is the last of the Church Orders proper. The long series of
pseudo-Apostolic codes closes with a crescendo in the claim to
authority natural in a dying type of literature. Whatever its

origin it owes its survival to its popularity and circulation in the Monophysite Churches. It is found in use in Syria and Egypt, the classic homes of Church Orders, whence it has spread to Mesopotamia and Abyssinia.*

What is important here is that T. among other sources made use of an excellent codex of the *Apostolic Tradition*. But it has made use of it in a peculiar way. The author of T. has added to Hippolytus so much of his own composition as to have produced to all intents and purposes a different work. But he has also succeeded in treating his source with remarkable respect. Nearly 50 per cent. of Hippolytus' actual wording has been introduced into the later work, which often incorporates whole sentences bodily from the *Apostolic Tradition*. But T. has so farced and expanded Hippolytus' prescriptions that it is quite impossible to detect what is his own and what is from Hippolytus without very careful comparison with other texts. In several cases he has faithfully retained every word of a verse of Hippolytus, but introduced words and phrases of his own well nigh between each of them. The result is that T. is the most laborious of our documents to collate.

Nevertheless the labour is well worth doing. The MS. which T. used was an outstandingly good one, and the perverse sort of fidelity with which T. reproduces it has preserved many valuable readings. Instances have already been given where T. is preferable to L. and alone preserves the ancient text, and others will be found throughout the work. The comparison of T.'s text with L.'s for the baptismal creed will sufficiently show both its defects and virtues.

T.	L.
Let him that baptiseth him say, laying his hand on him thus: (1) "Dost thou believe in God the Father Almighty?"	

---

* It must be remembered that almost the whole of the *popular* Christian literature of Asia Minor has been lost to sight under the Turkish flood. It is probable that the Church Orders, though they practically disappear from official Greek ecclesiastical literature in the fifth century (except *Ap. Const.*) did have a certain circulation in Asia Minor, but we cannot now detect it.

T.	L.
Let him that is being baptised say "I believe".	*(missing as far as)* manum habens in caput eius inpositam baptizet semel.
Let him *forthwith* baptise him once.	
Let *the priest* also say:	Et postea dicat:
(2) "Dost thou believe *also* in Christ Jesus the Son of God *who came from the Father who is of old with the Father*,	Credis in Christum Iesum filium Dei
(3) Who was born *of* Mary the Virgin *by* the Holy Ghost,	qui natus est *de* spiritu sancto *ex* Maria uirgine
(4) Who was crucified in the days of Pontius Pilate and died,	*et* crucifixus sub Pontio Pilato et mortuus est *et sepultus*
(5) and rose up the third day,	et resurrexit die tertia
(6) (7) living from the dead,	uiuus a mortuis
(8) and ascended into heaven,	et ascendit in caelis
(9) and sat on the right hand	et sedit ad dexteram
(10) of the Father, and comes to judge the living and the dead?"	patris uenturus iudicare uiuos et mortuos?
But when he saith "I believe" let him baptise him a second time.	Et cum ille dixerit: Credo iterum baptizetur.
And also let him say:	Et iterum dicat:
(11) "Dost thou believe in the Holy Ghost	Credis in spiritu sancto
(12) in the Holy Church?"	*et* sanctam ecclesiam
(13) *(om.)*	et carnis resurrectionem?

Looking at the variants: (2) "who came from the Father, etc." in T. is pure interpolation. Neither T. nor L. has exactly preserved Hippolytus' construction in (3). T. is supported by Ar.E.S. as well as by K. against L. in omitting "and buried" in (4). Nor

does the phrase appear in any of those "credal" passages in
Ignatius, Justin and Irenaeus which have a bearing on the
phrasing of the second-century creed. It seems to be L. which is
interpolating here. The last clause, "the resurrection of the flesh",
is deliberately omitted by T. on the strength of a preposterous
theory it develops elsewhere (T. ii. 10) that no catechumen is
"to know a word about the resurrection" before baptism. (This
doctrine was in the very forefront of Christian propaganda
among the pagans throughout the history of the Church.)

On the other hand T. is the only text which has preserved the
antithetical τὸν γεννηθέντα...τὸν σταυρωθέντα in (3) and (4)
which is a noticeable feature of the Greek Roman Creed as late
as Marcellus of Ancyra. Like L., T. has preserved the primitive
Roman order "Christ Jesus" not "Jesus Christ" in (2) and the
curious "*living* from the dead" in (6) which remained in the
Spanish texts of the creed long after Rome had dropped it. Here
as elsewhere L. is the surer basis of the text, because it aims at
being simply a version and not an adaptation like T. But T.
serves everywhere to test L.'s readings and sometimes to correct
them.

It would, of course, be easy to take other passages in which T.
shows to less advantage. In the later part of its second book,
especially, T.'s use of the *Apostolic Tradition* becomes very
"scrappy", though this is a characteristic which might be
applied to the later portions of T. as a whole. From ii. 10 onwards it reads almost like an epitome. Where T. reproduces
Hippolytus at all it does so with remarkable fidelity to his
sentiments even where his wording is considerably expanded or
adapted. Only once, in reproducing *Ap. Trad.* ix. 3, does T.
deliberately contradict its source. Hippolytus, for reasons of
his own, had written of the deacon "He is *not* the counsellor
of the whole clergy", with the managing archdeacon of Rome
in his mind's eye. T. has rather a fondness for deacons, and
in protest has written, "*Let him be* the counsellor of the whole
clergy."

In many ways T. is the most important of our sources after L.
But the peculiarities of its use of Hippolytus are such that it

can only be used as a check on the more continuous texts of
L.Ar.E.S. Its habit of expanding by interpolating odd words
even when it is reproducing Hippolytus *verbatim* makes it
essential to compare it throughout with the texts which profess
to be mere translations in order to detect what is T.'s own invention and what its author has drawn from his MS. of Hippolytus. Once this has been done T. is of very great value. The
excellence of the MS. of the *Apostolic Tradition* which T. used
suggests that it was already an old one when T. was written. So
it comes about that T. is sometimes to be followed even against
L., which depends on a Greek MS. which can confidently be
assigned to the later half of the fourth century.* This is especially the case when T. is supported against L. by any of the other
texts. The number of occasions where the combination L.T. is
right against Ar.E.S. is also significant. Were T. more continuous in its use of Hippolytus it would certainly represent the
best of the texts available, and even in its present state its readings generally deserve careful consideration.

Though originally written in Greek T. is now extant only in oriental versions.
The earliest and best is the Syriac text made by James of Edessa at the end of
the seventh century A.D. Portions of this were published by Lagarde† and the
whole text by H. B. Ignatius Ephraem ¡i Rahmani, Uniat Patriarch of Antioch,
with a Latin version.‡ An English translation with copious notes and introduction by Prof. Cooper and the present Primus of Scotland appeared in 1902.§
All these are now out of print. The work also exists in an Arabic recension still
unpublished, and in Ethiopic, also unpublished. Some readings of the Arabic
T. from a MS. in the Borgian Collection of the Vatican Library are given by
Rahmani in his edition of the Syriac. A collation of photographs of part of
this Borgian MS. with MSS. of Ethiopic T. in the British Museum makes it
clear that the latter is a translation from the Arabic not the Syriac. It is
probable that both T.Ar. and T.Eth. come from a lost Coptic version and not
from the original Greek, and it is at least certain that they are independent of
the Syriac, which seems on the whole much more faithful to the original than
the small portions of the Arabic hitherto published. The Liturgy only of T.Eth.
was published by the late Bishop J. M. Harden (*J.T.S.* xxiii. 44). It is practically identical with the current Abyssinian "Anaphora of our Lord".

* The Greek codex underlying L. contains the *Apostolic Church Order*, which in
its present form can hardly be older than c. A.D. 300 and might well come from
c. A.D. 325–350. A margin of time must be allowed for *Ap. Ch. O.* to gain a circulation
and some repute before it could be included in a collection with genuine third-
century works like the *Ap. Didascalia* and *Tradition*.
† *Rel. jur. eccl. ant. Syr.*, Vienna, 1856. Cf. an attempted restoration of the Greek,
Rel. jur. eccl. ant. Graece, 1856, pp. 80–89.
‡ *Testamentum D.N.J.C.*, Maintz, 1899.
§ *The Testament of our Lord*, J. Cooper and A. J. Maclean, Edinburgh, 1902.

iv. The Apostolic Constitutions (A.)

This is the longest, and at least so far as concerns the liturgy of its eighth book, the most widely known of the Church Orders. It professes to consist of "Constitutions" laid down by the Apostles jointly or severally and recorded by St Clement of Rome. It comes in reality from the pen of some ingenious and well-read Syrian of the region of Antioch in the later fourth century whom there is very good reason to suppose a full-blown Arian.* He is now generally identified with the writer who interpolated the Ignatian Epistles.†

Books i–vi consist of a revision of the *Apostolic Didascalia*, in places capriciously emended and altered, but treated on the whole much less cavalierly than the documents underlying vii and viii. Bk vii. 1–32 is based on the *Didache* very much expanded and adapted. The rest of Bk vii is taken up with liturgical matter from a number of unknown sources, and a good part of it may be the author's free composition based on current practice rather than documents. Among other pieces there appears a markedly subordinationist version of the *Gloria in excelsis*.

Book viii opens with a discussion of *charismata*. Since the time of Lightfoot it has been customary to assume that this is based on the treatise of Hippolytus, Περὶ Χαρισμάτων, which both in the Statue-catalogue of his works and by the opening words of the *Apostolic Tradition* is closely associated with the latter work. But a careful comparison of *Ap. Const.* viii. 1 and 2 with passages in other books which undoubtedly come from the "Constitutor's" own pen reveals so very much which is characteristic of his markedly individual style that it seems highly doubtful if any trace of Hippolytus' Περὶ Χαρισμάτων is really to be found in it; if the "Constitutor" used the work he has undoubtedly recast it altogether. But in fact these two chapters

* This was established beyond reasonable doubt by Turner, *J.T.S.* xv. 53.
† There is a handy discussion of the characteristics of his style by Brightman, *L.E.W.* p. xxiv *sq.*, which is too little known. Schwartz, *Ueber die pseudoapostolischen Kirchenordnungen*, attempts to distinguish four separate hands in this group of writings, but his arguments were entirely disposed of by Turner, *J.T.S.* xvi. 54 *sq.*

might conceivably have been suggested by *Ap. Trad.* i. 1 quite apart from the Περὶ Χαρισμάτων.

The remainder of Bk viii is based more or less—chiefly less— on the *Apostolic Tradition*. It contains like its source an ordinal, an anaphora (of the fourth-century Syrian type), and a large variety of other ecclesiastical regulations, arranged roughly in the order of Hippolytus' treatise, from which it frequently draws words and phrases. But so much has been added, altered, omitted or expanded that *Ap. Const.* viii can hardly be called a new edition of Hippolytus. It is really a fresh work for which the *Apostolic Tradition* has supplied the general outline and a certain amount of the language. But the author was evidently not in the least concerned to preserve the *Apostolic Tradition* for its own sake. The remnants of its text are usually swamped with supplementary matter, *e.g.* in the anaphora, where words and phrases certainly referable to the *Apostolic Tradition* amount to about eight lines in all of an anaphora occupying nine pages in Brightman's *L.E.W.* In this eighth book, the most practical part of his work, the author's main guide was un- doubtedly current Antiochene practice, as was natural if he wished his book to influence his own contemporaries at Antioch. Where we know for certain that Antiochene practice in the fourth century differed from that laid down by Hippolytus, *e.g.* in ordaining presbyters *without* imposition of hands by the other presbyters but by the bishop alone, or in ordaining lectors *with* imposition of the bishop's hands, the *Apostolic Constitutions* follows Antiochene custom, not the *Apostolic Tradition*.

Nevertheless, though its use of Hippolytus is everywhere dis- continuous and generally very free, the *Apostolic Constitutions* has some value for the reconstruction of Hippolytus' Greek text wherever this can be detected underlying the "Constitutor's" verbiage. But it is as well to emphasise the fact that it only assumes this value on account of the inadequate materials other- wise available. No fair estimate of the reliance to be placed on it can be made without careful consideration of the "Constitu- tor's" treatment of other documents in Bks i–vii. This author was equipped with a perverse ingenuity in the maltreatment of earlier documents, while sometimes leaving the whole structure of their sentences intact, which has to be studied to be adequately appreciated. He everywhere fuses the language of his sources with phrases and sentiments entirely of his own devising. A certain tendency to what can only be called moral reproof of the "Constitutor" on this head is observable in the writings of scholars who have had to struggle with his exasperating habit of adapting texts. It is but fair to say that in this he only follows the general practice of other authors of similar documents, though with a competence and a consistent thoroughness which none of his rivals can claim. If his work succeeded—as it did—in retaining its public for a thousand years after all the other Church Orders had virtually disappeared from Greek ecclesiastical literature, that was because it deserved to do so. With its profuse and ingenious use of scripture, its verbose prayers and its inflated rhetoric, the *Apostolic Constitutions* was excellently adapted to catch the later Byzantine taste. And almost everything before it of any value in this class of document had been absorbed into it and presented afresh in compact and practical form by an able and pious, if plainly heretical, editor. It is not only the climax but also the summary of the Church Orders.

So far as concerns its use of Hippolytus, the following observations may be made. The *Apostolic Tradition* has been treated, if possible, more rudely than any of the other sources of which this writer made use. Only about half the text of Hippolytus is represented at all in the *Apostolic Constitutions*, whereas the "Constitutor's" omissions from the *Didache* and *Didascalia* are small and unimportant. What does remain of Hippolytus is frequently summarised in language which, while reminiscent of the original, is not identical. In the *Didache* and the *Didascalia* the "Constitutor" has reproduced his sources with much greater fidelity. I have, I think, succeeded in extracting from the text of the "Constitutor" everything which may be said to bear traces of Hippolytus' wording. The surrounding matter of the "Constitutor's" own invention has been largely omitted, which gives a wholly misleading impression of the extent of his adherence to his source. Much less than a quarter of Bk viii has in fact any verbal connection with the *Apostolic Tradition*. And in those parts of it which do rest on the latter and in part preserve its language, caution is necessary to detect the frequent small changes of case and construction which the "Constitutor" has made. Words and phrases reproduced do not necessarily represent exactly Hippolytus' Greek.

The standard text is that of F. X. Funk (*Didascaliae et Constitutiones Apostolorum*, 2 vols., Paderborn, 1905), a beautiful book to work with, even though its text is sometimes susceptible of improvement.* There is an English translation in the *Library of the ante-Nicene Fathers*.

v. The "Epitome of Apostolic Constitutions, Bk viii" (Ep.) or "Constitutions through Hippolytus"

Neither of the titles by which this work is known accurately represents its contents. On the one hand it is not, strictly speaking, an *Epitome* of *Ap. Const.* viii so much as a series of extracts, some of them a little altered, but most of them given in the exact words of the *Apostolic Constitutions*. On the other, the title "Constitutions of the Holy Apostles through Hippolytus concerning Ordinations" is restricted by those MSS. in which it is found to the second only of the five chapters into which the work is divided. Its extension by some modern writers to the whole work seems to be due to an unfortunate theory put out by Achelis and patronised for a time by Harnack that the *Epitome* is really a source or first draft of *Ap. Const.* viii. The title of the whole work in the MSS., *Epitome*, was therefore regarded by them as misleading. But there is now no question that the *Epitome* is dependent on and later than the *Apostolic Constitutions*, and the title *Epitome* has therefore a certain convenience as emphasising this dependence.

The importance of the *Epitome* lies solely in this: that the "Epitomator" was aware that *Ap. Const.* viii made use of the *Apostolic Tradition*, and in three or four passages—the election of the bishop, the prayer for the consecration of a bishop, the

* Turner has shown that all MSS. except Vat. 1506 (Funk's MS. d) "tone down" the original Arianism of the work. The peculiar readings of d are generally placed by Funk in the *apparatus*.

appointment of a lector and (perhaps) for the regulation concerning concubinage with slaves in xvi. 24*b*—has for reasons no longer obvious preferred to reproduce Hippolytus' own text rather than the adapted text in his usual source. Clearly the original Greek text of the *Apostolic Tradition* lay before the "Epitomator" besides the *Apostolic Constitutions*, and in a MS. which still retained the author's name.

That the *Epitome* is later than the *Apostolic Constitutions* is obvious; how much later there is no satisfactory means of telling. The excellence of the text which it extracted from the *Apostolic Constitutions* suggests a fairly early date, but the oldest known MSS. are of the eleventh century. It is extant in a large number of MSS. differing considerably among themselves as to the portions of the *Apostolic Constitutions* reproduced, which suggests a long but not authoritative career for the work in the underworld of Greek canonical literature. We are equally in the dark as to its place of origin. The portions of the *Apostolic Constitutions* which it omits consist almost entirely of prayers and liturgical matter, which the "Epitomator" presumably thought superfluous as not being those in use in his own Church. But since it is probable that they were never in use quite in this form in any Church this gives no clue.

In a single MS. of this work, *Vienna, Hist. Gr.* vii, there are found two additional fragments of the *Apostolic Tradition*, from xxv. 1 and xxxvi. 6 respectively. This MS. is the only one to preserve the full Greek text of another Church Order, the *Apostolic Church Order*. Though it is only of the twelfth century its contents suggest derivation from an older MS., probably of Syrian origin.* Reliance on the obsolete matter of the Church Orders to the extent found in this MS. is unusual in Greek canonical collections, and indicates a non-Constantinopolitan origin for this one.

The *Epitome* is alone among our sources in offering us one or two continuous passages of Hippolytus' Greek text. It is unfortunate that even here one should have to point out that

---

* It contains extracts from the *Quaestiones* of Anastasius of Sinai, a writer on canon law popular in Syria in the eighth and ninth centuries.

Hippolytus has undergone slight but tendencious modification. In the prayer for the consecration of a bishop (iii. 3) it is the two *Greek* texts which have for opposite doctrinal reasons differently modified the words of their original and the translations which have preserved Hippolytus' own wording. This is one more caution against trusting too exclusively to any one source in the present state of our materials.

The Greek text of the *Epitome* was first printed in full by Lagarde (*Rel. jur. eccl. ant. Gr.*, Vienna, 1856, pp. 1–18) and has been several times reprinted since, by Pitra and others. I have used here that of F. X. Funk (*op. cit.* ii. 72 *sq.*). There is also a Syriac version, and Horner (*op. cit.* p. viii) speaks of an Arabic version, but of these I have no knowledge. There is no English version of the *Epitome*.

vi. The Canons of Hippolytus (K.)

With this document we really pass out of the Church Orders into a somewhat different group of writings. But since K. is largely based on the *Apostolic Tradition*, which is conventionally placed within them, it is convenient and usual to class K. as a Church Order.

In reality it belongs to an age when collections of Canons had become the recognised authority on Church usage and the fiction that all prescriptions on Church Order of necessity derived from the Apostles had been abandoned. But canonical literature in Egypt continued to cover itself with the venerated names of the past. Similar sets of Canons attributed to Athanasius, Basil, Gregory of Nyssa and other Doctors are known, and seem to represent much the same state of things. They are all in part based upon genuine extracts from the works of the Fathers whose names they bear, very freely adapted; a date in the late fifth or sixth century and an Egyptian origin seems attributable to all of them. K. is therefore not an isolated document, even though it really stands outside the Church Orders.

A hesitation to place it in its proper setting of these later Egyptian canonical collections, which are still very imperfectly known,* has obscured the character of K. in modern study.

* The only texts of some of them are German versions or summaries in Riedel's pioneer *Kirchenrechtsquellen*. *Canons of Athanasius* has been edited by Riedel and Crum, London, 1904.

Achelis arrived at the unfortunate conclusion that K. was the original of the whole group of Church Orders (*Ap. Trad., Ap. Const., Ep., Test.*) which contain Hippolytean matter, and from K. he supposed all the others to derive. K. is in fact the latest of the group and his theory was fruitful of impossible conclusions. Though it is now universally abandoned this false start seems in some way still to secure K. more consideration from scholars than its real character and date would justify.

K. is no more than a drastic re-casting of the *Apostolic Tradition*, which it has used with great freedom, altering the whole bearing of much in its original and shuffling the order of some of the parts. Thus *e.g.* Hippolytus' remarks concerning the cemetery (*Ap. Trad.* xxxiv) become in K. 24 regulations about sick persons sleeping in churches in the hope of a miraculous cure. The "tiles" which in the *Apostolic Tradition* close the *loculus*-grave in the catacomb are transformed in K. into "earthen-ware vessels" accidentally broken in the service of the sick, and the cemetery-watchman into "the steward of the Church". Nevertheless, faint but distinct traces of Hippolytus' wording are apparent in the passage in spite of these curious alterations, once it is realised that K. 24 is based on *Ap. Trad.* xxxiv. Sometimes it is only by examination of the context in the passages preceding and following parts of K. which at first sight appear to be quite independent compositions, that one can see how a passage of the *Apostolic Tradition* has suggested the very different contents of K. In such cases K. is of value rather as a witness to the fact that the passage in question stood in the MS. of the *Apostolic Tradition* used by its author than as evidence for particular readings. In any case K. has so greatly altered Hippolytus' wording that it can as a rule be used only as a secondary witness to reinforce other texts, but for this it is distinctly useful. Where L. is wanting and Ar.E.S. have edited the original text K. several times accords with T. in demonstrating that Ar.E.S. are not authentic, in passages where without K. we could not be sure that it is Ar.E.S. and not T. which are at fault. (A notable instance of this will be found at xxi. 2.)

The *Apostolic Tradition* is not the only older document on

which K. has drawn. Dom Connolly has shown good reason to believe that its author knew the Egyptian Liturgy of St Mark[*] and also the Syrian *Apostolic Didascalia*;[†] while Riedel[‡] has shown that he also used the questionably Athanasian *De Virginitate*. It seems possible also that he knew the *Apostolic Constitutions*. In the list of trades forbidden to Christians (*Ap. Trad.* xvi. 15), the *Apostolic Constitutions* (viii. 32. 9) has an interpolated text thus: "gladiator, a runner on the race course, trainer of gladiators, one who takes part in Olympic games". The second and fourth of these trades are not in Hippolytus' original list. K. has interpolated these two trades at the same point as the *Apostolic Constitutions* and in the second case retains the same Greek word (ὀλυμπικός) transliterated in its Arabic text. This point of contact between the *Apostolic Constitutions* and K. might be due to each being based on MSS. containing a similar interpolation, but a second point of contact cannot be so accounted for. The *Apostolic Constitutions* (viii. 25. 1) glosses Hippolytus' comment on the rules for the probation of widows (*Ap. Trad.* xi. 3) "for often the passions even grow old with one who gives place to them" with the words "if they are not restrained with a tighter rein". K. (15) reproduces the *Apostolic Constitutions*' gloss word for word, not with reference to the widows, but in connection with the trades forbidden to Christians in *Ap. Trad.* xvi. 21 *sq.*

If K. thus shows a knowledge of the *Apostolic Constitutions* it can hardly be older than the fifth century. The end of the fifth or the sixth century seems on the whole a reasonable date to assign to its composition. Its title, with that of *Ep.* ii, is the latest indication we have that the *Apostolic Tradition* was still circulating under its author's name.

One interesting point about K. is a curious tendency it shows at intervals to a sort of theoretical "presbyterianism". Thus where Hippolytus (*Ap. Trad.* ii. 5) orders "let one of the bishops who are present at the request of all lay his hands on him who is

---

[*] *So-called Eg. Ch. O.* p. 120.
[†] *Ibid.* p. 76; cf. Connolly, *Did. Apostolorum*, p. lxxxvi.
[‡] *Theologische Studien und Kritiken*, 1903, p. 338 *sq.*

ordained bishop", K. (2) orders "let one of the bishops *and presbyters* who are present, etc." Later on, however, K. (4) carefully reproduces Hippolytus' caution (*Ap. Trad.* ix. 7) that a presbyter "has no power" to ordain. Yet K. insists in the same passage that a presbyter is in all things equal to the bishop "except for the throne and the (power of) ordination"; and the presbyter, according to K., is to be ordained with exactly the same prayer as that used for the consecration of a bishop, except that the word "bishop" is to be changed to "presbyter". In this last case the author of K. is the victim of a confusion in the text of *Ap. Trad.* viii. 2 which has deceived modern authors also, but which is, I think, entirely dissipated by a discovery of Prof. Turner's which I have incorporated in the text and the note at this point. Nevertheless attempts have been made to see in K.'s blunder further evidence for "the well-known fact that the introduction of the monarchical episcopate came later in Egypt than elsewhere".* The alleged "fact" is dubious enough when judged by historical evidence, and K. does no more than repeat what had been said by writers from regions where the monarchical episcopate undoubtedly existed in the first century.† Such language was almost a commonplace in the fourth and fifth centuries. But I venture to think that it was not then a survival of something old but a mistake from something new. The primitive Christian presbytery, like the Jewish presbytery from which it derived, was a corporate judicial and administrative body, and the bishop as *ruler* of his church was simply its president, a presbyter among his fellow-presbyters. The primitive Christian presbyter, like his Jewish prototype, *had as such no liturgical functions* (cf. the presbyter's ordination-prayer in the *Apostolic Tradition*). But the ἐπισκοπή, the bishop's own office as bishop,

* Easton, *Ap. Trad.* p. 79. This author also cites Ar.S. as supporting K. in this. What they do is to insert Hippolytus' rubric at viii. 1 *verbatim* as far as "praying and saying", which they omit together with the subsequent prayer, as they have previously omitted the bishop's ordination-prayer at iii. 1 together with the preceding "saying". It does not seem to be more than clumsiness.

† *E.g.* St Jerome, *Ep.* 146: *Quid enim facit excepta ordinatione episcopus quod presbyter non faciat?* St Chrysostom, *Hom.* xi, in i Tim. iii. 8: τῇ χειροτονίᾳ μόνῃ ὑπερβεβήκασι καὶ τούτῳ μόνον δοκοῦσι πλεονεκτεῖν πρεσβυτέρους—a very steep statement! Cf. *e.g.* Ambrosiaster, *In* i *Tim.* iii. 10; *Quaest. Vet. et Nov. Test.* ci, etc., for similar passages.

was from the first *primarily liturgical*, like the deacon's (cf. their ordination-prayers in Hippolytus). The history of the episcopate is in one sense the history of the steady breaking down of its primitive liturgical monopoly. It was inevitable that as the Church grew this should be so by the mere necessity of numbers. By the fourth century only the power of ordaining remains a strictly episcopal preserve, and attempts were even being made (Ischyras, Aedesius, the Council of Ancyra) to extend that to presbyters. In the end the presbyters did break down the episcopal monopoly so far as minor orders were concerned. But all this is something *new*, not contemplated by ancient documents like the *Apostolic Tradition* or the *Didascalia*. So far as I can see there is nothing in the *Apostolic Tradition* which directly suggests that there is any liturgical function a presbyter can perform which a deacon cannot, except for the one privilege of joining in the imposition of hands in the ordination of a presbyter, a natural right of the presbyter since by derivation the *ruling* presbyterate was a corporate body. But in return for this parcelling out of his liturgical functions among the presbyters the bishop had by the fourth century practically monopolised the whole governmental power of the old corporate presbytery. The two offices had by then become in appearance assimilated to a large extent, though not in fact because the bishop has gained very largely in practical power by the exchange. It was, however, natural that the resemblance should be noted and emphasised, and this is done for the first time by fourth-century writers. I believe this history of the process can be illustrated at considerable length from almost every ecclesiastical document from Clement of Rome onwards. What is here important is that K. by its very attempt to assimilate the presbyter to the bishop betrays its late date.

Like all the other documents we have here discussed K. rests on a Greek original. It is now extant only in Arabic, but it is clear that a lost Coptic version intervenes between the Arabic and the original Greek.* Though Wansleb drew attention to K. as early as the seventeenth century, it was only in 1870 that the full text was published by Bishop D. B. von Haneberg with a

---

* Riedel, *Kirchenrechtsquellen*, p. 195.

Latin translation.* From v. Haneberg's text H. Vielhaber prepared a fresh
Latin version for Achelis' essay (*T.U.* I. vi. 4), parts of which were reprinted
as an appendix to the earlier editions of Duchesne's *Christian Worship*. A
German version from better and older MSS. was given by W. Riedel in his
Kirchenrechtsquellen des Patriarchats Alexandrien and it is his text which has
been used here.

* *Canones S. Hippolyti Arabice*, Münster, 1870.

Symbols used in the Text

The following symbols are used in the text:

⟨ ⟩ = Words or phrases having no authority from any version but introduced into the English translation to assist the sense.

[ ] = Words or phrases having authority from one or more versions but probably forming no part of the original Greek.

⌐ ⌐ = Words or phrases having authority from one or more versions, but not all, yet probably forming part of the original Greek.*

Greek words in ( ) within the English text are found transliterated in the Sahidic and/or Bohairic versions. They usually, but not invariably, come from Hippolytus' own Greek text.

Abbreviations

A. = *Apostolic Constitutions*, Bk viii, ed. F. X. Funk. Paderborn, 1905. i. 460 *sq.*

Achelis = H. Achelis, *Die Canones Hippolyti. (Texte und Untersuchungen, VI.)* Leipzig, 1891.

Ar. = Arabic version of *Ap. Trad.* ed. G. Horner, *Statutes of the Apostles.* London, 1904. 95 *sq.* [ed. Périer, Patrologia Orientalis 8, 4 (1912).]

Boh. = Bohairic version of *Ap. Trad.* ed. H. Tattam, *The Apostolical Constitutions, etc.* London, 1848.

Connolly = Dom R. H. Connolly, *The So-called Egyptian Church Order and Derived Documents. (Cambridge Texts and Studies,* viii. 4.) Cambridge, 1916.

Cooper and Maclean. *The Testament of our Lord* (Eng. tr.), J. Cooper and A. J. Maclean. Edinburgh, 1902.

E. = Ethiopic version of *Ap. Trad.* ed. Horner, *op. cit.* 10 *sq.* (and collations 365 *sq.*).

Easton = *The Apostolic Tradition of Hippolytus* (Eng. tr.), B. S. Easton. Cambridge, 1934.

Ep. = *Epitome of Ap. Const.* Bk viii, ed. Funk, *op. cit.* ii. 72 *sq.*

J.T.S. = *Journal of Theological Studies.*

†Jungklaus = E. Jungklaus, *Die Gemeinde Hippolyts* (German tr.). Leipzig, 1928.

K. = *Canons of Hippolytus* (German tr.), W. Riedel. *Die Kirchenrechtsquellen des Patriarchats Alexandrien.* Leipzig, 1900. 200 *sq.*

L. = Latin version of *Ap. Trad.* ed E. Hauler, *Didascaliae Apostolorum Fragmenta Veronensia Latina.* Leipzig, 1900. 101 *sq.*

S. = Sahidic version of *Ap. Trad.* ed. P. de Lagarde. *Aegyptiaca.* Göttingen, 1883. 248 *sq.*

S.² = Fragments of a second MS. of S. ed. Horner, *op. cit.* 461 *sq.*

Schwartz = E. Schwartz. *Ueber die pseudoapostolischen Kirchenordnungen.* Strassburg, 1910. [= *Gesammelte Schriften* 5 (1963), 192–273.]

T. = *Testamentum Domini* (text), ed. I. E. Rahmani. Mainz, 1899.

---

* Italicised words in such brackets are more doubtful.

† There appears to be some confusion about this edition. It originally appeared as Bd 46, Hft 2 of the *Texte und Untersuchungen* series (IV Reihe, i Bd, 2 Hft). But the real 46. 2. seems to be F. Loofs' *Theophilus v. Antiochien adv. Marcion.*

THE APOSTOLIC TRADITION

✦———✪———✦

i. ⟨Prologue⟩

L.E.(T.A.)

1 We have, then, set forth what was to be said concerning
spiritual gifts such as God has from the beginning bestowed on
men according to His own will in presenting to Himself that
image ⟨of Himself⟩ which had gone astray.

2 And now, "through the love which He had for all the
saints", having come to our most important topic, we turn to
⟨the subject⟩ of the Tradition which ⌜is proper for⌝ the Churches,

2. Cf. Eph. i. 15.

L. (p. 101). 1 Ea quidem quae
uerba [l. uerbo] fuerunt digne [l.
digna] posuimus de donationibus
quanta quidem Dē a principio se-
cundū propriam uoluntatem praestitit
hominibus offerens sibi eam imaginem
quae aberrauerat. 2 Nunc autem ex
caritate, quā in omnes sanctos habuit,
producti ad uerticem traditionis quae
catecizat ad ecclesias perreximus,

A. viii. 3. 1. Τὰ μὲν οὖν πρῶτα τοῦ
λόγου ἐξεθέμεθα περὶ τῶν χαρισμάτων ὅσαπερ ὁ θεὸς κατ᾽ ἰδίαν
βούλησιν πάρεσχεν ἀνθρώποις....
2. νυνὶ δὲ ἐπὶ τὸ κορυφαιότατον*
τῆς ἐκκλησιαστικῆς διατυπώσεως ὁ λόγος ἡμᾶς ἐπείγει.

  * The original was probably κορυφήν;
cf. Connolly, p. 160 sq., Sah. Hept. 63 has
κεφαλαίον.

---

1. The versions have made meagre use of this Prologue, probably by reason of the
obscurity of its archaic ideas. It is found in full in L., and has left traces in A. (inf.)
and T. i. 14 and 18. There is also an Eth. version (Horner, p. 162) but so confused and
corrupt as to be of little assistance. This Eth. Prologue is found in the Sinodos out of
place, in an interpolated chapter containing a series of prayers based on Pt ii of Ap.
Trad. This whole chapter is missing from Ar.S., which strongly suggests that it was
omitted in the common archetype from which Ar.E.S. derive, and has found its way into
E. from an independent source.

2. we turn to] perreximus L.; Turning to the Churches T. (? original = προτρέ-
ποντες. | which is proper for] traditionis quae catecizat L.; this is meaningless. Frere,
J.T.S. xvi. 32, suggests = an error of κατήχει for καθήκει; T. evidently read καθήκει.
T.(Syr.) i. 14 has: "Turning to the Churches...speak to every man as is helpful to
him": T.(Ar.): "Build up the Churches and ordain for them the offices which suit
each man." E: . . . which befits the Churches.

3   in order that those who have been rightly instructed may hold fast to that tradition which has continued until now, and fully understanding it from our exposition may stand the more firmly ⟨*therein*⟩.

4   ⟨*This is now the more necessary*⟩ because of that ⌐apostasy⌐ or error which was recently invented out of ignorance and ⟨*because of certain*⟩ ignorant men.

5   The Holy Ghost bestows the fulness of grace on those who believe rightly that they may know how those who are at the head of the Church should teach the tradition and maintain it in all things.

L. 3 ut [*h*]ii qui bene ducti [*l.* docti] sunt eam quae permansit usq̄ nunc traditionem exponentibus nobis custodiant et agnoscentes firmiores maneant, 4 propter eum qui nuper inuentus est per ignorantiam lapsus uel error et hos qui ignorant, 5 praestante sc̄o sp̄u perfectam gratiam eis qui recte credunt, ut cognoscant quomodo oportet tradi et custodiri omnia eos qui ecclesiae praesunt.

T. i. 18. 3, 4 But it shall be spoken…to those who are fixed and firm and do not fall away and keep my commandments and this tradition, that they may remain standing and strong in Me, 5 the Holy Ghost bestowing on them His grace that they may believe rightly, that they may…know the things of the Spirit.

⟨Part I. Of the Clergy⟩

ii. ⌐Of Bishops⌐

L.Ar.E.S.T.A.Ep. (K.)

Election

1   Let the bishop be ordained ⌐being in all things without fault⌐ chosen by all the people.

L. 1 Episcopus ordinetur electus ab omni populo; 2 quique cum nomina-   A. viii. 4. 2. *Cf.* Ep. в′. iii. 3. Ἐπί-σκοπον χειροτονεῖσθαι διατάσσο-

---

4. apostasy.] T., fall away, *suggests* ἀπόστασις *or* ἀποστασία *as the original of* L. lapsus. (*Cf.* E. unawares they slipped away.) *The word would fit Hippolytus' view of the Church's desertion of his own teaching.*

5. tradi et custodiri *in* L. *appear to represent verbs in the Middle Voice.*

Titles. Of the Clergy. *No version retains this. But Pt ii in T. retains* "Of the Laity" *which suggests a similar heading for Pt i. The chapter-headings resemble one another in* L.T.Ar.E.S., *but they are such as would naturally be suggested by the contents, and may not be original.*

Of the Bishops *so* S. Of the ordination of Bps Ar.E. (*and so* A.?). *All titles in* L. *have been effaced, being originally inscribed in a red paint more fugitive than the black ink of the text. Hauler here conjectures* ⟨De episcopo⟩ (? +ordinando). *There would be space for* ⟨De episcopis⟩ *as in* S., *but hardly for* ordinando.

1. being—fault] *so* Ar.S.T.A.Ep. (?K.); *om.* LE.

Confirmation

2 And when he has been proposed and found acceptable to all, the people shall assemble on the Lord's day together with the presbytery and such bishops as may attend.

Consecration

3 With the agreement of all let ⌜the bishops⌝ lay hands on him and the presbytery stand by in silence,

4 And all shall keep silence praying in their heart for the descent of the Spirit.

5 After this one of the bishops present at the request (ἀξιοῦν) of all, laying his hand on him ⌜who is ordained bishop⌝, shall pray thus, saying:

tus fuerit et placuerit omnibus conueniet populum una cum praesbyterio et his qui praesentes fuerint episcopi, die dominica.

L. 3 Consentientibus omnibus inponant super eum manus et praesbyterium adstet quiescens. 4 Omnes autem silentium habeant orantes in corde propter discensionem sps; 5 ex quibus unus de praesentibus episcopis ab omnibus rogatus inponens manum ei qui ordinatur episcopus, oret ita dicens:

μαι...ἐν πᾶσιν ἄμεμπτον...ὑπὸ παντὸς τοῦ λαοῦ ἐκλελεγμένον. οὗ ὀνομασθέντος καὶ ἀρέσαντος (ἀρεσθέντος Ep.), συνελθὼν ὁ λαὸς ἅμα τῷ πρεσβυτερίῳ καὶ τοῖς παροῦσιν ἐπισκόποις...ἐν ἡμέρᾳ κυριακῇ (+συνευδοκείτω Ep.).

A. viii. 4. 6. καὶ σιωπῆς γενομένης εἷς τῶν πρώτων ἐπισκόπων ἅμα καὶ δυσὶν ἑτέροις πλησίον τοῦ θυσιαστηρίου ἐστώς, τῶν λοιπῶν ἐπισκόπων καὶ πρεσβυτέρων σιωπῇ προσευχομένων, τῶν δὲ διακόνων τὰ θεῖα εὐαγγέλια ἐπὶ τῆς τοῦ χειροτονουμένου κεφαλῆς ἀνεπτυγμένα κατεχόντων λεγέτω...

2. And—assembled] om. E. | to all] om. A.Ep. | on the Ld's day] the Sabbath E.; within the week of his ordination K. | presbytery] +and the deacons Ar.E.S.
3. the bishops] om. L. | in silence] subst. waiting S.
4. heart] so L.S.; pl. Ar.E.T. | for the descent] L. propter might mean "on account of", suggesting that this is the actual consecration. Cf. T. (inf.). Possibly the original was ὑπέρ. | T. supplies a prayer for this first imposition of hands thus: "Let the bishops lay hands on him saying: 'We lay hands on the servant of God, who has been chosen in the Spirit by the true and pious appointment (κατάστασις translit.) of the Church, which alone has the principality and is not dissolved, of the invisible living God, and for the delivering of true judgement and divine and holy revelations, and of divine gifts and faithful doctrines of the Trinity, by the Cross, by the Resurrection, by the incorruptibility in the holy Church of God.' After this one bishop, commanded by the other bishops, shall lay hands on him saying his calling of appointment thus:"—followed by T.'s version of iii. 1. ("Calling of appointment" =ἐπίκλησις καταστάσεως implying that iii. contains the consecration.) A. omits this first imposition.
5. After this] so L. (=ἐκ τούτων) T.; om. Ar.E.S. | bishops] +and presbyters K. | present] Ar.E.S. subst. while all stand (πάντων στάντων for παραστάντων) | at the request of] L.T.Ar.E.S. seem to take ἀξιούμενος as "being requested", but A. (εἰς τῶν

iii. ⌐Prayer for the Consecration of a Bishop.⌐

L.Ep.E.T.A.K.

1 "O God and Father of our Lord Jesus Christ, Father of mercies and God of all comfort", "Who dwellest on high yet hast respect unto the lowly", "who knowest all things before they come to pass";

2 Who didst give ordinances unto Thy church "by the Word of Thy grace"; Who "didst foreordain from the beginning" the race of the righteous from Abraham, instituting princes and priests and leaving not Thy sanctuary without ministers; Who from the foundation of the world hast been pleased to be glorified in them whom Thou hast chosen;

3 ⌐And⌐ now pour forth that Power which is from Thee, of "the princely Spirit" which Thou didst deliver to Thy Beloved Child

L. (p. 103). 1 Dš et pater dm̄ nostri Ieū Chn̄, pater misericordiarum et Dš totius consolationis qui in excelsis habitas et humilia respicis, qui cognoscis omnia antequam nascantur, 2 tu qui dedisti terminos in ecclesia per uerbum gratiae tuae praedestinans ex principio genus iustorum Abraham, principes et sacerdotes constituens et scm̄ tuum sine ministerio non derelinquens, ex initio saeculi bene tibi placuit in his quos elegisti ⟨lau⟩dari.

Ep. Β΄. iv. 1. Ὁ Θεὸς καὶ Πατὴρ τοῦ κυρίου ἡμῶν Ἰ. Χ. ὁ πατὴρ τῶν οἰκτιρμῶν καὶ θεὸς πάσης παρακλήσεως, ὁ ἐν ὑψηλοῖς κατοικῶν καὶ τὰ ταπεινὰ ἐφορῶν, ὁ γινώσκων τὰ πάντα πρὶν γενέσεως αὐτῶν· σὺ ὁ δοὺς ὅρους ἐκκλησίας διὰ Λόγου τοῦ χάριτός σου, ὁ προορίσας τε ἀπ' ἀρχῆς γένος δίκαιον ἐξ Ἀβραάμ, ἄρχοντάς τε καὶ ἱερεῖς καταστήσας, τό τε ἁγίασμά σου μὴ καταλιπὼν ἀλειτούργητον, ὁ ἀπὸ καταβολῆς κόσμου εὐδοκήσας ἐν οἷς ἡρετίσω δοξασθῆναι·

1. Cf. 2 Cor. i. 3; Ps. cxii, 5 & 6. 2. Cf. Acts xx. 32; Eph. i. 5.
3. Cf. Ps. l. 14.

L. 3 nunc effunde eam uirtutem quae a te est, principalis spš quem

Ep. καὶ νῦν ἐπίχεε τὴν παρὰ σοῦ δύναμιν τοῦ ἡγεμονικοῦ πνεύματος, ὅπερ

πρώτων) and K. as "being thought worthy" or "chosen". | who is ord. bp] so L. (?A.); om. Ar.E.S.T.K. | thus] om. S. | saying] om. Ar.S.

Title. εὐχὴ χειροτονίας ἐπισκόπου Ep. and so T. Some MSS. of A. have ἐπίκλησις χειρ. ἐπισκόπων, but the best (Funk's d) εὐχὴ ἐπὶ χειρ. ἐπισκόπου. L., Title effaced. E., no title and no fresh section. Ar.S. omit the whole chapter.

1. God and Father] and om. E.

2. ordinances] sing. E.; illumination T. (?ὁροῦν for ὅρους). | unto Thy church] the ch. T.E.; of Thy ch. Ep.A.; in the ch. L. | from Abraham] from om. L. | sanctuary] ἁγίασμα has troubled some of the translators. T.E. rightly render sanctuary (cf. L.).

3. And] om. L. | which is from Thee] om. A. | princely] holy E. | wh. Thou didst deliver to thy Bel.] so L.E.T. (to Thy Holy One, T.); wh. by Thy Bel. Thou didst

Jesus Christ, which He bestowed on Thy holy Apostles who established the Church which hallows Thee in every place to the endless glory and praise of Thy Name.

4 ⌐Father⌐ "who knowest the hearts [of all]" grant upon this Thy servant whom Thou hast chosen for the episcopate to feed Thy holy flock and serve as Thine high priest, that he may minister blamelessly by night and day, that he may unceasingly [behold and] propitiate Thy countenance and offer to Thee the gifts of Thy holy Church,

5 And that by the high priestly Spirit he may have authority "to forgive sins" according to Thy command, "to assign lots" according to Thy bidding, to "loose every bond" according to the authority Thou gavest to the Apostles, and that he may please

dedisti dilecto filio tuo Ieū Chrō quod donauit sanctis apostolis qui constituerunt ecclesiam per singula loca, sanctificationem tuam in gloriam et laudem indeficientem nomini tuo.
4 Da cordis cognitor pater super hunc seruum tuum quem elegisti ad episcopatum pascere gregem sanctam tuam et primatum sacerdotii tibi exhibere sine repraehensione seruientem noctu et die, incessanter repropitiari uultum tuum et offerre dona sancta⟨e⟩ ecclesiae tuae,

διὰ τοῦ ἠγαπημένου σου παιδὸς 'Ι. Χ. δεδώρησαι τοῖς ἁγίοις σου ἀποστόλοις οἳ καθίδρυσαν τὴν ἐκκλησίαν κατὰ τόπον ἁγιάσματός σου εἰς δόξαν καὶ αἶνον ἀδιάλειπτον τοῦ ὀνόματός σου. ⟨Δός Α.⟩ καρδιωγνῶστα πάντων ⟨δὸς Ep.⟩ ἐπὶ τὸν δοῦλόν σου τοῦτον ὃν ἐξελέξω εἰς ἐπισκοπὴν ⟨ποιμαίνειν τὴν ποίμνην⟩ σου τὴν ἁγίαν καὶ ἀρχιερατεύειν σοι, ἀμέμπτως λειτουργοῦντα νυκτὸς καὶ ἡμέρας ἀδιαλείπτως τε ⟨ἐξ⟩ιλάσκεσθαι τῷ προσώπῳ σου καὶ προσφέρειν σοι τὰ δῶρα τῆς ἁγίας σου ἐκκλησίας,

4. Cf. Acts i. 24. 5. Cf. Jn. xx. 23: Acts i. 26; Is. lviii. 6; Mt. x. 1; Eph. v. 2.

L. (p. 105). 5 spū primatus sacerdotii habere potestatem dimittere peccata secundum mandatum tuum, dare sortes secundum praeceptū tuum,

Ep. καὶ τῷ πνεύματι τῷ ἀρχιερατικῷ ἔχειν ἐξουσίαν ἀφιέναι ἁμαρτίας κατὰ τὴν ἐντολήν σου, διδόναι κλήρους κατὰ

---

bestow on Thy holy App....Ep.K. (to avoid subordinationism); princely Sp. who serves Thy Bel. (ὅπερ διακονεῖται τῷ ἡγ.) A. (to emphasise subord.). | on Thy holy App.] so T.A.Ep.; on us Thy holy App. E.; on the holy App. L. | the Ch. which hallows Thee] so L.Ep.; Send...to every place that singeth "Holy" to Thee E.; in the place of Thy holiness E. | of Thy Name] to Thy N. L. The ref. is to the "hallowing of the Name", cf. Lord's Prayer. On this verse cf. Additional Note, p. 86.
4. Father] so L.T.; God A.; om. Ep.E.K. | of all] so Ep. (fr. Acts i. 24); om. L.E.T.A. | upon] so all. | episcopate] so all exc. A. (ἐπίσκοπον). | feed Thy holy flock] om. feed Thy flock Ep., and joins holy with episcopate. As restored inf. Ep. does not entirely agree with A. | night and day] day and night T.E. | behold and] so E.T.; om. L.Ep.A. | and propitiate] om. T.; repropitiari L. supports ἐξιλάσκεσθαι (A.) agst. ἱλάσκ. (Ep.). | to Thee] om. L. | of Thy holy Ch.] in Thy holy Church E.
5. And] om. L. | to assign—bidding] to give the ordination of Thine ordinance E. | bond] pl. T.; +of iniquity E.K. | the App.] Thine App. E.T.

Thee in meekness and a pure heart, "offering" to Thee "a sweet-smelling savour",

6   through Thy Child Jesus Christ our Lord, through Whom to Thee be glory, might and praise, to the Father and to the Son with ⟨the⟩ Holy Spirit now [and ever] and world without end. Amen.

soluere etiam omnem colligationem secundum potestatem, quam dedisti apostolis, placere autem tibi in mansuetudine et mundo corde, offerentem tibi odorem suauitatis. 6 per puerum tuum lem̄ Chr̄m̄ per quem tibi gloria et potentia et honor, patri et filio cum spū scō, et nunc et in saecula saeculorum. Amen.

τὸ πρόσταγμά σου, λύειν τε πάντα σύνδεσμον κατὰ τὴν ἐξουσίαν, ἣν ἔδωκας τοῖς ἀποστόλοις εὐαρεστεῖν τέ σοι ἐν πραότητι καὶ καθαρᾷ καρδίᾳ, προσφέροντά σοι ὀσμὴν εὐωδίας διὰ τοῦ παιδός σου Ἰησοῦ Χριστοῦ, τοῦ κυρίου ἡμῶν, μεθ' οὗ σοι δόξα, κράτος, τιμὴ σὺν ἁγίῳ πνεύματι νῦν [καὶ ἀεὶ] καὶ εἰς τοὺς αἰῶνας τῶν αἰώνων. Ἀμήν.

iv. ⟨The Liturgy⟩

L.Ar.E.S.T.A.K.

Kiss of Peace

1   And (δέ) when he has been made bishop (ἐπίσκοπος) let every one offer him the kiss of peace (εἰρήνη) saluting (ἀσπάζεσθαι) him, for he has been made worthy ⟨of this⟩.

Offertory

2   To him then let the deacons (διάκονος) bring the oblation (προσφορά) and (δέ) he with all the presbyters (πρεσβύτερος) laying his hand on the oblation (πρ.) shall say giving thanks (εὐχαριστῶν *sic*):

L. (p. 106). 1 Qui cumque factus fuerit episcopus omnes os offerant pacis, salutantes eum, quia dignus effectus est. 2 Illi uero offerant diacones oblationes, quique inponens manus in eam cum omni praesbyterio dicat gratia[n]s agens:

6. our Lord] so Ep.E.T.; *om.* L. | through whom] with whom Ep. (*to avoid subordinationism*). | glory, might and praise] so L.Eᵖ.E.; δόξα, τιμὴ καὶ σέβας A.; praise, glory and might T. | with the H.S.] in the H.S.A. | and ever] Ep. *only.*
Title. No version has a fresh heading or section at this point.
1. When he—bishop] Ar.E.S. *differ a little from* L. *but both appear to represent* ἐπισκόπῳ δὲ γενομένῳ | saluting him] *om.* T. | for—worthy] *om.* Ar.S.T. (A.).
2. To him—oblation 1°] *om.* T. | deacons] so L.Ar. (1 *MS.*) S.A.; *sing.* E.K.Ar. (1 *MS.*) | oblation 1°] so S.E.; *pl.* L. (*but* eam *inf.*) Ar.K. | hand] so Ar.E.S.T.K.;

3 The Lord be with you. And the people (λαός) shall say: And with thy spirit. [*And the bishop shall say:*] Lift up your hearts. [*And the people shall say:*] We have them with the Lord. [*And the bishop shall say:*] Let us give thanks unto the Lord. [*And the people shall say:*] ⟨*It is*⟩ meet and right. And forthwith he shall continue thus:

3 Dn̄s uobiscum; et omnes dicant: et cum sp̄u tuo. Susum [*sic*] corda. Habemus ad dom̄. Gratias agamus dn̄o. Dignum et iustum est. Et sic iam prosequatur.

S.A.K. Ὁ κύριος μετὰ [πάντων] ὑμῶν (*om.* ὑμῶν K.). ℟. ⌈καὶ⌉ (*om.* S.) μετα τοῦ πνεύματός σου. ℣. Ἄνω ὑμῶν τὰς καρδίας. ℟. Ἔχομεν πρὸς τὸν κύριον. ℣. Εὐχαριστήσωμεν τῷ κυρίῳ [τὸν κύριον S.]. ℟. Ἄξιον καὶ δίκαιον.

L.E.T.(A.)

Canon

4 We render thanks unto thee, O God, through Thy Beloved Child Jesus Christ, Whom in the last times Thou didst send to us ⟨*to be*⟩ a Saviour and Redeemer and the Angel of Thy counsel;
5 Who is Thy Word inseparable ⟨*from Thee*⟩, through Whom Thou madest all things and in Whom Thou wast well-pleased;
6 ⟨*Whom*⟩ Thou didst send from heaven into ⟨*the*⟩ Virgin's womb and Who conceived within her was made flesh and demonstrated to be Thy Son being born of Holy Spirit and a Virgin;

L. (*p.* 106). 4 Gratias tibi referimus, Ds̄, per dilectum puerum tuum Iem̄ Chrm̄ quem in ultimis temporibus misisti nobis saluatorem et redemptorem et angelum uoluntatis tuae; 5 qui est uerbum tuum inseparabilem per quem omnia fecisti et bene placitum tibi fuit; 6 misisti de caelo in matricem uirginis (γέγονεν ἐν μήτρᾳ παρθένου A.) quiq̄ in utero habitus incarnatus est et filius

---

pl. L. | oblation 2°] *so* L. (eam) Ar.E.S.; *pl.* K. (T. on the loaves wh. have been put on the altar). | with all the presbs.] *om.* T.

3. You]+all S.; *om.* you *and subst.* all K. *Both* S. *and* K. *transliterate the Gk. of these* ℣. *and* ℟. | And the Bp *etc.*] *These rubrics are found with slight variants in all but* L. | And forthwith] *so* L. (iam) T.A. (ἐξῆς); *om.* Ar.E.S. | he] *so* L.Ar.S.: the bishop E.T.; ἀρχιερεύς A. | continue] *so* L.; say Ar.E.T.A.; continue thus and say what *etc.* S. | thus] *subst.* what comes after this in the custom of the (+ holy S.) oblation (προσφ. S.) Ar.S. *and omit the prayer following.*

In a few cases A. *has adapted phrases from the first part of this prayer which are here inserted after the relevant phrases in* L.

4. We render thanks] *so* L.T. (*probably* εὐχαριστίας ἄγομεν *rather than* εὐχαριστοῦμεν). | God] Lord E. | and Redeemer] *om.* T. Angel] *cf.* Isa. ix. 5.

5. inseparable] *so* L., who is from thee E.; who is Son of counsel and of promise T. | wast] *so* L.E.T., art *Easton.*

6. (the) Virgin's womb] *so* L.E.; a virgin womb T. (? εἰς μήτραν παρθένου [*cf.* A. *sup.*], T. *reading* πάρθενον). | and who conceived] and *om.* T. | conceived—flesh] E. *transposes these clauses.*

7 Who fulfilling Thy will and preparing for Thee a holy people stretched forth His hands for suffering that He might release from sufferings them who have believed in Thee;

8 Who when He was betrayed to voluntary suffering that He might abolish death and rend the bonds of the devil and tread down hell and enlighten the righteous and establish the limit and demonstrate the resurrection:

9 Taking bread ⟨and⟩ making eucharist [*i.e.* giving thanks] to Thee said: Take eat: this is My Body which is broken for you [*for the remission of sins*]. Likewise also the cup, saying: This is My Blood which is shed for you.

10 When ye do this [ye] do My "anamnesis".

11 Doing therefore the "anamnesis" of His death and resurrec-

tibi ostensus est ex spū scō et uirgine natus; 7 qui uoluntatem tuam conplens (τὸ θέλημά σου ἐπλήρωσε A.) et populum sanctum tibi adquirens extendis (*sic*) manus cum pateretur ut a passione liberaret (ἵνα πάθους λύσῃ A.) eos qui in te crediderunt.

L. 8 qui cumque traderetur uoluntariae passioni ut mortem soluat et uincula diaboli dirumpat et infernum calcet et iustos inluminet et terminum figat et resurrectionem manifestet, 9 accipiens panem gratias tibi agens dixit: Accipite, manducate: hoc est corpus meum, quŏd pro uobis confringetur. Similiter et calicem dicens: Hic est sanguis meus qui pro uobis effunditur; 10 quando hoc facitis, meam commemorationem facitis. 11 Memores igitur mortis et resurrectionis

A. viii. 12. 33. προδοσίᾳ τοῦ τὴν κακίαν νοσήσαντος...ἵνα πάθους λύσῃ καὶ θανάτου ἐξέληται τούτους δι᾽ οὓς παρεγένετο, καὶ ῥήξῃ τὰ δεσμὰ τοῦ διαβόλου...

τοῦτο ποιεῖτε εἰς τὴν ἐμὴν ἀνάμνησιν. ...μεμνημένοι τοίνυν τοῦ πάθους αἰτοῦ καὶ τοῦ θανάτου καὶ τῆς ἐκ

7. for Thee] *so* L.E.; *om.* T; *Easton renders* for himself. | for suffering] *so* E.T.; cum pateretur L. (? = πάθει *in both cases*) | from sufferings] *so* T.; the sufferers E.; a passione L. (*Easton by his death*).

8. enlighten] *so* L.; guide into light T.; lead forth E. (? *original* ἐκφωτίζειν). | limit | *probably of hell* (ὅρος).

9. bread] + and gave it to His disciples T. | making euch, to Thee] *om.* T. | Take] + and E. | is broken] θρυπτόμενον A. *not* κλώμενον *as in* 1 *Cor.* ii. 24 | for the rem. of sins] *so* T.A. *and two late MSS. of* E.; *om.* L. *and older MSS. of* E. | Likewise also *etc.*] T. *subst.* Also the cup of wine which He mixed He gave for a type of the Blood which He shed for us.

10. ye do] *so* L. (*pr.* indic.); do (*pr.* imperative) E.T. ποιεῖτε *can mean either.* | "anamnesis"] T. *has* my resurrection, *error of* ἀνάστασιν *for* ἀνάμνησιν. *The word transl.* "*do*" *in Greek, Syriac and Ethiopic can just as well mean* "*offer*". *Cf. Note on* "*anamnesis*".

11. His death] *so* L.A. *and older MSS. of* E.; thy death and thy res. T. *and* 1 MS.

tion we offer to Thee the bread and the cup making eucharist to Thee because Thou hast made us worthy to stand before Thee and minister as priests to Thee.

12 And we pray Thee that thou wouldest send Thy Holy Spirit upon the oblation of Thy holy Church Thou wouldest grant to all ⌐Thy Saints⌐ who partake to be united [to Thee] that they may be fulfilled with the Holy Spirit for the confirmation of ⟨their⟩ faith in truth.

13 that ⌐we⌐ may praise and glorify Thee through Thy [Beloved] Child Jesus Christ through whom glory and honour ⟨be⟩ unto Thee with ⟨the⟩ Holy Spirit in Thy holy Church now ⌐and for ever⌐ and world without end. Amen.

eius offerimus tibi panem et calicem gratias tibi agentes quia nos dignos habuisti adstare coram te et tibi ministrare.

νεκρῶν ἀναστάσεως...προσφέρο-μέν σοι...τὸν ἄρτον τοῦτον καὶ τὸ ποτήριον τοῦτο, εὐχαριστοῦντές σοι δι' αὐτοῦ ἐφ' οἷς κατηξίωσας ἡμᾶς ἑστάναι ἐνώπιόν σου καὶ ἱερατεύειν σοι.

L. 12 Et petimus ut mittas s̄p̄m̄ tuum s̄c̄m̄ in oblationem sanctae ecclesiae; in unum congregans des omnibus qui percipiunt sanctis in repletionem s̄p̄s̄ s̄o̅ī ad confirmationem fidei in veritate. 13 ut te laudemus et glorificemus per puerum tuum Īē̄m̄ Ch̄r̄m̄ per quem tibi gloria et honor patri et filio cum s̄c̄ō̄ s̄p̄u̅ in sancta ecclesia tua et nunc et saecula saeculorum. Amen.

A. καὶ ἀξιοῦμέν σε ὅπως...

ἵνα οἱ μεταλαβόντες αὐτοῦ βεβαιω-θῶσιν...πνεύματος ἁγίου πλη-ρωθῶσι....

ὅτι σοὶ πᾶσα δόξα, σέβας καὶ εὐχαριστία, τιμὴ καὶ προσκύνησις, τῷ πατρὶ καὶ υἱῷ καὶ τῷ ἁγίῳ πνεύματι, καὶ νῦν καὶ ἀεὶ καὶ εἰς τοὺς...αἰῶνας τῶν αἰώνων. Ἀμήν.

---

of E. | because] ἐφ' οἷς A. and so T. (literally transl. into Syriac).
   12. On the difficulties of the text here cf. Note. | pray thee] + Lord and we beseech Thee some MSS. of E. | that Thou wouldest send etc.] so L.; to send Thy H.Sp. upon this oblation of Thy Ch. E.; om. T. The epiclesis in A. seems to be derived from another source. | to all Thy Saints who partake] so L.; to all who partake of Thy holy things (ἁγίων for ἁγίοις) T.; for holiness E. Cf. Note. | to Thee] so T.; om. L.E.
   13. that we] so L.; they T.E. | praise and glorify] so L.E.; raise a doxology T. | through] and to T. | Beloved] so T.; om. L.E. Cf. vi. 4. | with the H.Sp.] so L.; om. E.; with Thy H.Sp. T. | in Thy holy Ch.] so L.T.; in the E. | now and] om. T. | and for ever] so E.; om. L.T.; but cf. vi. 4.
   For other textual materials see Note.

v. ⟨*Blessing of Oil*⟩

L.E.(T.K.)

1   If any one offers oil, he [*i.e., the bishop*] shall make eucharist [*or, render thanks*] as at the oblation of bread and wine. But he shall not say word for word ⟨*the same prayer*⟩ but with similar effect, saying:

2   ⌜O God⌝ who sanctifiest ⌜this⌝ oil, as Thou dost grant unto all who are ⌜anointed⌝ and receive of it ⌜the hallowing⌝ wherewith Thou didst anoint kings ⟨*and*⟩ priests and prophets, so ⟨*grant that*⟩ it may give strength to all that taste of it and health to all that use it.

L. 1 Si quis oleum offert secundum panis oblationem et uini et non ad sermonem dicat, sed simili uirtute gratias referat dicens:

2. L.	E. (*Horner, p.* 141).
Ut oleum hoc sanctificans das Ds san⟨ct⟩itatem utentibus [*l. unctis*] et percipientibus, unde uncxisti reges sacerdotes et profetas, sic et omnibus gustantibus confortationem et sanitatem utentibus illud praebeat.	Having sanctified oil Thou shalt grant to all who are anointed or receive it that ⟨*with*⟩ which Thou anointedst priest and prophets, and in like manner strengthen those and all who taste, and sanctify them who receive it.

vi. ⟨*Blessing of Cheese and Olives*⟩

L.(T.K.E.)

1   Likewise if any one offers cheese and olives he shall say thus:
2   Sanctify this solidified milk, solidifying us also unto Thy charity.

L. (*p.* 108). 1 Similiter si quis caseum et olivas offeret, ita dicet: 2 Sanctifica lac hoc quod quoagulatum est, et nos conquaglans tuae caritati. 3 Fac a tua

---

1. E. *is confused in this verse but seems to represent the same Gk as* L. T. *subst.* If the priest offers oil for the healing of the sick let him say thus quietly, *placing the vessel before the altar, followed by a different prayer.* K. *has only,* if oil be there, he shall pray over it in the same way, *with no prayer.* A. (viii. 29. 3) *gives a prayer for blessing oil and water for the sick which has no points of contact with* L.E.

2. L.E. *are both very confused in this prayer.* E. *omits* kings.

⟨O God⟩ *om.* E. | this] *om.* E. | who are anointed] *so* E. utentibus L. (*error,* χρησθεῖσι *for* χρισθεῖσι) | hallowing] L. sanitatem *read* sanctitatem. *The next clause* unde uncxisti, *etc., shows that something conferred on* Kgs, Priests, *etc., is meant. Either* sanitatem *is a copyist's error, or the original translator read* ἀγίασμα *as* ὑγίασμα. | kings] *om.* E. | health] *so* L.; sanctify E. (*error* ἀγίασον *for* ὑγίασον).

1, 2, 3. L. *alone preserves these three verses, but* T. *attests their genuineness by intro-*

3 Grant also that this fruit of the olive depart not from Thy sweetness, ⟨*this fruit*⟩ which is the type of thy fatness which Thou hast caused to flow from the Tree* for the life of them that hope in Thee.

4 But in every blessing shall be said: To Thee be glory, to the Father and to the Son with ⟨*the*⟩ Holy Spirit in the holy Church now and for ever and world without end. Amen.

dulcitudine non recedere fructum etiam hunc oliuae qui est exemplū tuae pinguidinis, quam de ligno fluisti in uitam eis, qui sperant in te. 4 In omni uero benedictione dicatur: Tibi gloria, patri et filio cum sc̄o spū in sancta ecclesia et nunc et semper et in omnia saecula saeculorum. ⟨*Amen.*⟩

vii. [*Spurious. Communion Prayers*]

E. only

The bishop shall say:

And again we beseech Thee, Almighty God, the Father of our Lord Jesus Christ, to grant us to receive with blessing this holy mystery: and that He may not condemn any of us, but cause worthiness in all them who take the reception of the holy mystery, the Body and the Blood of Christ, Almighty Lord, our God.

The deacon shall say: Pray ye. ⟨*Here should follow the Lord's Prayer.*⟩

And the bishop shall say: God Almighty, grant to us the reception of Thy holy mystery as our strengthening; nor condemn any among us, but bless all through Christ, through Whom to Thee with Him and with the Holy Spirit be glory and might now and always and for ever and ever. Amen.

The deacon shall say: As ye stand, bow down your heads.

The bishop shall say: Eternal God, the knower of that which

---

ducing the phrase oil which is the type of thy fatness *into the blessing of oil which it substitutes for verse* V. 2.

4. L.K.E. *all preserve this, but only* L. *in full;* T. *omits.* | E. *has only* And the people shall say: as it was, is and shall be to generation of generation and to age of age. Amen.—*which it appends to verse* 2. | in every blessing] at the end of every prayer K. | in the holy ch. now and for ever] *om.* K. | Amen] *not in* L. *Probably written in red ink and so effaced like the titles.*

* "Tree" here seems to mean the Cross, not the olive tree. But *cf.* R. H. Charles, *Apocr. and Pseud.* ii. p. 143–4 and *Laudate* xiv. p. 231 sq.

is secret and that which is open, to Thee Thy people bowed down their heads, and to Thee they bent the hardness of heart and flesh, look from Thy worthy dwelling-place, bless them both men and women, incline Thine ear to them and hear their prayer, and strengthen ⟨them⟩ with the might of Thy right hand, and protect ⟨them⟩ from evil sickness, be their guardian for both body and soul, increase to them and to us also Thy faith and Thy fear, through Thine only Son, through Whom to Thee etc. Amen.

And the deacon shall say: Let us attend.

And the bishop shall say: Holiness to holy ones.

And the people shall say: One Holy Father, one Holy Son, one is the Holy Spirit.

The bishop shall say: The Lord ⟨be⟩ with you all.

And the people shall say: With thy Spirit.

And then they shall lift up their hands for glorifying; and the people shall come in for the salvation of their souls, that their sin may be remitted.

The Prayer after they have communicated:

God Almighty, the Father of our Lord Jesus Christ, we give Thee thanks because Thou hast imparted to us the reception of the holy mystery: let it not be for guilt or condemnation, but for the renewal of soul and body and spirit, through Thine only Son through Whom to Thee etc. *And the people shall say:* Amen.

And the presbyter shall say: The Lord be with you. *The laying on of hands after they have received:*

Eternal God, Almighty, the Father of the Lord and our Saviour Jesus Christ, bless Thy servants and handmaids, protect and help and prosper ⟨them⟩ by the power of Thine Archangel. Keep and confirm in them Thy fear by Thy greatness; provide that they shall both think what is Thine and believe what is Thine and will what is Thine; grant them peace without sin and anger through Thine only Son through Whom etc.

The people shall say: Amen.

And the bishop shall say: The Lord be with you all.

And the people shall say: With thy Spirit.

And the deacon shall say: Go forth in peace.

And with that the Oblation is finished.

viii. ⌜Of Presbyters⌝

Officiants   L.Ar.E.S.(A.Ep.T.K.)

1 And (δέ) when a presbyter is ordained (χειροτονεῖν) the bishop shall lay his hand upon his head, the presbyters also touching him. And he shall pray over him according to the aforementioned form which we gave before over the bishop, praying and saying:

Ordination

2 O God and Father of our Lord Jesus Christ—⟨*as far as* "*of thy Name*" (iii. 3) *but continuing*⟩—Look upon this Thy servant and impart to him the spirit of grace and counsel, "that he may share" in the presbyterate "and govern" Thy people in a pure heart.

2. Cf. 1 Cor. xii. 28.

L. (*p.* 108). 1 Cum autem praesbyter ordinatur, inponat manum super caput eius episcopus, contingentib̄ etiam praesbyteris et dicat secundum ea q̄ praedicta sunt, sicut praediximus super episcopum, orans et dicens: 2 Dś et pater Dm̄ī nostri Ieū Chr̄ī, ⟨——⟩ respice super seruum tuum istum et impartire spm̄ gratiae et consilii, praesbyteris ut adiuuet et gubernet plebem tuam in corde mundo,

A. viii. 16. 2. Ep. Β′ v. 1. πρεσβύτερον χειροτονῶν, ὦ ἐπίσκοπε, τὴν χεῖρα ἐπὶ τῆς κεφαλῆς ἐπιτίθει αὐτός, τοῦ πρεσβυτερίου παρεστῶτός σοι καὶ τῶν διακόνων, καὶ ἐπευχόμενος λέγε...

A. viii. 16. 4. ...ἔπιδε ἐπὶ τὸν δοῦλόν σου τοῦτον...εἰς πρεσβυτέριον ἐπιδοθέντα, καὶ ἔμπλησον αὐτὸν πνεῦμα χάριτος καὶ συμβουλίας τοῦ ἀντιλαμβάνεσθαι καὶ κυβερνᾶν τὸν λαόν σου ἐν καθαρᾷ καρδίᾳ,

Title. So S., *and* L. *has room only for* de praesbytero *or* -teris. περὶ χειροτονίας πρεσβυτέρων A. *and* E.; π. χ. πρεσβυτέρου Ep. *Others no title.*

1. And] *om.* Ar.E. | when] *so* L.Ar.K.; *if* E.S. (Let a presb. be ordained T.) | when a presb. is ordained] when the bp will ord. a presb. he shall *etc.* Ar.E.S. (*inversion due to lack of proper pass. forms in Sahidic; and so frequently*). | bishop] + himself A. (*in protest against the idea of presbs. laying on hands*). | hand] *pl.* S. | touching him] *subst.* standing by with the deacons A. (*in protest*); touching and holding him T. | over him] *om.* L. | over the bishop] *so all exc.* E. *om.* (ἢ ὑπὲρ ἐπισκ. = concerning the bp). | praying and saying] *om.* Ar.S. *with the remainder of the Chapter.* | *Cf. Notes on the confusion caused by this verse.*

2. O] My E. | and Father] the Father T.E. | as far as——continuing] *The omission or early loss of some such rubric has caused all the confusion in the versions.* | impart] *so* L.E.; make him partaker of T.; ἔμπλησον A.Ep. | may share in the presbyterate] *so* Turner *emends, cf. Note.* praesbyteris ut adiuuet *makes poor sense;* prob. = error πρεσβυτερίῳ ἀντιλαμβάνεσθαι (*cf.* A.) *for* πρεσβυτερίου ἀντ. E. *subst.* and the gift of holiness *for that* he may share in the prbte. | and govern] that he may be able to govern E. | *Tidner reads* consilii praesbyterii ut]

3 As Thou didst look upon the people of Thy choice and didst command Moses to choose presbyters whom Thou didst fill with ⌜the⌝ spirit which Thou hadst granted to Thy minister,

4 So now, O Lord, grant that there may be preserved among us unceasingly the Spirit of Thy grace, and make us worthy ⌜that in faith we may minister to Thee⌝ in singleness of heart praising Thee

5 Through Thy Child Christ Jesus through Whom to Thee be glory, might ⟨and praise⟩, to the Father and to the Son with ⟨the⟩ Holy Spirit ⌜in the holy Church⌝ now and ⌜for ever and⌝ world without end. Amen.

4. Cf. Eph. vi. 5.

L. (p. 109). 3 sicuti respexisti super populum electionis tuae et praecepisti Moysi ut elegeret praesbyteros, quos replesti de s͞p͞u tuo quod tu donasti famulo tuo; 4 et nunc, d͞n͞e, praesta indeficienter conseruari in nobis s͞p͞m gratiae tuae et dignos effice ut credentes tibi ministremus in simplicitate cordis laudantes te 5 per puerum tuū Chrm Iem, per quem tibi gloria et uirtus, patri et filio cum s͞p͞u s͞c͞o in sancta ecclesia et nunc et in saecula saeculorum. Amen.

A. viii. 16. 4. ὃν τρόπον ἐπεῖδες ἐπὶ τὸν λαὸν ἐκλογῆς σου καὶ προσέταξας Μωϋσεῖ αἱρήσασθαι πρεσβυτέρους, οὓς ἐνέπλησας πνεύματος. καὶ νῦν, κύριε, παράσχου, ἀνελλιπὲς τηρῶν ἐν ἡμῖν τὸ πνεῦμα τῆς χάριτός σου, ὅπως, πλησθεὶς ἐνεργηγμάτων ἰατικῶν καὶ λόγου διδακτικοῦ ἐν πραότητι παιδεύῃ σου τὸν λαὸν καὶ δουλεύῃ σοι εἰλικρινῶς ἐν καθαρᾷ διανοίᾳ...καὶ τὰς ὑπὲρ τοῦ λαοῦ σου ἱερουργίας ἀμώμους ἐκτελῇ διὰ τοῦ χριστοῦ σου, μεθ' οὗ σοι δόξα, τιμὴ καὶ σέβας καὶ τῷ ἁγίῳ πνεύματι εἰς τοὺς αἰῶνας· Ἀμήν.

---

3. with the spirit] so A.Ep.; Thy sp. L.; the Holy Sp. E. | minister]+Moses E. (ὁ θεράπων alone is quite usual for Moses. Cf. Lightfoot on 1 Clem. 4).

4. The punctuation at the end of 2 and 3 follows T. not L.A., as yielding better sense. | grant—grace] so L.A.Ep. Rather differently in E., but apparently reflecting the same Greek. | make us worthy] vouchsafe to us E.; make him worthy T. | that in faith—Thee] so L.; subst. while Thou fillest us with Thy worship E.; being filled with Thy wisdom to feed Thy people T.; πλησθεὶς...λόγου διδακτικοῦ ἐν πραότητι παιδεύῃ σου τὸν λαόν...A. This quasi-agreement of the versions suggests that something has been altered in L., but it seems hopeless to restore it. | praising Thee] so L.T.; to glorify Thee E. (cf. A.). | in singleness of heart] so L.; in our heart E.; in holiness of heart T. (cf. A.).

5. Christ Jesus] The Greek order, and that wh. is primitive in the Roman Creed. | and praise] from iii. 7. The two doxologies are clearly meant to be the same | with] καί A. | in the holy Church] so L.E., om. TA. | for ever and] om. L.; cf. iii. 6. | Amen] + Let both the priests and people give him the Peace with an holy kiss T. by analogy with the newly consecrated bishop iv. 1.—Let all the people say, Amen and Amen, and, He is worthy of it. E.

ix. ⌐Of Deacons¬

Ordination

1 And (δέ) a deacon when he is ⌐appointed¬ (καθιστάναι) shall be chosen according to what has been said before, the bishop [*alone*] laying hands on him [*in the same manner*]. Nevertheless we order that the bishop alone shall lay on hands at the ordaining of a deacon for this reason:

Functions

2 that he is not ordained (χειροτονεῖν) for a priesthood, but (ἀλλά) for the service (ὑπηρεσία) of the bishop that he may do [*only*] the things commanded by him.

3 For he is not (οὐδέ) [*appointed to be*] the fellow-counsellor (σύμβουλος) of the [*whole*] clergy (κλῆρος) but to take charge ⟨*of property*⟩ and to report to the bishop whatever is necessary.

L. 1 Diaconus uero cum ordinatur eligatur secundum ea quae praedicta sunt, similiter inponens manus* episcopus [*solus*]. Sicuti et praecipimus in diacono ordinando solus episcopus inponat manus propterea, 2 quia non in sacerdotio ordinatur, sed in ministerio episcopi, ut faciat ea quae ab ipso iubentur; 3 non est enim particeps consilii in clero, sed curas agens et indicans episcopo quae oportet,

---

Title. So S.T.; *space only for* de diacono *or* -is *in* L.; περὶ χειροτονίας διακόνων A., *and so* Ar.E.; π. χ. διακόνου. Ep.

1. And] *om.* Ar. | a den when he is apptd] when the bp will appt (ordain E.) a den Ar.E.S. | apptd] *so* T.A.S.; ordained L.Ar.E. *This part of the sentence seems to refer to election not ordination, and A.S. retain* καθιστάναι, *probably rightly.* | alone 1°] *so* L.E.Ar.; *om.* A.S. (T. *paraphr.*). *It seems unnecessary here.* | in the same manner] L. *only, om. caet.* | Nevertheless] L. sicuti et = καὶ ὡς. *I have emended Hauler's punctuation here.* | we order that] L. praecipimus. (*So MS. Hauler unnecessarily changes to* praecepimus.) | for this reason] *so* L. *But* Ar.E.S.: Why have we ordered that the bp alone is he who shall lay on hds on the den? The reason of this is this.

2. only] *so* T. *om. caet. It seems required.*

3. he is not] T. *om.* not, *deliberately. He has a high opinion of deacons.* | appointed to be] *so* Ar.E.S.K.; *om.* L.T. | whole] *so* Ar.S.T.; *om.* L.E. | charge] + of the sick Ar.S.T.; *om.* L.E. *The original sense seems to be as above.* | necessary] + about them (*i.e. the sick*) S.; take charge of what is nec. and report to the bp Ar.E. (+ about it. Ar.).

* *Hauler reads:* manus episcopus solus sicuti et praecepimus. In diacono....

4 L.

he does not receive the Spirit which is common to ⟨all⟩ the presbyterate, in which the presbyters share, but that which is entrusted to him under the bishop's authority.

Ar.E.S.

Nor (οὐδέ) is he appointed (καθιστάναι) to receive the Spirit of seniority which the presbyters share (μετέχειν)

Ar.	E.	S.
but to give attention and to be worthy of the bishop's trust and to be diligent about what is fitting.	but to occupy himself with that which is proper that the bishop may trust him and that he may acquaint the bishop with what is fitting.	but to be worthy (ἄξιος) for the bishop to trust (πιστεύειν) him with the things which it is fitting.

5 Wherefore the bishop alone shall make (χειροτονεῖν S.) the deacon.

Presbyters' ordination

6 But upon the presbyter the ⟨other⟩ presbyters also lay their hands because of the similar Spirit ⟨which is⟩ common to ⟨all⟩ the clergy.

L. (p. 109). 4 non accipiens communem praesbyteri⟨i⟩ spm eum cuius participes praesbyteri sunt, sed id quod sub potestate episcopi est creditum. 5 Qua de re episcopus solus diaconum faciat,

L. 6 super praesbyterum autem etiam praesbyteri superinponant manus propter communem et similem	S. 6 But (δέ) as for the presbyter the bishop shares (μετέχειν) with him, he lays hand on him because it is the

---

4. *There seems to be some corruption about this verse in* L. *Hauler suggests that* id quod *may refer to* spiritum (*the translator thinking of* πνεῦμα), *but this scarcely helps the sense, and* the spirit common to the presbyterate in which the presbyters share *does not look right.* Ar.E.S. *on the other hand looks like an amended text.* T. *omits the whole passage as derogatory to deacons.*

5. the bishop]+is he who E. | make] *so* L.; ordain Ar.E.S.

6, 7, 8. Ar.E.S. *have here an edited text, but* Ar.E. *is so confused as not to be worth citing.* S. *is given below. The imposition of hands by presbyters together with the bishop at the ordination of a presbyter seems to have troubled the Eastern text, the custom being unknown in the East.*

7 For (γάρ) the presbyter has authority (ἐξουσία) only for this one thing, to receive. But he has no authority to give ⌈holy orders⌉ (κλῆρος).

8 Wherefore he does not ordain (καθιστάναι S.) ⟨a man⟩ to orders (κληρικός) but ⟨by laying on hands⟩ at the ordination of a presbyter he [only] blesses (lit. seals σφραγίζειν) while the bishop ordains (χειροτονεῖν).

cleri spm. 7 Praesbyter enim huius solius habet potestatem ut accipiat; dare autem non habet potestatem. 8 Quapropter clerum non ordinat; super praesbyteri uero ordinatione consignat episcopo ordinante.

same spirit (πνεῦμα) which comes upon him. 7 For (γάρ) the presbyter receives only. He has no authority (ἐξουσία) to give holy orders (κλῆρος). 8 For this cause he is not to appoint (καθ.) a cleric (κληρικός). The presbyter only seals* (σφραγίζειν) while the bishop lays on hands (χειροτονεῖν).

Ordination of deacon

9 Over a deacon, then, let him say thus:

⌈Prayer of Ordination of a Deacon⌉

L.E.T.(A.Ep.K.)

10 O God who hast created all things and hast ordered them by the Word, Father of our Lord Jesus Christ whom Thou didst send to minister Thy will and reveal unto us Thy desire;

11 grant the ⌈Holy⌉ Spirit of grace and earnestness and diligence upon this Thy servant whom Thou hast chosen to minister to Thy church and to bring up in holiness to Thy holiness that

L. (p. 110). 9 Super diaconum autem ita dicat: 10 Ds qui omnia creasti et uerbo perordinasti, pater dñi nostri Ieu Chrī, quem misisti ministrare tuam uoluntatem et manifestare nobis tuum desiderium, da spm scm gratiae et sollicitudinis et industriae in hunc seruum tuum, quem elegisti ministrare ecclesiae tuae et offerre....(def.)

---

9. om. Ar.E.S. | him] the bishop T. | Title. so E.T.Ep. (εὐχὴ χειροτονίας διακόνου).
10. om. Ar.S. | ordered] so L.; adorned T. (κοσμεῖν in both cases). | minister] (διακονεῖν) + according to E.
11. om. Ar.S. | Holy] so L.; om. E.T. | earnestness] om. E. | upon] so L. (cf. iii. 4); in T.; unto E. | bring up] offer L.E.T. (ἀναφέρειν). L. breaks off with this word. | in holiness to Thy holiness] so T.; in Thy holy of holies E. Easton renders in Thy holy sanctuary. | by Thine ordained high priests] so E.; from the inheritance of Thine

* So MS. B.M.Or. 3580, f. 28, but B.M.Or. 1320 (the usual MS. of S.) reads: he only seals the presbyter.

which is offered to Thee by Thine ordained high priests ⌜to the glory of Thy Name;⌝ so that ministering blamelessly and in purity ⟨of heart⟩ he may by Thy goodwill be found worthy of this [high and] exalted office, praising Thee,

12 through Thy Child Jesus Christ [our Lord] through whom to Thee with Him ⟨be⟩ glory, might and praise with the Holy Spirit ⟨in the holy Church⟩ now and ever and world without end. Amen.

A. viii. 18 *substitutes a different prayer, whose close offers slight points of contact with that above:* καὶ καταξίωσον αὐτόν, εὐαρέστως λειτουργήσαντα τὴν ἐγχειρισθεῖσαν αὐτὸν διακονίαν...ἀμέμπτως...μείζονος ἀξιωθῆναι βαθμοῦ....

x. ⌜Of Confessors⌝

Ar.E.S.T.(K.A.Ep.)

The confessor a presbyter without ordination, but not a bishop

1 But (δέ) if a confessor (ὁμολογητής) has been in chains in prison for the Name, hands are not laid on (χειροτονεῖν) him for the diaconate (διακονία) or the presbyter's (πρεσβύτερος) office. For he has the office (τιμή) of the presbyterate by his confession (ὁμολογία). But if he be appointed (καθ.) bishop, hands shall be laid on him.

E. (*p.* 145). If the Confessor has been in prison in chains for the Name [of Christ] they shall not lay hand on him for the diaconate, for that is the honour of a deacon, but ⟨for⟩ the honour of the presbyterate—though

A. viii. 23. 2. ...περὶ ὁμολογητῶν. ὁμολογητὴς οὐ χειροτονεῖται, γνώμης γὰρ τοῦτο καὶ ὑπομονῆς· τιμῆς δὲ μεγάλης ἐπάξιος ὡς ὁμολογήσας τὸ ὄνομα τοῦ θεοῦ καὶ τοῦ Χριστοῦ.... ἐὰν δὲ χρεία αὐτοῦ ᾖ εἰς ἐπίσκοπον ἢ πρεσβύτερον ἢ

---

high priests T. | to the glory—Name] so E.; *om.* T. | purity of heart] in pure life E.; purely T. | by Thy goodwill] *so* T.; and Thy honour E. (*except one good MS.* in Thy counsel). | be found—office] *so* T.; he may obtain the exalted E. (*one late MS. adds* priesthood). *It is a common trick of Syriac translators to render one Greek word by two Syriac synonyms;* high and *is bracketed in the text as not represented in* E. | *The last half of this v. cannot be restored with any certainty from the available materials.*

12. *Doxology as found in* E. *except:* our Lord] *bracketed as not found in any other doxology in* Ap. Trad. | in the holy Church] *supplied from Hippolytus' customary form.* | T. *has:* through Thy only-begotten Son our Lord Jesus Christ by whom praise and might be to Thee for ever and ever. The People ⟨*answer*⟩: Amen.

Title. περὶ ὁμολογητῶν Ar.E.A.Ep.K.; *sing.* S.; *no title* T. E.A. *have drastically edited* 1 *and* 2, *cf. inf.* Ar.S.T. *as text above.*

1. in chains in prison] *so* T.; in prison in chains E.; *om.* in prison Ar.S. | the Name]+of the Lord Ar.S.; of Xt. E.; of God T.; τοῦ θεοῦ καὶ τοῦ Χριστοῦ A.; τοῦ θεοῦ Ep. | office] Ar.E.T. *all translate* honour, *but rank* K. | presbyterate] κλῆρος *transliterated* T.

Lesser Confessors

2 And (δέ) if he be a confessor (ὁμ.) who was not brought before a public authority (ἐξουσία) nor (οὐδέ) punished (κολάζειν) with chains nor (οὐδέ) condemned (κατακρίνειν) to any penalty (καταδίκη) but (ἀλλά) was only by (κατά) chance derided for the Name, though he confessed (ὁμολογεῖν), hands shall be laid on him for every order (κλῆρος) of which he is worthy.

Extempore Prayer

3 And (δέ) the bishop shall give thanks (εὐχαριστεῖν) according to (κατά) the aforesaid ⟨models⟩.

4 It is not altogether (οὐ πάντως) necessary (ἀνάγκη) for him to recite the very same words which we gave before as though studying to say them by heart in his thanksgiving (εὐχαριστία) to God; but (ἀλλά) let each one pray according to (κατά) his own ability.

5 If indeed (μέν) he is able to pray suitably (ἱκανῶς) with a grand and elevated prayer (προσευχή), this is a good thing (ἀγαθόν). But (δέ) if on the other hand he should pray and recite a prayer (προσευχή) according to a brief form, no one shall prevent (κωλύειν) him. Only (μόνον) let his prayer be correct and right [*in doctrine*] (ὀρθόδοξος).

he hath the honour of the presbyterate by that which he confessed— the bishop shall ordain him, having laid his hand upon him.

διάκονον, χειροτονεῖται. εἰ δέ τις ὁμολογητὴς μὴ χειροτονηθεὶς ἁρπάσῃ ἑαυτῷ ἀξίωμά τι τοιοῦτον ὡς διὰ τὴν ὁμολογίαν, καθαιρείσθω καὶ ἀποβαλλέσθω.

---

2. for the Name] +and he was punished with a punishment of house Ar.; +of his Lord E.; +of our Lord and he was punished *etc.* (*as in* Ar.) S. | though] *so* S.; yet Ar.E.; but only hath T. | hands shall be laid on him *etc.*] *so* Ar.S.; he is counted worthy of the laying on of hand, for he receiveth the prayer of the clergy T.

3. *Easton supplies* in all ordinations *after* give thanks.

4. Ar.E. *have edited this verse:* It *is* necessary for him to recite what we have already said [+reading Ar.] clearly and carefully and giving thanks to God according as it is possible for each to pray. *Easton's view that this* "*makes the passage senseless*" *seems unjust. It merely reflects later practice, the recital of a fixed liturgy by every celebrant with such feelings of devotion as God may grant.*

5. indeed] *om.* Ar.E. | suitably] fluently Ar. (*al.* calmly); with devotion E. | and elevated] *om.* S. | this is a good thing] *so.* S. *and some MSS. of* E.; and is a good man Ar. E.(*al.*). | recite a prayer] speak praise Ar.E. | according to a brief form] *so I understand* S. (*lit.* in measure — ? κατὰ μέτρον); as he can Ar.; with moderation E. | shall prevent him] shall be prevented Ar.E. | Only] *om.* Ar.E. | let his prayer be] from praying who is correct and right Ar.E. | let his pr. be orthodox] *so* S. *The last word has a suspicious ring in* S. Ar.E. *reflect* ὀρθος.

xi. ⌐Of Widows⌐

Ar.E.S.T.(A.Ep.K.S².)

Appointment of Widows

1 When a widow (χήρα) is appointed (καθ.) she is not ordained (χειροτονεῖν) but (ἀλλά) she shall be chosen by name.

2 But if she lost her husband a long time previously, let her be appointed (καθ.).

3 But if she lately lost her husband, let her not be trusted (πιστεύειν). And (ἀλλά S.) even if she is aged let her be tested (δοκιμάζειν) for a time (χρόνος) for ⌐often⌐ (πολλάκις γάρ) the passions (πάθος) [*even*] grow old with him who gives place for them in himself.

Not ordained

4 Let the widow (χήρα) be instituted (καθ.) by word only and ⟨*then*⟩ let her be reckoned among the ⟨*enrolled*⟩ widows. But (δέ) she shall not be ordained, because she does not offer the oblation (προσφορά) nor has she a ⟨*liturgical*⟩ ministry (λειτουργία).

A. viii. 25. 1. ...περὶ χηρῶν. χήρα οὐ χειροτονεῖται, ἀλλ᾽ εἰ μὲν ἐκ πολλοῦ ἀπέβαλεν τὸν ἄνδρα,...κατατασσέσθω εἰς τὸ χηρικόν (*cf. v.* 4) εἰ δὲ νεωστὶ ἀπέβαλεν τὸν ὁμόζυγον μὴ πιστευέσθω ἀλλὰ χρόνῳ... κρινέσθω· τὰ γὰρ πάθη ἐσθ᾽ ὅτε καὶ συγγηρᾷ ἀνθρώποις, μὴ ὑπὸ κρείττονος χαλινοῦ εἰργόμενα.

Title. περὶ χηρῶν A.Ep.S.T. Of the appointment of ww. Ar.; Of the ordination of ww. E. S. (B.M.Or. 1320) *arranges capp.* xi–xiv *thus: Reader, Subdeacon, Widow, Virgin; but the order of* Ar.E.T.A.Ep.K. *and of the Coptic fragments in* B.M.Or. 3580 (S²) *is clearly original.*

1. When] *so* Ar.S.; If E.; Let a w. be apptd. T. | she is not] *so* A.Ep.; she shall not be Ar.E.S.K. (*om.* T.). | chosen by name] *so* Ar.E.S.; she shall not be ordained but prayer sh. be made over her K. (T. *omits the whole verse, but in the actual practice it prescribes it follows* K.'s *rule.*)

2. If she lost—previously] *so* A.Ep.; If her husband died *etc.* Ar.E.S. (*with slight variants*); If for a long time past she have abided without a husband T. | let her be appointed] *so* Ar.E.S.T., *but* A. *fuses with v.* 4.

3. But if—husband] *so* A.Ep.; But if it was one whose husband lately died Ar.E.; But if she has not abided long since her husband died S. (εἰ δὲ νεωστί; A. *is clearly represented in* Ar.E., *but* S. *is paraphrasing throughout this passage.*) | let her not be trusted] *so* Ar.E.A.Ep.; trust her not S. | And even] *om.* Ar. | let her be tested] *so* Ar.E.A.Ep.; let them test her S. | for a time] many days E. | often] *so* S.; *om.* Ar.E.; sometimes A. | even] *so* S.A.; *om.* Ar.E. | who gives place—himself] Ar.S.; for lust will contend with those who are ordained to a place E.; +If they are not restrained with a tighter rein A. (*om.* Ep.). K. *reproduces* A.'s *gloss verbally in another connection* (K. xv. 207).

4. Has she a ministry] does she conduct S.

5 But (δέ) ordination (χειροτονία) is for the clergy (κλῆρος) on account of their ⟨liturgical⟩ ministry (λειτουργία). But (δέ) the widow (χήρα) is appointed (καθ.) for prayer, and this is ⟨a function⟩ of all ⟨Christians⟩.

xii. ⌐Of the Reader⌐
Ep.Ar.E.S.(T.K.A.)

The Reader (ἀναγνώστης) is appointed (καθ.) by the bishop's handing to him the book. For he does not have hands laid upon him (χειροτονεῖν S.).

Ep. Β´. viii. περὶ ἀναγνώστου. ἀναγνώστης καθίσταται ἐπιδιδόντος αὐτῷ βιβλίον τοῦ ἐπισκόπου· οὐδὲ γὰρ χειροθετεῖται. A. Gives a prayer and orders a laying-on of hands, T. an exhortation without imposition of hands.

xiii. ⌐Of Virgins⌐
Ar.E.S.T.K.(A.Ep.)

⌐The Virgin is not appointed but voluntarily separated and named.⌐ A Virgin (παρθένος) does not have an imposition of hands, for personal choice (προαίρεσις) alone is that which makes a virgin.

T. i. 46. A male or female virgin is not instituted or appointed by man, but is voluntarily separated and named. But a hand is not laid upon him* as for virginity. For this separation is of ⟨his⟩ own free will.

K. viii. 50. Nor shall a bachelor be ordained ⟨to holy orders⟩ unless witness first be borne to him by his neighbours.... Nor shall hand be laid on any one as for virginity, except when having reached mature age....

Title. So all, exc. Ar. om. Ep. has for some reason abandoned A. for this cap. and returned to the text of Ap. Trad.
The Reader etc.] To the R. who is ordained (sic) the Bp shall give E. | the book] so Ep.Ar.T.; the gospel K.; book of the Apostle and praying over him S.; the Scripture E. | For he does not have etc.] so Ep.Ar.T.K.; he shall not lay hand upon him E.S. |χειροτονεῖν] so S. Cf. Ep.
Title. So all, exc. T. which reads: Of male and female Vv.
The Virgin—named] No such clause in Ar.E.S.(A.Ep.), but something of this kind seems indicated in T.K. The sense would be: "There can be no question of appointing any one to be a virgin, but if they choose this state for themselves, there is a public recognition of this self-dedication. (Cf. xi. 1.) There is no laying-on of hands because it is a purely personal matter, not a public ministry." The apparent repetition would easily cause one clause to be dropped, but both are really required. | A Virgin does not have etc.] cf. T.K. sup.: hand shall not be placed on a virgin Ar.S.; he shall not lay h. on a v. E.; παρθένος οὐ χειροτονεῖται A.Ep. | personal choice] so S., cf. T.; inmost heart Ar.; heart E.; γνώμης γάρ ἐστι τὸ ἐπαθλον A.Ep.

* T. contemplates virgins of both sexes. E.S. phrase everything in the fem.

xiv. ⌜Of Subdeacons⌝

Ar.E.S.(T.A.K.Ep.)

Hands shall not be laid on a subdeacon (ὑποδιάκονος) but he shall be named that he may serve the deacon.

xv. ⌜Of a gift [*of healing*]⌝

Ar.E.S.T.A.K.

If any one among the laity appear to have received a gift of healing by a revelation, hands shall not be laid upon him, because the matter is manifest.

A. viii. 26. 2. ὁ γὰρ λαβὼν χάρισμα ἰαμάτων δι᾽ ἀποκαλύψεως ὑπὸ θεοῦ ἀποδείκνυται, φανερᾶς οὔσης πᾶσιν τῆς ἐν αὐτῷ χάριτος.

Title. So Ar.E.T.A.; *sing.* S.; περὶ χειροτονίας ὑποδιακόνου Ep.

Hands shall not be laid on] *so* Ar.; He shall not l. h. on E.; They sh. not l. h. on S.; Let a subdcn be appointed...the bishop praying over him T. (*and adds a prayer but no imp. of hands*); ὑποδιάκονον χειροτονῶν, ἐπιθήσεις ἐπ᾽ αὐτῷ τὰς χεῖρας A. (*with a prayer but not that in* T.); A subdeacon ⟨shall be appointed⟩ after the same manner as the Reader K. | he shall be named] a name shall be put upon him Ar.; he shall make mention over him of the (Divine) Name E.; they shall name him S. | he may] *so* S.; they may Ar.E. | serve] follow Ar.S.; minister to E. (=ἀκολουθεῖν *in all texts*).

Title. So Ar.E.S.; Of gifts of healing K.; Of a gift T.; *no title* A.

If] *so* Ar.E.T.; Whenever S. | appear] *so* T. (=ἐὰν φανῇ); says Ar.E.S.K. (=ἐὰν φῇ). | to have] *so* T. (λαβών, *cf.* A.); I have received Ar.E.S.K. (ἔλαβον). | by a revelation] *so* Ar.S.A.; and revelation E.; or revelation T. | because] *so* Ar.S.T. (ὡς); until E.K. (ἕως). | the matter is manifest] the deed is manifest T.K.; the deed itself will make it manifest whether he speaks the truth Ar.E.S. *In this cap.* T.'s *text*, ἐὰν τις φανῇ ἐν τῷ λαῷ λαβὼν χάρισμα ἰαμάτων καὶ (*l.* δι᾽) ἀποκαλύψεως οὐ χειροθετεῖται, ὡς φανερὸν τὸ πρᾶγμα, *seems to be original, and* Ar.E.S. *an edited version.* E.K.'s *reading,* ἕως φανερόν, *implies that the proved charismatic is to be ordained.* A. *precedes this by a regulation that the Exorcist, regarded as a specialised kind of healer, is not to be ordained.*

Part II. ⌜Of the Laity⌝

xvi. ⟨*Of New Converts*⟩

Ar.E.S.T.A.K.(Ep.)

Hearers to be questioned

1 Those who come forward for the first time to hear the word shall first be brought to the teachers ⌜at the house⌝ before all the people (λαός) come in.

2 And let them be examined as to the reason (αἰτία) why they have come forward ⌜to the faith⌝ (πίστις). And (δέ) those who bring them shall bear witness for them whether they are able to hear.

3 Let their life (βίος) and manner of living be enquired into, [*whether* (ἤ) *he has a wife and*] whether he is a slave or free.

Of Slaves

4 If he be the slave of a believer and his master permit him, let him hear. If his master do not bear witness to him, let him be rejected.

A. viii. 32. 2. οἱ πρώτως προσιόντες...διὰ τῶν διακόνων προσαγέσθωσαν τῷ ἐπισκόπῳ ἢ τοῖς πρεσβυτέροις, καὶ τὰς αἰτίας ἐξεταζέσθωσαν οὗ χάριν προσῆλθον....οἵ τε προσενεγκόντες μαρτυρείτωσαν αὐτοῖς.... ἐξεταζέσθωσαν δὲ αὐτῶν καὶ οἱ τρόποι καὶ ὁ βίος καὶ εἰ δοῦλοί εἰσιν ἢ ἐλεύθεροι.

A. viii. 32. 3. καὶ ἐὰν ᾖ τις δοῦλος, ἐρωτάσθω οὗ δεσπότου καὶ ἐὰν πιστοῦ δοῦλος ᾖ, ἐρωτάσθω ὁ κύριος αὐτοῦ εἰ μαρτυρεῖ αὐτῷ· ἐὰν δὲ μή, ἀπο-

---

Part II. T. *here opens Bk ii with* Of laymen *thus, which has no connection with the rest of the sentence and probably represents an old title.* T. *is alone in making a specially marked division after* xv.

Title. Of—Converts] *I conj. this from the versions:* Of new men (? = περὶ καινῶν) who come in to the faith Ar.S.; Of new men who wish to be baptised E.; Of those who wish to become Xtns K.; περὶ κανόνων A.Ep. (*so all MSS.*). Ar.E.S. *diverge a good deal from the other texts here.*

1. Those who—first time] *so* T.A.Ep.; Those who come in as new Ar.; New persons who are to be baptised E.; Let those who sh. be brought in to the new faith S. | at the house] *so* T. *only but probably authentic. Cf. Notes.* | before—come in] *om.* T.

2. let them be examined] *so* T.A.K.; they shall examine them Ar.E.S. | reason] *so* Ar.E.S.; all the reason T.; the reasons A.Ep. (+ of the thing, namely S.). | to the faith] *so* Ar.E.S.K.; *om.* T.A. | hear] + the word E.S.

3. manner of living] *so* A.; conversation T.; occupation K. (*which is perhaps what is meant*); *subst.* of what sort it is Ar.E.S. | whether—wife] *so* Ar.E.S.; *om.* T.A.K. (*it is clearly out of place*); + or a woman if she has a husband E. | whether he is a slave or free] *so* T.A.K.; *om.* Ar.E.S.

4. witness to him] + that he is good S.

5   If his master be a heathen (ἐθνικός) let him be taught "to please his master" that there be no scandal (βλασφημία).

Of Marriage

6   If a man have a wife or a woman a husband, let them be taught the man to be contented with his wife and the woman to be contented with her husband.

7   A man who is unmarried let him be taught not to commit fornication (πορνεύειν) but either (ἀλλὰ ἤ) to marry lawfully (κατὰ νόμον) or to abide ⟨steadfast⟩.

Energumens

8   But if there be one who has a devil, let him not hear the word from the teacher until he be cleansed.

5. Cf. Tit. ii. 9.

βαλλέσθω, ἕως ἂν ἑαυτὸν ἄξιον ἐπιδείξῃ τῷ δεσπότῃ· εἰ δὲ μαρτυρεῖ αὐτῷ προσδεχέσθω. εἰ δὲ ἐθνικοῦ ᾖ οἰκέτης, διδασκέσθω εὐαρεστεῖν τῷ δεσπότῃ, ἵνα μὴ βλασφημῆται ὁ λόγος. εἰ μὲν οὖν ἔχει γυναῖκα ἢ ἡ γυνὴ ἄνδρα, διδασκέσθωσαν ἀρκεῖσθαι ἑαυτοῖς· εἰ δὲ ἄγαμοί εἰσιν, μανθανέτωσαν μὴ πορνεύειν, ἀλλὰ γαμεῖν νόμῳ. [εἰ δὲ ὁ δεσπότης αὐτοῦ, πιστὸς ὢν καὶ εἰδὼς ὅτι πορνεύει οὐ δίδωσιν αὐτῷ γυναῖκα ἢ τῇ γυναικὶ ἄνδρα, ἀφοριζέσθω.] ἐὰν δέ τις δαίμονα ἔχῃ, διδασκέσθω μὲν τὴν εὐσέβειαν, μὴ προσδεχέσθω δὲ εἰς κοινωνίαν πρὶν ἂν καθαρισθῇ· εἰ δὲ θάνατος κατεπείγοι, προσδεχέσθω.

⌐Of the crafts and professions (ἐπιστήμη) ⟨forbidden to Christians⟩⌐

9   [They shall enquire about the crafts and occupations of those who are brought for instruction.]

---

5. that there be no scandal] so Ar.E.S.; om. T. A. conforms to Tit. ii. 5.
6. or a woman a husband] om. T. and alters the rest of this verse.
7. or to abide steadfast] to remain as becomes him Ar.; to remain according to the law S.: let him abide in the Lord T.; om. E. (ἠ μένειν seems indicated as original).
8. from the teacher] so T.Ar.; of instruction E.S. Cf. A.
Title. So Ar.E.S.: no title T.K., but a fresh chapter.
9. Ar.E.S. only. om. T.A.K. | They shall enquire] so S.: om. Ar.E. | about] so S.; besides Ar.E. | for instruction] so Ar.E.; to be appointed (καθιστάναι) S. This seems to be an interpolation, repeating xvi. 3a.

Immoral

10 If a man be a pander (πορνοβοσκός) who supports harlots (πόρνη) either (ἤ) let him desist or (ἤ) let him be rejected.

Idolatrous

11 If a man be a sculptor or (ἤ) a painter (ζωγράφος), he shall be taught not to make idols (εἴδωλον). If he will not desist, let him be rejected.

12 If a man be an actor (θεατρικός) or one who makes shows (ἐπίδειξις) in the theatre (θέατρον), either (ἤ) let him desist or (ἤ) let him be rejected.

Schoolmaster

13 If a man teach children worldly knowledge, it is indeed (μέν) well if he desist. But (δέ) if he has no other trade (τέχνη) by which to live, let him have forgiveness.

Circus

14 A charioteer (ἡνίοχος) likewise (ὁμοίως) ⌜or one who takes part in the games (ἀγωνίζεσθαι) or who goes to the games (ἀγών)⌝, either (ἤ) let him desist or (ἤ) let him be rejected.

A. viii. 32. 7. εἴ τις πορνοβοσκός, ἢ παυσάσθω τοῦ μαστροπεύειν ἢ ἀποβαλλέσθω. πόρνη προσιοῦσα ἢ παυσάσθω ἢ ἀποβαλλέσθω. εἰδωλοποιὸς προσιὼν ἢ παυσ. κτλ. τῶν ἐπὶ σκηνῆς, ἐάν τις προσίη ἀνὴρ ἢ γυνή...ἢ παυσάσθωσαν κτλ.

---

10. *There is much confusion in some of the versions as to the list which follows, owing to misunderstandings and omissions due to changes and differences of environment. Thus A. omits the refs. to the painter, schoolmaster, magistrate, etc., because it was compiled when these avocations were no longer in conflict with the plain duty of a Christian while E., Ar. and K. have found difficulties in those items which refer to the circus and amphitheatre, which had no meaning in their day and neighbourhood. I have not tried to note all the variations of order, etc., but to reconstitute so far as possible what Hippolytus wrote. The list is that of S. checked by the others.*
a pander who supports harlots] so S.; a harlot (al. a fornicator, πόρνος) or a pander T.; a pander...and a harlot A.; who supports harlots om. Ar.E. | let him desist—rejected] om. E.

11. painter] om. A. | If he will not] let them (him A.) desist or let them be S.A.

12. So S. *The other versions summarise or adapt.*

13. om. A. | worldly knowledge] so T.E.; om. Ar.S. | desist]+from the thing S. | by which to live] so T.E.K.; om. Ar.S. | forgiveness]+he who goes (caused to go, E.) to the sacrifices of idols let him desist etc. Ar.E.

14. charioteer] om. Ar.E.K. (*but* Ar. *subst.* a potion-maker or one who teaches the making of potions). | or one who—goes to the games] om. Ar.E.A. (*but cf.* A. *inf.*) K. | one who] om. S.

Amphitheatre

15 A man who is a gladiator (μονομάχος) or a trainer of gladiators (μον.) or a huntsman (κυνηγός) ⟨in the arena⟩ or one concerned with wild-beast shows (κυνηγίον) or a public official (δημόσιος) who is concerned with gladiatorial shows (μονομάχιον), either let him desist or let him be rejected.

Idolatry

16 If a man be a priest of idols (εἴδωλον) or a keeper of idols (εἰδ.), either let him desist or let him be rejected.

Servants of the Pagan State

17 A soldier who is in authority (ἐξουσία) must be told not to execute men; if he should be ordered to do it, he shall not do it. He must be told not to take the military oath. If he will not agree, let him be rejected.

18 A military governor (ἐξουσία) or a magistrate (ἄρχων) of a city who wears the purple ⟨toga⟩, either let him desist or let him be rejected.

19 If a catechumen (κατηχούμενος) or (ἤ) a baptised Christian

A. viii. 32. 9. ...ἡνίοχος ἢ μονομάχος ἢ σταδιοδρόμος ἢ λουδεμπιστὴς ἢ ὀλυμπικὸς ἢ χοραύλης ἢ κιθαριστὴς ἢ λυριστὴς ἢ ὁ τὴν ὄρχησιν ἐπιδεικνύμενος ἢ κάπηλος, ἢ παυσάσθωσαν κτλ. 15. θεατρομανίᾳ εἴ τις πρόσκειται ἢ κυνηγίοις ἢ ἱπποδρομίοις ἢ ἀγῶσιν, ἢ παυσάσθω κτλ.

A. viii. 32. 10. στρατιώτης προσιὼν διδασκέσθω "μὴ ἀδικεῖν, μὴ συκοφαντεῖν,

15. who is a gladiator] *om.* Ar.E.; +ἢ σταδιοδρόμος *etc.* A.; +runner, teacher of music, comedian, ὀλυμπικός (*transliterated*) K. (*cf.* A.). | trainer of gladiators] *lit.* one who teaches gladiators to fight S.; one who teaches wrestling T.; teaches war and fighting Ar.É.; teaches savagery K. | huntsman—μονομάχιον] T. *summarises:* a huntsman of the public treasury (δημοσίου *for* δημόσιος) *and om. the gladiatorial shows.*

16. *om.* A. | or a keeper of idols] *om.* E.

17. who is in authority] *i.e. an officer in the army;* or one in authority T.; *om.* A. | must be told] *so* T. (? διδασκέσθω): *subst.* let him not execute Ar.; they shall not receive, and if indeed they did receive him if he was ordered to kill men E.; cause him not to execute S.; he shall not do it] *so* Ar.E.; cause him not to hasten to the work S. | He must oath] *lit.* and cause him not to swear S.; and he shall speak no hard word K.; *om.* Ar.E.T. If he will not agree] *lit.* If not Ar.; being unwilling S.; ἀντιλέγων A.

18. *om.* A. | military governor] *lit.* one who has authority (ἐξουσία) over the sword Ar.S.; a magistrate with a sword E.; an overseer with a sw. K.; *om.* T.A.

19. *om.* A. | baptised christian] πιστὸς τοῦ λαοῦ T. | him] *so* T.; them Ar.E.S. | For he has despised God] *so* T.S. (they have S.); Surely they have removed far from God Ar.; because it is far from God E.

(πιστός) wishes to become a soldier ⟨*i.e. a volunteer*⟩, let him be cast out. For he has despised (καταφρονεῖν) God.

Immorality

20 A harlot or a sodomite [*or one who has castrated himself*] or one who does things which may not be spoken of, let them be rejected for they are defiled.

Magic

21 A magician (μάγος) shall not even be brought for consideration (κρίσις).

22 A charmer or an astrologer (ἀστρολόγος) or an interpreter of dreams or a mountebank [*or a clipper of fringes of clothes*] or a maker of amulets, let them desist or let them be rejected.

Concubinage

23 If a man's concubine (παλλακή) be ⌐a⌐ slave, let her hear ⌐on⌐

ἀρκεῖσθαι δὲ τοῖς διδομένοις ὀψωνίοις" (Lk. iii. 14)· πειθόμενος προσδεχέσθω, ἀντιλέγων δὲ ἀποβαλλέσθω.

A. viii. 32. 11. ἀρρητοποιός, κίναιδος, βλάξ, μάγος, ἐπαοιδός, ἀστρολόγος, μάντις, θηρεπῳδός, λῶταξ, ὀχλαγωγός, περιάμματα ποιῶν, περικαθαίρων, οἰωνιστής...χρόνῳ δοκιμαζέσθωσαν, δυσέκνιπτος γὰρ ἡ κακία· παυσάμενοι οὖν προσδεχέσθωσαν, μὴ πειθόμενοι δὲ ἀποβαλλέσθωσαν.

A. viii. 32. 12. παλλακή τινος ἀπίστου δούλη, ἐκείνῳ μόνῳ σχολά-

---

20. harlot] *om.* A. (*ins. v.* 10); *ins.* pander *here* K. (*om. in v.* 10). | sodomite] *so* A.K.; dissolute man Ar.S.T. (+ or a drunkard T.); pitiless man E. | or one—himself] *so* S.; *om. caet.* | or one who does] or indeed any other who does S. | for defiled] *om.* A.
21. even] *om.* T. | be brought for] does not come for T. | for consideration] *so* S.T.; into the ranks of the faithful Ar.E. (E. *applies this to* 20, *and* (?) *includes the* μάγος *in* 22).
22. charmer] ἐπαοιδός A.; *om.* Ar.E. | astrologer] + user of the astrolabe Ar.; + diviner by the sun (? = μάγος) E. | astrologer] + μάντις A.; νεκρόμαντις T. *After* μάντις T.A. (= θηρεπῳδός) *and* K. *all agree in adding* snake-charmer. | interpreter of dreams] *om.* A. (*but* οἰωνιστής *later*). | mountebank] ὀχλαγωγός A., *but in the sense of* one who collects a crowd, *not* sedition-monger *as* Ar.E. | clipper] Ar.E.S. *have here some hopeless corruption;* or one who sells clothes from the grave-diggers Ar.: one who puts on [*al.* sells] clothes for lascivious ornaments [*al.* for forearms] E.: or him (*sing.*) who spoil (*pl.*) the fringes of tunics who are the stammerers (ψελλιστής) S. *The other versions go from* ὀχλαγωγός *to* amulet maker. | amulets] potions E.
23. *Before this vers.* Ar.E. *insert a title.* Of concubines E.; Of the c. Ar.; *om. caet.* | man's] unbeliever's A. | a slave] *so* T.A.E. (*some MSS.*); his sl. Ar.E.(*al.*)S. | on condition that] *so* S.E. (and if E.); *om.* Ar.T. | on cond. that—her children] *om.* A. |

condition that⌐ (εἰ μέν) she have reared her children, and if she consorts with him alone. But if not let her be rejected.

24a If a man have a concubine (π.), let him desist and marry legally (κατὰ νόμον); and if he will not, let him be rejected.

24b ⌐And if a baptised woman consort with a slave, either let her desist or let her be rejected.⌐

25 [If we have omitted anything, decide ye as is fit; for we all have the Spirit of God.]

25. 1 Cor. vii. 40.

ζουσα προσδεχέσθω· εἰ δὲ καὶ πρὸς ἄλλους ἀσελγαίνει, ἀποβαλλέσθω. 13. πιστὸς ἐὰν ἔχῃ παλλακήν, εἰ μὲν δούλην, παυσάσθω καὶ νόμῳ γαμείτω, εἰ δὲ ἐλευθέραν, ἐκγαμείτω αὐτὴν νόμῳ· εἰ δὲ μή, ἀποβαλλέσθω. [Ep. Γ. 13. + ἐὰν δὲ καὶ πιστὴ δούλῳ συναφθῇ, ἢ παυσάσθω κτλ.]

xvii. ⌐Of the time (χρόνος) during which they shall hear the word after ⟨abandoning these⟩ crafts and professions (ἐπιστήμη)⌐

Ar.E.S.T.A.K.

1 Let a catechumen (κατηχουμένος) be instructed for three years.

2 But (δέ) if a man be earnest (σπουδαῖος) and persevere (προσκαρτερεῖν) well in the matter, ⌐let him be received⌐, because it is not the time (χρόνος) that is judged, but (ἀλλά) the conduct (τρόπος).

A. viii. 32. 16. ὁ μέλλων κατηχεῖσθαι τρία ἔτη κατηχείσθω· εἰ δὲ σπουδαῖός τις ᾖ καὶ εὔνοιαν ἔχῃ περὶ τὸ πρᾶγμα, προσδεχέσθω, ὅτι οὐχ ὁ χρόνος, ἀλλ' ὁ τρόπος κρίνεται.

if she consorts with] so Ar.S. (kept to S.); if she did not approach another man E. | But] om. S. | if not] if there was another man E.

24a. desist] separate from her T. | legally] κατὰ νόμον S.; νόμῳ A. | not]+then S.

24b. Found only in Ep. Γ'. 13. But cf. A. viii. 34. 13 πιστὸς ἢ πιστὴ δούλοις συναφθέντες ἢ ἀφιστάσθωσαν ἢ ἀποβαλλέσθωσαν, which is also reproduced by Ep. Δ'. xxiv. 13.

25. om. T.A.K.; hab. Ar.E.S. It seems to be an interpolation imitated from xxxviii. 4. | anything] so Ar.E.; any other work S. | decide ye as is fit] so Ar.E.; the works will instruct your sight S.

Title. So E. Of the time for hearing the word after their occupations Ar.; Of the time of those who hear the word after the crafts and professions S.; no title T.A.K.

1. a catechumen] so T.A.K.; pl. Ar.E.S. | be instructed for three years] so A.T. (not less than three years T.); spend three years hearing the word Ar.E.S.

2. matter] cf. A. Ar.E.S.T. all transl. work. | let him be received] so A.; let him be baptised T.; om. Ar.E.S. | because] so T.A.; om. Ar.E.S. | it is not—conduct] so A.; for it is not the time that is judged, but the will of faith T.; they do not judge him by time but his conduct alone shall judge for him Ar.E.S.

xviii. ⌜Of the Catechumen's Prayer and his Kiss⌝

Ar.E.S.T.

Catechumens pray apart

1 Each time (ὅταν) the teacher finishes his instruction (καθη-γεῖσθαι, *sic*) let the catechumens (κατ.) pray by themselves apart from the faithful (πιστός).

And women apart from men

2 And let the women stand in the assembly (ἐκκλησία) by themselves [*apart from the men*], both (εἴτε) the baptised women (πιστός) and (εἴτε) the women catechumens (κατ.).

Kiss of peace

3 But (δέ) after the prayer is finished the catechumens (κατ.) shall not give the kiss of peace (εἰρήνη), for (γάρ) their kiss is not yet pure.

4 But (δέ) the baptised (πιστός) shall embrace (ἀσπάζεσθαι) one another, men with men and women with women. But (δέ) let not men embrace (ἀσπ.) women.

Women to veil their heads

5 Moreover (δέ) let all the women have their heads veiled with a scarf (πάλλιον) but (ἀλλά) not with a veil [*lit. thing*, εἶδος] of linen only, for that is not a ⟨sufficient⟩ covering (κάλυμμα).

A. viii. 11. 9. (*Cf.* 4 *sup.*) καὶ ὁ διάκονος εἰπάτω πᾶσιν· "Ἀσπάσασθε ἀλλή-λους ἐν φιλήματι ἁγίῳ," καὶ ἀσπαζέσθωσαν οἱ τοῦ κλήρου τὸν ἐπίσκοπον, οἱ λαϊκοὶ ἄνδρες τοὺς λαϊκούς, αἱ γυναῖκες τὰς γυναῖκας.

Title. So Ar.E.S. (*om. and his Kiss* S.); *no title* T. (*This definition of the contents of* xviii *is very inadequate.*)

1. Each time] *so* S.; When Ar.E.; After T. | his] *so* S.; the Ar.E. | his instruction] *om.* T.

2. stand] + in a place Ar.; + as they pray in a place E.; + in a place as they pray quite S. | apart from the men] *so* T.; *om.* Ar.E.S.

3. after the prayer] *so* T.; when they finish (finished Ar.) the prayer Ar.S.; if the pr. is finished E. | not give *etc.*] *so* Ar.S.; the women catechumens shall give the peace to one another, and men to men and women to women T.; the cats. shall not kiss with the faithful E. | for—pure] *om.* T.

4. baptised] *fem.* Ar. | men, women] *sing.* S.

5. let all the women] every woman T. | not] *om.* S. | a ⟨sufficient⟩ covering] *so* S.; what is suitable Ar.; what is allowed them E.; *om.* T. (*adapting the whole sentence*).

xix. ⌐Of the Imposition of Hands on the Catechumens⌐

Ar.E.S.T.K.(A.)

The teacher to lay hands on catechumens

1 After the prayer [*of the catechumens*] let the teacher lay hands upon them and pray and dismiss them. Whether (εἴτε) the teacher be an ecclesiastic (ἐκκλησιαστικός) or (εἴτε) a layman (λαϊκός) let him do the same.

Baptism by blood

2 If any ⌐one being a⌐ catechumen should be apprehended for the Name, let him not be anxious about ⟨*undergoing*⟩ martyrdom. For (γάρ) if he suffer violence and be put to death before baptism, he shall be justified having been baptised in his own blood.

A. viii. 32. 17. ὁ διδάσκων εἰ καὶ λαϊκὸς ᾖ, ἔμπειρος δὲ τοῦ λόγου καὶ τὸν τρόπον σεμνός, διδασκέτω· "ἔσονται" γὰρ "πάντες διδακτοὶ θεοῦ" (Is. liv. 13).

xx. ⌐Of those who are to receive baptism (βάπτισμα)⌐

Scrutiny   Ar.E.S.T.(K.)

1 And (δέ) when they are chosen who are set apart to receive baptism (βάπτισμα) let their life (βίος) be examined, whether

---

Title. So Ar.E.; Of the manner of laying hand on S.; *no title* T.K.A. *Again this only describes some of the contents.*

1. of the catechumens] *so* T.; *om.* Ar.E.S.K. | teacher] *so* Ar.E.S.K.; bishop or presbyter T. | the same] *so* Ar.E.; thus S.; whether—same *om.* T. *The versions are not clear as to the order of the words here. The above follows* Ar.

2. one being a] *so* T. (εἰ τις κατηχ.); If a cat. E.S.K.; If he was arrested (*om.* catech.) Ar. | Name] *so* T.; +of the Lord Ar.S.; +of our Lord Jesus Xt. E. | about martyrdom] about the testimony E.S.; his testimony Ar.| For] *so* E.S.; *om.* Ar.; but T. | if he suffer—death] *so* T.K.; if he was overpowered and put to death Ar.; if they overpower and injure and kill him E.; If it should be that they offer violence and put him to death S. | before baptism] *so* K.; without receiving the laver T.; before obtaining the pardon of his sins Ar.; before he receives baptism for the forgiveness of sins E.; before his sins have been forgiven S. | he shall be justified] *so* Ar.E.S.T.; he sh. be buried with all the martyrs K. | having been *etc.*] *so* T.; for (γάρ) he was baptised in his own blood (*om.* own Ar.) Ar.E.S.

Title. Of him who is baptised Ar.E.; Of those who will receive baptism S.; *no title* T.

1. when] Ar.E.S.; if T.K. | are chosen] *so* T.; have been ch. Ar.E.S. | set apart] *so* S.; if they are separately chosen who are to be bapt. T.; one (+who E.) has been chosen or is made ready to be baptd. Ar.E. | let their life be examined] *lit.* their life having

they lived piously (σέμνως) while catechumens (κατ.), whether "they honoured the widows" (χήρα), whether they visited the sick, whether they have fulfilled every good work.

2 If those who bring them bear witness to them that they have done thus, ⌜then⌝ let them hear the gospel (εὐαγγέλιον).

Exorcisms

3 Moreover (δέ), from the day they are chosen, let a hand be laid on them and let them be exorcised (ἐξορκίζειν) daily. And when the day draws near on which they are to be baptised, let the bishop ⟨himself⟩ exorcise each one of them, that he may be certain that he is purified.

4 But (δέ) if there is one who is not purified (καθαρός) let him be put on one side because he did not hear the word of instruction with faith (πίστις). For the [evil and] strange spirit remained with him.

Maundy Thursday

5 ⌜And⌝ (δέ) let those who are to be baptised (βαπτίζειν) be instructed to wash and cleanse themselves on the fifth day of the week (σάββατον).

1. Cf. 1 Tim. v. 3.

---

been examined S.; let them be examined T.; let him be ex. concerning his life Ar.; they sh. ex. their life E. | piously] *so* S.; chastely Ar.; in the fear of God E.; (examined as to) how they lived T.

2. If] *so* Ar.E.; When S.; Let them be borne w. to by those who bring T. | that—thus] *om.* T. | then] *so* S.K.; *om. caet.* | then—gospel] *so* S.; And when they hear the g. let a hand be laid on them T. (*and so with variants* Ar.E.).

3. day 1°] *so* T.Ar.; time E.S. | are chosen] *so* T.; were Ar.E.; will be S. | chosen] *so* T.; brought Ar.; set apart E.S. (ἐκλέγειν ? = *the original*). | let them be exorcised] *so* T.; and ex. them Ar.; in exorcising them S.; and instruct them E. | day 2°] *pl.* T.| one of them]+separately T. | be certain] *lit.* be persuaded T. (πείθεσθαι); know Ar.E.S. | he is purified] *so* T.; *pl.* Ar.E.S.

4. not] +good (καλός) and S. | put on one side] *so* Ar.E.S.; removed from the midst T. | of instruction] *so* E.T.; *om.* Ar.S. | For—with him] *so* T. (evil and *is probably* T.'s *expansion*); Because it is not possible that an alien should be baptised Ar.; Because it is not proper to do to an alien E.; Because it is never poss. for the alien to be concealed S.

5. And] *so* S.E.; *om.* Ar.T. | those who are] + set apart to be S. | cleanse themselves] cleanse their heads (!) T.; and free themselves S.; and pray Ar.; and be exorcised E.; and eat K. (καθαρίζεσθαι?, or *original*). | day of] *om.* S.

6 And (δέ) if any woman be menstruous she shall be put aside and be baptised another day.

Friday and Saturday in Holy Week

7 Those who are to receive baptism (βάπτισμα) shall fast (νηστεύειν) on the Friday (παρασκευή) and on the Saturday (σάββατον). And (δέ) on the Saturday (σάββ.) the bishop shall assemble those who are to be baptised in one place, and shall bid them ⌐all⌐ to pray and bow the knee.

8 And laying his hand on them he shall exorcise every evil spirit to flee away from them and never to return to them ⌐henceforward⌐. And when he has finished exorcising, let him breathe on ⌐their faces⌐ and seal (σφραγίζειν) their foreheads and ears and noses and ⟨then⟩ let him raise them up.

The Paschal Vigil

9 And they shall spend all the night in vigil, reading the scriptures ⌐to them⌐ and instructing (καθηγεῖσθαι, sic) them.

10 Moreover (δέ) those who are to be baptised shall not bring any other vessel, save (εἰ μή τι) that which each will bring with him for the eucharist (εὐχαριστία). For (γάρ) it is right for every one to bring his oblation (προσφορά) then.

---

6. woman] + among them Ar.E. | she shall be put aside etc.] so Ar.E.S.; om. T. altering to: let her take in addition another day washing and bathing beforehand.

7. Friday and on the Saturday] so T.; Friday of the Sabbath S.; and on the Sat. om. Ar.E. | the bp shall—place] so Ar.E.T.K.; when they who will be baptd. have assembled in one place by the direction (γνώμη) of the bp S. | all] om. T.K. | knee] + facing east K.

8. laying] let him lay T.; having laid Ar.E.S. | every evil—henceforward] om. T.| henceforward] so Ar.E.; om. S. | on their faces] so Ar.S.; on them E.T. | and seal—up] om. E. | foreheads and ears and noses] so Ar.E.S.; forehead, nose, heart and ears T.; breast, forehead, heart and ears K.

9. And—vigil] om. E. | the night] so S.T.; their n. Ar. | the scriptures] so T. and E. (1 MS.); om. Ar.E.(al.)S. | to them] om. T.

10. Moreover] om. T. | those] sing. Ar. | shall not—eucharist] so S.; shall not bring anything else with them save one loaf for the euch. T.; sh. not bring in with him any vessel, but each one sh. give thanks Ar.; sh. not bring with them any ornament of gold nor ring nor gem of any kind, but every one of them shall give thanks E. | For it is right—then] om. T. | every one] so Ar.; him who was (is E.) worthy E.S. | oblation] pl. E.

xxi. ⌐Of the conferring (παράδοσις) of Holy Baptism (βάπτ.)¬

(L.)Ar.E.S.(Boh.)T.K.

Blessing of font

1 And (δέ) at the hour when the cock (ἀλέκτωρ) crows they shall first ⟨of all⟩ pray over the water.

2 ⌐*When they come to the water, let the water be pure and flowing.*¬

The Neophytes

3 And (δέ) they shall put off their clothes.

4 And (δέ) they shall baptise (βαπτίζειν) the little children first. And if they can answer for themselves, let them answer. But if they cannot, let their parents answer or (ἤ) someone from their family (γένος).

5 And next they shall baptise the grown men; and last the women, who shall [all] have loosed their hair and laid aside the gold ornaments (κόσμησις) [which they were wearing]. Let no one go down to the water having any alien object (εἶδος ἀλλότριον) with ⌐them¬.

Title. So S.; Of the Order of Bapt. Ar.E.K.; *no title* T.
   1. T. *om. this verse, but elsewhere orders that Bapt. shall be administered on Holy Sat. at midnight.*
   2. *So* T. *only.* K. *is corrupt, but the words* pure flowing stream *are certain in its version.* Ar.E.S. *have:* Let the water flow along into the tank (κολυμβήθρα) or be poured down into it. Let it be thus if there be no necessity (ἀνάγκη) [E. *renders* ἀν. scarcity]; *but if there be any necessity [+continuous and sudden* S. *only]* use (χρᾶσθαι) *any water you shall find. This seems to be an edited version. The Jewish and early Xtn. practice was to require "living water" for bapt. Generally a stream or the sea was used. The prepared "tank" of* Ar.E.S. *smacks of the "baptistery", an innovation not earlier than the third century. The "necessity" of* Ar.S. *probably refers to emergency, sickness, persecution, etc., rather than "drought" as in* E. *The independent support of* K. *justifies the acceptance of* T. *as the primitive form of the rubric.* [The reading of Ar.E.S. may well be right. *H.C.*]
   3. *om.* T. | And] *om.* Ar. | clothes] +and be baptised naked E.
   4. they shall baptise] you shall b. S. | if they can answer] *sing.* Ar. | themselves] himself +and take oath Ar. | family] *so* Ar.E.S.; houses T. (K. *paraphrases*).
   5. they shall baptise]you sh. b.S. | women, who shall]*om.* shallS. | all]*om.* Ar.T. | and laid aside] *so* Ar.S.K. (T. *paraphrases*); And they shall be forbidden to wear their ornaments and their gold E. | gold] +and silver S.; +and other K. | which they were wearing] *om.* T.K. *and* 1 *MS. of* Ar. | go down—having] take down S. | with them] *so* E.S.K.; with him T.; *om.* Ar.

Consecration of Holy Oils

6 And (δέ) at the time determined for baptising (βαπτίζειν) the bishop shall give thanks (εὐχαριστεῖν) over the oil and put it into a vessel (σκεῦος) and ⌐it is called⌐ the Oil of Thanksgiving (εὐχαριστία).

7 And (δέ) he shall take [also] other oil and exorcise (ἐξορκίζειν) over it, and it is called Oil of Exorcism (ἐξορκισμός).

8 And let a deacon carry the Oil of Exorcism and stand on the left hand [of the presbyter] ⟨who will do the anointing⟩. And another deacon shall take the Oil of Thanksgiving and stand on the right hand.

Renunciation

9 And when the presbyter takes hold of each one of those who are to be baptised, let him bid him renounce (ἀποτάσσεσθαι), saying:

I renounce (ἀποτάσσ.) thee, Satan (σατανᾶς), and all thy service and all thy works.

1st Anointing

10 And when he has said this let him anoint him with the Oil of Exorcism saying:

Let all evil spirits depart far from thee.

---

6. And at—baptising] *so* S.; *om.* K.; And at the time when they are baptd. Ar.; And whenever they baptise E.; But when they are about to receive the oil for anointing T. | and—vessel] *so* S.; *om.* T.; which he put in a v. Ar.; which is in a v. E. | it is called] *so* E.; *om.* T.; and we call it Ar.; and call it S.; which is the K. | Oil of Thanksgiving] *so* Ar.S.K.; *om.* T.; mystic oil E.

7. also] *so* S.; *om.* Ar.E.K.T. | exorcise] + Satan E. | over] in E. | it is called] *so* E.; and call it Ar.S.

8. deacon 1°] presbyter K. (*and so later*). | of Exorcism] wh. has been exorcised from every unclean Spirit E. | presbyter] bishop K. | of the presbyter] *om.* T. | right hand] + of the presbyter S.; + of the bishop K.

9. takes] *so* T.; has taken Ar.E.S. | of those—baptised] *om.* T. | service] angels E.; thy service and thy shows and thy pleasures and all thy works T. | thy works] thy unclean works Ar.E.; thy retinue K.

10. said this] *so* Ar.E.T.K.; renounced all these S. | let him anoint] let the presbyter an. K. | anoint him] be anointed T. | of Exorcism] *subst.* wh. he has made pure fr. all evil E. | Let—from thee] *subst.* I anoint thee with this oil of exor. for a deliverance from every evil and unclean spirit and for a deliverance from every evil T. | evil spirits] evil *om.* S. | far] *so* Ar.S.; *om.* E.K.

(Adherence)

[10*a*   *And also turning him to the East, let him say:*

I consent to Thee, O Father and Son and Holy Ghost, before whom all creation trembleth and is moved. Grant me to do all Thy wills (sic) without blame.]

Baptism

11   Then after these things let him give him over to ⌜the presbyter⌝ who stands at the water [*to baptise*];

(Adherence)

[11*a*   *And a presbyter takes his right hand and he turns his face to the East. Before he descends into the water, while he still turns his face to the East, standing above the water he says after receiving the Oil of Exorcism, thus: I believe and bow me unto Thee and all Thy service, O Father, Son and Holy Ghost. And so he descends into the water.*]

11.   And let them stand in the water naked. And (δέ) let ⌜a⌝ deacon likewise (ὁμοίως) go down with him into the water.

(Adherence)

[11*b*   *And (δέ) let him say to him and instruct him: Dost thou believe (πιστεύειν) in one God the Father Almighty (παντοκράτωρ), and His only-begotten (μονογενής) Son Jesus Christ our Lord and our Saviour, and His Holy Spirit (πνεῦμα), Giver of life to all creatures, the Trinity of one Substance (τριὰς ὁμοούσιος), one Godhead, one Lordship, one Kingdom, one Faith, one Baptism in the Holy Catholic (καθολική) Apostolic (ἀποστολική) Church (ἐκκ.) for*

[10*a*. *So* T. *only. An interpolation.*]
11. Then after these things] *so* T.K.; *subst.* And thus Ar.E.S. | to the presbyter] naked to the bp or to the presb. E.S.; to the bp Ar. | who stands at the water to baptise] *so* S.; who stands at the water of the baptistery Ar.; at the water of baptism E.; who baptises T.; who st. at the water K.
[11*a*. K. *only. An interpolation.*]
11. likewise] *so* S.T.; *om.* Ar.E. | a deacon] *all the texts have* the. | down] *om.* S. | into the water] *om.* T.
[11*b*. Ar.E.S. *only. An interpolation.* | to him] *om.* E. | instruct him] *so* Ar.E.; helping him to say it S. | Dost thou believe] *so* Ar.; I believe E.S. | one] Ar.E.; the only true S. | His Holy Spirit] *so* S. *and* Ar. (1 *MS*.); the H.Sp.E. *and* Ar. (1 *MS*.). | one Godhead] *so* S.; Trinity of one coequal Godhead Ar.E. (*fusing the two clauses*). | Holy Catholic] *so* E.S. (Holy *after* Apost. S.); *om.* Ar. | Apostolic] *om.* Ar. | for life] *so* S. *and*

*life eternal [Amen]? And he who is baptised shall say ⌜again⌝
thus: Verily, I believe.]*

Profession of Faith and Baptism

12   And [*when*] he [*who is to be baptised*] goes down to the
water, let him who baptises lay hand on him saying thus:
   Dost thou believe in God the Father Almighty?
13   And he who is being baptised shall say:
   I believe.
14   Let him forthwith baptise him once, having his hand laid
upon his head.
15   And after ⟨*this*⟩ let him say:
   Dost thou believe in Christ Jesus, the Son of God,
   Who was born of Holy Spirit and the Virgin Mary,
   Who was crucified in the days of Pontius Pilate,
   And died, [*and was buried*]

L. (*p.* 110).   14 ...manum habens in caput eius inpositam baptizet semel.

L. (*p.* 110).   15 Et postea dicat: Credis in Chrm̄ Iem̄ filium Dī, qui natus est
de spū scō ex Maria uirgine et crucifixus sub Pontio Pilato et mortuus est [*et*

Ar. (one *MS.*); *om.* E. (1 *MS.*) *and* Ar. (1 *MS.*); *and* E. (*al.*). | Amen] *so all. It seems
unnecessary after an interrogative Creed.* | he who is baptised] *so* Ar.E.; *he who re-
ceives, let him also say* S. | again] *so* E.S. (*lit. also* S.); *om.* Ar. *The formula probably
consisted originally of three questions with an assent to each. The first two replies and the
second two questions have disappeared in all three texts. Cf.* 12–18 *inf.* | thus] *so* Ar.E.;
according to (κατά) *all these things* S. | Verily] *so* Ar.E.; *Thus* S.
   12. And when—thus] Ar.E.S. *have an edited version of this rubric:* And he who
baptises (gives S.) shall put his hand on the head of him who receives and dip him
thrice declaring these things every time Ar.S. And thus he shall baptise him and
lay his hand on him, and on him that answers for him. And he shall dip him thrice
and he who is baptised shall declare each single time that he is dipped E. | when]
so T.; *om.* Ar.E.S.K. | who is to be baptised] *so* T.; *om.* Ar.E.S.K. | him who baptises]
so T.; *the presbyter* K. | Dost—almighty] *so* T.K.; *om.* Ar.E.S. (!).
   13. *So* T.K.; *om.* Ar.E.S.
   14. baptise—head] *so* L. (*which begins again here*) K.; *om.* T.Ar.E.S.
   15. after] *so* L.Ar.E.; *also* T.; *the second time* K.; *om.* S. | him] *the presbyter* T. |
say] + again E.S.; + to him Ar.E.; *subst.* ask him K. | Christ Jesus] *in this* (*the Gk.*)
order L.T.E.; *Jesus* Xt. K.; *Jesus* Xt. *our Lord* Ar.S.; In the Name of Xt. J. our
Lord E. | the Son of God] *so* L.T.K.; *the only Son of God the Father* Ar.E.S. | Who
was born—Mary] *so* L. *exc.* of H. Sp. *and;* Who came from the Father, who is of
old with the Father, who was born of Mary the Virgin by the Holy Sp. T.; Whom
the V. M. bore of the H. Sp., who came for the salvation of the race of man K.; that
he became man by an incomprehensible (*om.* incomp. S.) miracle from (in S.) the
H. Sp. and from Mary the (+ holy S.) Virgin without seed of man Ar.E.S. | of Holy
Spirit and the] from Sp. of the L. | Who was crucified] Who T.K.; and L.Ar.E.S.

And rose the third day living from the dead
And ascended into ⌜the⌝ heaven⌜s⌝,
And sat down at the right hand of the Father,
And will come to judge the living and the dead?

16 And when he says: I believe, let him ⌜baptise him⌝ the second time.

17 And again let him say:

Dost thou believe in ⟨the⟩ Holy Spirit in the Holy Church,
And the resurrection of the flesh?

18 And he who is being baptised shall say: I believe. And so let him ⌜baptise him⌝ the third time.

2nd Anointing

19 And afterwards when he comes up [*from the water*] he shall

sepultus] et resurrexit die tertia uiuus a mortuis et ascendit in caelis et sedit ad dexteram patris uenturus iudicare uiuos et mortuos? Et cum ille dixerit: Credo, iterum baptizetur.

L. 17 Et iterum dicat: Credis in spū scō et sanctam ecclesiam et carnis resurrectionem? 18 Dicat ergo qui baptizatur, Credo: et sic tertia uice baptizetur.

L. 19 Et postea cum ascenderit ungueatur a presbytero de illo oleo quod

---

crucified] + for us K.S. | And died] *so* L.T.Ar.E.; Who died K.; He died S. | died] + by His own will for our salvation Ar.E.S. | and was buried] L. *only.* | the third day] *om.* Ar.E.S.; *subst.* from the dead Ar.E. | living] *so* L.T.; *om.* K.Ar.E.S. | from the dead] *so* L.T.K.; *subst.* on the third day Ar.E.S.; + and released the captives Ar.S. | heavens] *so* L.Ar.E.S.; heaven T.K. | of the Father] of His good (ἀγαθός) Father in the height S. | And will] And *om.* L. | will come] comes T.S.; + again K.S. | dead] + at His appearing and His kingdom Ar.E.S.

16. *om.* Ar.E.S. | baptise him] *so* T.K.; be baptised L.

17. And—say] *om.* Ar.E.S. | Holy Spirit] Holy, good (+ and sanctifying S.) Spirit who gives life (+ to all things S.) Ar.E.S. | Spirit] + who proceeds from the Father and the Son K. | in the Holy Church] *so* T.Ar.E.S.; and the Holy Church L.; K. *omits the whole clause.* | *After the word* Church *two ff. are missing in* B.M.Or. 1320, *the only available MS. of* S. *Horner supplies a Coptic text from Tattam's Bohairic version.* | And—flesh] *so* L. *only; om.* K.T. (T. *deliberately, cf. p.* lxix); *om.* Boh. *also, apparently accidentally, since* Ar.E. *have:* And dost thou believe in the resurrection of the flesh wh. shall happen to all men and the kingdom of the heavens and eternal judgement?

18. L.T. *agree verbally in this verse except:* baptise him] *so* T.K.; be baptised L. | And—believe] And he shall answer for all those things saying: Amen, I believe Ar.E. (*and om.* And so—time); Again let him say, I believe Boh. (*and om.* And so—time *as* Ar.E.); If he says I believe, let him baptise him the third time. Each time he says therewith: I baptise thee in the Name of the Father and of the Son and of the Holy Ghost, the coessential Trinity K.

19. And—comes up] *so* T.Ar.E.; And—has come up L.; And let them go up Boh. | up] + from the water Ar.E.Boh.K. | he shall be anointed] the presb. sh. anoint him

be anointed by the presbyter with the Oil of Thanksgiving (εὐχ.) saying:

I anoint thee with holy oil in the Name of Jesus Christ.

20 And ⌐so⌐ each one drying himself [*with a towel*] they shall ⌐now⌐ put on their clothes, ⌐and after this let them be together in the assembly⌐ (ἐκκλησία).

sanctificatum est, dicente: Ungueo te oleo sancto in nomine Ieū Chrī. 20 Et ita singuli detergentes se iam induantur et postea in ecclesia ingrediantur.

xxii. ⟨*Confirmation*⟩

L.Ar.E.Boh.T.(K.)

Imposition of hands

1 And (δέ) the Bishop shall lay his hand upon them invoking and saying:

O Lord God, who didst count these [*Thy servants*] worthy ⌐of deserving⌐ the forgiveness of sins by the laver of regeneration, ⌐make them worthy to be filled with⌐ Thy Holy Spirit and send upon them Thy grace, that they may serve Thee according to Thy will; [*for*] to Thee ⟨is⟩ the glory, to the Father and to the Son with ⟨the⟩ Holy Ghost in the holy Church, both now ⌐and ever⌐ and world without end. Amen.

L. 1 Episcopus uero manu illis inponens inuocet dicens: Dñe Dś, qui dignos fecisti eos remissionem mereri peccatorum per lauacrum regenerationis ⟨........⟩ spū⟨s⟩ scī, inmitte in eos tuam gratiam, ut tibi seruiant secundum uoluntatem tuam; quoniam tibi est gloria, patri et filio cum spū scō in sancta ecclesia et nunc et in saecula saeculorum. Amen.

Ar.E.Boh.K. | of Thanksgiving] *so* T.Ar.Boh.K.; sanctified oil L.E. (1 *MS.*); mystic oil E.(*al.*). | with holy oil] with an unction in holy oil Boh. | holy] *om.* T. | in the Name of Jesus Christ] *so* L.T.Boh.; *om.* Ar.E.; in the Name of the Father and of the Son and of the Holy Ghost K.

20. And so—clothes] *om.* T. | so] *so* L.Boh.; then Ar.K.E. (*most MSS., om. al.*). | each one—himself] *subst.* having anointed each one of the rest Boh. | drying himself] *om.* Ar.E.; he (the presb.) dries him K.Boh. | with a towel] *so* K.Boh.; *om. cæt.* | now] *so* L. *only.* | put on their clothes] he (the presb.) puts on his clothes K.Boh. | and after—assembly] *so* T. *only* (*cf. p.* lv *for regarding this as original*); and after-wards let them go in (*sic*) the Church L.Ar.E.Boh. (*om.* afterwards Boh.); and leads him then into the Church K.

No titles in any version.

1. invoking] *so* L.T.; praying Ar.E.K. (=ἐπικαλῶν *in both cases*); *subst.* with great desire Boh. | Thy servants] T. *only.* | of deserving] *so* L.T.; *om.* Ar.E.Boh.K. | by the laver of regeneration] *so* L.T.Ar.E.; *subst.* unto the age which comes Boh. | make them—with] *so* T.Ar.E.Boh.K.; *om.* L. *which is corrupt here.* | upon them] *subst.* down Boh. | for to Thee] *so* L.; *om.* for T.Ar.E.Boh.K. | is] *so* L. *only*; be Ar.E.Boh. (? =σοὶ ἡ δόξα *in both cases*). | and ever] E. *only.* | T. *subst. quite another doxology.*

Confirmation

2 After this pouring ⌐the consecrated⌐ oil [*from his hand*] and laying ⌐his hand⌐ on his head, he shall say:

I anoint thee with holy oil in God the Father Almighty (παντοκράτ.) and Christ Jesus and the Holy Ghost.

3 And sealing (σφραγίζειν) ⌐him⌐ on the forehead, he shall give him the kiss [*of peace*] and say:

The Lord be with you.

And he who has been sealed shall say:

And with thy spirit.

4 And so he shall do to each one ⌐severally⌐.

Prayers of the Faithful

5 Thenceforward they shall pray together with all the people. But they shall not previously pray with the faithful before they have undergone all these things.

Kiss of Peace

6 And after the prayers, let them give the kiss of peace.

L. 2 Postea oleum sanctificatum infunde⟨n⟩s de manu et inponens in capite dicat: Ungueo te sc̄o oleo in dn̄o patre omnipotente et Chr̄o Īeū et sp̄u sc̄o. 3 Et consignans in frontem offerat osculum et dicat: Dn̄s tecum. Et ille qui signatus est dicat: Et cum sp̄u tuo.

L. (*p.* 111). 4 Ita singulis faciat. 5 Et postea iam simul cum omni populo orent, non primum orantes cum fidelibus, nisi omnia haec fuerint consecuti. 6 Et cum orauerint de ore pacem offerant.

---

2. After this] *so* L.K.; *om.* Boh.; And afterwards Ar.E.; Similarly T. | consecrated] *so* L.; *om.* T.; Oil of Thanksgiving Ar.Boh.; mystic oil K.; oil of anointing K. *These look rather like independent interpolations, and* T. *may be right in omitting the word, though doubtless the "Oil of Thanksgiving" of* xxi. 6 *is meant.* | from his hand] *so* L.; upon his hand Ar.E.Boh.; T. *has* pouring the oil and placing his hand on his head (ἔλαιον ἐκχέων χεῖρα ἐπιτιθεὶς ἐπὶ τῇ κεφαλῇ *for* L.'s ἐλ. ἐκχ. χειρὸς ἐπιτ. κτλ.) *which is perhaps supported by* Boh.: pouring oil of Tksgvng. upon his hand and laying his hand on his head. T. *represents the rite as found in Tertullian Didascalia, etc., and is the right reading.* | I anoint] Anointing I anoint T. | with holy oil] *so* L.Ar.E.; *om.* T.; with an unction in holy oil Ar.Boh. | in God] *so* T.Boh.; in the Name of God Ar.E. | God] *so* Ar.E.Boh.T.; in Dn̄o L. (? *error for* Dō). | the Father] *om.* T.| Christ Jesus] *so* L.Ar.E.; J. Xt. T.Boh.

3. him] *so* T.Boh.; all of them Ar.E.; *om.* L. | kiss of] *om.* T. | of peace] *so* Boh.; the peace T.; *om.* L.Ar.E. | with you]+all E.

4. *om.* Ar.E.; Thus all the rest severally shall do Boh. | he shall do] *om.* T. | each one]+of the baptised K. | severally] *om.* L.

5. Thenceforward—people] *so* L.T. Ar.E.Boh. *have confused the text of this verse but do not appear to witness to any Gk. variant.* | But they shall—these things] *om.* T.

6. *om.* T. | give the kiss of peace] say peace with their mouth Boh.

xxiii. ⟨*The Paschal Mass*⟩

L.Ar.E.S.(Boh.)T.(K.)

Offertory and Consecration

1 And then let the oblation ⌜at once⌝ be brought by the
deacons to the bishop, and he shall eucharistize (εὐχαριστεῖν)
⌜first⌝ the bread into the representation, [*which the Greek calls
the antitype*] of the Flesh (σάρξ) of Christ; ⌜and⌝ the cup mixed
with wine for the antitype, [*which the Greek calls the likeness*] of
the Blood which was shed for all who have believed in Him;

Milk and Honey

2 and milk and honey mingled together in fulfilment of the
promise which was ⟨*made*⟩ to the Fathers, wherein He said I
will give you a land flowing with milk and honey; which Christ
indeed gave, ⟨*even*⟩ His Flesh, whereby they who believe are
nourished like little children, making the bitterness of the
⟨*human*⟩ heart sweet by the sweetness of His word (λόγος);

L. (*p.* 112). 1 Et tunc iam offeratur oblatio a diaconibus episcopo et gratias
agat panem quidem in exēplum (quod dicit Grecus antitypum) corporis Chrī;
calicem uino mixtum propter antitypum (quod dicit Graecus similitudinem)
sanguinis, quod effusum est pro omnibus, qui crediderunt in eum;

L. (*p.* 112). 2 lac et mel[*le*] mixta simul ad plenitudinem promissionis quae
ad patres fuit, qua[*m*] dixit terram fluentem lac et mel, quam et dedit carnem
suam Chrs, per quam sicut paruuli nutriuntur qui credunt, in suauitate uerbi

1. at once] *so* L. *only.* | be brought by] *so* L.T.; let the deacons bring Ar.E.Boh. |
deacons] *sing.* T. | he shall eucharistize—Him] *This archaic passage has given trouble
to the versions.* L. *has felt obliged to insert the notes which the Greek, etc.* T. *abbreviates
thus:* And so let the Shepherd give thanks: but the bread is offered for a type of my
Body. Let the cup be mixed with wine; Ar.E. *correct the theology:* Let the Bp give
thanks over the bread and the cup, ⌜the bread⌝ (*om.* Ar.) that it may become the
Body of Xt. and ⌜the cup, the wine mixed, that it may become⌝ (*om.* Ar.) His Blood
which was (He Ar.) shed for all of us who believe in Him Ar.E. And he sh. give
thanks over the bread because that ⟨*is*⟩ the form of the Flesh (σ.) of Xt. and a cup
of wine because it is the Blood of Xt. wh. will be shed for all who believe in Him
Boh. | first] L. quidem (μέν). | and] *om.* L.
2. *om.* T. | and 1°] *so* E.Boh.; *om.* L.; as for Ar. | together] + and he shall make
them drink of it Ar.E. | promise] *pl.* Boh. | was ⟨made⟩] *so* L.; *om.* Boh.; wh. He
promised Ar.E. | to the Fathers] of the F. Boh. | wherein He said] qua[*m*] dixit L.;
saying to them Ar.; saying E.; for He said Boh. | I will give] *om.* L. | honey] S.
begins again after this word. | which Christ indeed gave] *so* L.; *subst.* to us by wh. we
are nourished by Him as little children for they who believe were begotten by Him
Ar.E. (*slight variants* E.); wh. He gave to us to nourish us with it like little children
S. | making *etc.*] *so* L.Ar.E.; It will cause the bitterness of the heart to be dissolved
by the sweetness o the word S.

Water

3   water also for an oblation for a sign of the laver, that the
inner man also, which is psychic, may receive the same ⟨*rites*⟩
as the body.

4   And the bishop shall give an explanation (λόγος) concerning
all these things to them who receive.

Communion

5   And when he breaks the Bread in distributing to each a fragment (κλάσμα) he shall say:

The Bread of Heaven in Christ Jesus.

6   And he who receives shall answer: Amen.

7   And the presbyters—but if there are not enough ⟨*of them*⟩
the deacons also—shall hold the cups (ποτήριον) and stand by
in good order (εὐταξία) and with reverence: first he that holdeth
the water, second he who holds the milk, third he who holds the
wine.

amara cordis dulcia efficiens; 3 aquam uero in oblationem in indicium lauacri,
ut et interior homo, quod est animale, similia consequa[n]tur sicut et corpus.

L. (*p.* 112). 4 De uniuersis uero his rationem reddat episcopus eis qui
percipiunt; 5 frangens autem panem singulis partes porrigens dicat: Panis
caelestis in Chrō Iēu. 6 Qui autem accipit respondeat: Amen.

L. (*p.* 112). 7 Praesbyteri, uero si non fuerint sufficientes, teneant calices
et diacones et cum honestate adstent et cum moderatione: primus qui tenet

---

3. *om.* Ar.S.K.; *ut sup.* L.; Let the cup be mixed with wine and water, for it is
a sign of blood and water, so that also the inner man, that wh. is of the soul (= τὸ
ψυχικόν) may be counted worthy of those things wh. are like those things of the
body T.; And the water also of the oblation he sh. shew in the bread like the
inward part of the man who is soul as well as body E. | psychic] animale L. (*cf.* T.)
4. *om.* T. | give an explanation] make a covenant Ar. | to them] with him Ar.;
to all E.; to him S. | who receive] who are baptised Ar.(*sic*)E.S. (shall be bapt. S.).
5. when] + the bishop Ar.E.S. | to each] + of them Ar.E.S. | he shall say] *so* L.;
let him give and say Ar.E.; he shall give saying S. | say] + This is Ar.E.S. | in Christ
Jesus] *so* L.; the Body of Xt. Ar.E.; the Body of Xt. Jesus S. | T. *subst. for this:* Let
him who giveth say: The Body of Jesus Xt. the Holy Spirit, for the healing of soul
and body. *The editors Cooper and Maclean would emend this to* which is of the Holy
Sp., *inserting* DMN *in the Syriac text on the strength of the Abyssinian Anaph. of
O. L., but there is no need. The 2nd Person of the Trinity was still occasionally referred
to as* πνεῦμα *in the fourth century.*
6. answer] say T.; answer and say Ar.E.
7. *om.* T. | And the presbyters—deacons] If there is no prb. let the deacon
Ar.E.S. | and with reverence] *om.* Ar.E.S. | first—wine] *om.* Ar.S.; The first who has
the honey and the second who has the milk; [and he who gives the cup shall say:
"In God the Father Almighty."] And the third who has the wine E. (*confusing
with v.* 8).

8   And they who partake shall taste of each ⟨*cup*⟩, he who gives
⟨*it*⟩ saying thrice: ˷

   In God the Father Almighty;
and he who receives shall say: Amen.

9   **And in the Lord Jesus Christ;**
⟨*and he shall say: Amen.*⟩

10   And in ⟨*the*⟩ **Holy Spirit** [*and*] **in the Holy Church;**
and he shall say: Amen.

11   So shall it be done to each one.

12   And when these things have been accomplished, let each
one be zealous (σπουδάζειν) to perform good works and to
please God, living (πολιτεύεσθαι) righteously, devoting himself
to the Church, performing the things which he has learnt,
advancing (προκόπτειν) in the service of God.

13   And (δέ) we have delivered to you briefly these things
concerning Baptism and the Oblation because (ἐπειδή) you
have already been instructed (καθηγεῖσθαι) concerning the re-

aquam, secu.dus qui lac, tertius qui uinum. 8 Et gustent qui percipie ɪt de
singulis ter, dicente eo qui dat: In Dō patre omnipotenti. Dicat autem qui
accipit: Amen. 9 Et dnō Īeū Chrō ⟨; *et dicat: Amen.*⟩ 10 et spū scō [*et*] sancta
ecclesia. Et dicat: Amen. 11 Ita singulis fiat.

   L. (*p.* 113). 12 Cum uero haec fuerint, festinet unusquisque operam bonam
facere...(*def.*).

8, 9, 10. *This unfamiliar custom has troubled the versions badly. T. omits altogether,
while Ar.E.S. all garble it in such a way that it is not worth while to cite them.*

   9. and he shall say: Amen] *om.* L (*apparently*).

   10. and in 2°] *so* L., *but, it may be, in error; possibly the original was in* (*cf.* xxi.
17).

   12. And] *om.* Ar.S. | accomplished] *om.* L. | works] *so* Ar.E.S.T.; *sing.* L. *L. breaks
off with this word.* T. *om. the rest of this verse and from this point onwards omits more
and more of the Ap. Trad.* | to please] *so* S.; what pleases Ar.E. | living righteously]
om. Ar. | devoting himself to] *so* S.; finding time to go to Ar.; and united
with E.

   13. briefly] *so* S.; openly Ar.E. | concerning]+the holy S. | the Oblation] the
holy Ob. S.; the ordinance of the Ob. E. | because you—instructed] *lit.* And we have
finished our instr. Ar.; and, lo, we have finished the instr. we give you E.; they have
already instructed you S. (*all three probably derive from a Sahidic inversion to avoid
a pass. verb in the original*). | the resurrection] *From this and the next verse* T. *has
derived the extraordinary notion that the doctrine of the resurrection is only to be taught
to the baptised, which it expresses openly here, but has already hinted at by om. the last
clause of the Creed.* And let them be taught also about the res. of the body; before
any one receiveth baptm. let no one know the word about the resurrection, for

surrection of the flesh (σάρξ) and the rest according to (κατά) the Scriptures.

14 But (δέ) if there is any other matter which ought to be told, let the bishop impart it secretly to those who are communicated. He shall not tell this to any but the faithful and only after they have first been communicated. This is the white stone (ψῆφος) of which John said that there is a new name written upon it which no man knows except him who receives [the stone (ψῆφος)].

14. cf. Rev. ii. 17.

⟨Part III. Church Observances⟩

xxiv. ⟨The Stational Mass⟩

E.T.K.

[On the reasons for accepting the genuineness of this Chapter, cf. Notes]

E.	T. (ii. 10).	K.
1 [*And on the sabbath and*] on the first day of the week the bishop, if it be possible, shall with his own hand deliver to all the people, while the deacons break the bread.	Let the deacons give ⟨*the bread*⟩ to the people in their hands.	On Sunday [*at the time of the holy oblation*] the bishop, if he be able, shall allow all the people to partake from his own hands.

this is the new decree (*i.e.* ψῆφος) which hath a new name that none knoweth but he who receiveth T. | and the rest] *om.* S. | acc. to the Scriptures] *lit.* as it was written Ar.E.; acc. to what is written S.

14. communicated] *so* Ar.E.; baptised S. | white stone] *so* S.; holy token Ar.; holy blessing (*error*) E. | knows] knew Ar. | receives] shall receive S. | the stone] *om.* Ar.E.

1. And on the sabbath and] *so* E., all *MSS.*, *but not represented in* K. *Saturday was not a liturgical day at Rome in the third century, but it has been so in the Ethiopic Church as far back as we can trace,* "the Jewish Sabbath" *ranking almost with* "the Christian Sabbath" *as a weekly commemoration. The clause here seems therefore to be an interpolation in E.*

E.

2 And the pres-
byters also shall
break the [*delivered*]
bread. And when-
ever the deacon ap-
proaches the pres-
byter he shall hold
out his ⟨*vessel*⟩ and
the presbyter him-
self shall take and
deliver to the peo-
ple with his hand.
3 ⌐On other days
they shall give as the
bishop shall direct.⌐

T. (ii. 10).

The deacon does
not give the obla-
tion to a presbyter.
Let him ⟨*hold out*⟩
the πίναξ (*translit.*)
or paten and let the
presbyter take.

K.

When a presbyter
is sick a deacon
brings him the my-
steries and the pres-
byter shall take
them for himself un-
aided.

xxv. [*Of Fasting* (νηστία)]

Ar.E.S.Gr.

1 Widows and virgins shall fast often and pray on behalf of
the Church. The presbyters when they wish and the laity
(λαϊκός) likewise shall fast.

Gr. 1 χῆραι καὶ παρθένοι πολλάκις νηστευέτωσαν καὶ εὐχέσθωσαν ὑπὲρ τῆς

---

2. E. delivered bread]. *There is confusion in all MSS. of* E. *here.* B.M.Or. 796,
in some ways the best MS., omits delivered *altogether.* | hold out] *so* E. (= ἀναγέτω).
Both MSS. of T. *read* open (? *a misreading* ἀνοιγέτω *for* ἀναγέτω). | E. vessel]
All MSS. of E. *here read* robe, *which is nonsense.* T.'s πίναξ *is clearly right.* E.'s *text
probably arises from a misreading of* Käs (=a vessel) *as a derivative of* Ḳasā (=to
dress) *in the Arabic version from which* E. *was made. I am indebted to* Dr *O. H. E.
Burmester for this suggestion.*
3. *Found only in* E., *but probably authentic.*
Title. So S.; Of widows and virgins and when the bishop ought to fast Ar.E.
The Greek text of xxv *and also of* xxvi. 1 *has been preserved in a fragmentary quotation
found by Funk in Vindob. cod. hist. gr.* 7, *f.* 12, *and first publ. by him Theolog.
Quartalschrift,* 1893, *pp.* 664–6, *and again Did. et Const. Ap.* ii. *p.* 112. *The Gk. has
no title and makes no division between* xxv *and* xxvi. T. *omits* xxv *entirely, but gives
much more stringent rules of its own on the matter elsewhere.*
1. Widows *etc.*] Ar.E. *precede this by:* And they shall do as we have often said.
Ar. *omits* Widows—Church. | on behalf of the Church] *so* Gr.; in the Ch. E.S. | the
laity] *so* Gr.S.; the deacons Ar.E.

2 The bishop cannot fast (νηστεύειν) except when all the people (λαός) also [*fast*].

ἐκκλησίας. πρεσβύτεροι, ἐπὰν βούλοιντο, καὶ λαϊκοὶ ὁμοίως νηστεύετωσαν.
2 ἐπίσκοπος οὐ δύναται νηστεύειν, ἐὰν μὴ ὅτε καὶ πᾶς ὁ λαός.

xxvi. ⟨*Of a Private Agape*⟩

Ar.E.S.Gr.T.(K.)

1 For often some one wishes to bring an offering, and he cannot be denied (ἀρνεῖσθαι) and (δέ) ⟨*the bishop*⟩ having broken ⟨*the bread*⟩ shall always (πάντως) taste of it, and eat with such of the faithful (πιστός) as are present.
2 And they shall take from the hand of the bishop one piece (κλάσμα) of a loaf before each takes his own bread, for (γάρ) this is "blessed ⟨*bread*⟩"; but it is not the eucharist (εὐχαριστία) as is the Body (σῶμα) of the Lord.

Gr. 1 ἔσθ᾽ ὅτε γὰρ θέλει τις προσενεγκεῖν, καὶ ἀρνήσασθαι οὐ δύναται· κλάσας δὲ πάντως γεύεται (*et def.*).

⌐Of the time of eating⌐

3 And (δέ) before they drink let each of those ⌐*of you*⌐ who are present ⌐*take a cup and give thanks* (εὐχαριστεῖν) *and drink*⌐, and so take your meal ⌐*being purified in this way*⌐.

L. (*p.* 113). 3 ...qui praesentes estis, et ita aepulamini. 4 Catecuminis

---

2. fast] *so* Ar.E.S. *bis*; *om.* Gr. 2°.
No title and no division in the texts.
1. For—offering] *so* Gr.; For—wishes to take some to the Church Ar.S.; Because if they bring that which it is proper to bring to the Ch. E. | taste] Gr. *ends with this word.* | and eat—present] *It is not clear who is the subject of* eat. Ar.E.S. *have simply* and he sh. eat with other believers who are with him and they shall take, *with no stop between* 1 *and* 2.
2. T. ii. 13. In the supper or feast let those who have come together receive thus from the shepherd as for a blessing. | but] and Ar.E.S. (δέ). | as is] *lit.* like Ar.E.S.
Title. So S.; Of the time when it is right to eat Ar.E. (*Perhaps the original was* Of ⟨*rules for*⟩ when they eat ⟨*together*⟩. *There is nothing about* "time" *in the text.*)
3. And] *om.* E. | drink] eat and drink anything at all E. | each of] *om.* E. | of you] *so* L.; *which begins again at this point*; *om.* Ar.S.T. *It is clear that* L. *read a quite different text of this verse to* Ar.E.S., *but in its incomplete state it does not permit us to correct the latter.* | take a cup—drink] *om.* L. | being purified in this way] *so* S.; and thus they are pure Ar.; for they are pure E.; *om.* L.

4 But (δέ) to the catechumens let exorcised bread be given; ⌐and they shall each offer⌐ a cup.

⌐That catechumens ought not to sit at table ⟨at the Agape⟩ with the faithful⌐

5 A catechumen shall not sit at table at the Lord's Supper (δεῖπνον).

6 And (δέ) at every ⌐act of offering⌐ let him who ⌐offers⌐ remember him who invited him, for to this end he [i.e. the host] petitioned that ⌐they might come⌐ under his roof.

⌐That it is right to eat with moderation (ἐπιστήμη) and temperately and not be drunken⌐

7 But (δέ) when you eat and drink ⌐do it⌐ in good order and not unto drunkenness, and not so that any one may mock ⌐you⌐, or that he who invites you may be grieved (λυπεῖν) by your disorder, but [rather] so that he may pray [to be made worthy] that the Saints may come in unto him. For He said, Ye are the salt of the earth.

7. Cf. Mt. v. 13.

uero panis exorcizatus detur et calicem singuli offerant. ⟨Title effaced⟩ 5 Cate-cuminus in cena dominica non concumbat.

L. 6 Per omnem uero oblationem memor sit qui offert eius qui illum uocauit; propterea enim depraecatus est, ut ingrediatur sub tecto eius. ⟨Title effaced⟩ 7 Edentes uero et bibentes cum honestate id agite et non ad ebrie-tatem, et non ut aliquis inrideat, aut tristetur qui uocat uos in uestra inquie-tudine, sed ut oret ut dignus efficiatur ut ingrediantur sancti ad eum. Uos, enim, inquit, estis sal terrae.

---

4. But] om. Ar.E. | exorcised bread] so L.; bread of exorcism (ἐξοργισμός) S.; bread of blessing Ar.E.; bread purified by prayer K. | and they shall each offer] om. Ar.E.S. This v. is represented in T. ii. 13: But let not a catechumen receive (the eulogion).

Title. sit at the table with] lit. eat with Ar.E.S. Title effaced in L.; no title T.K.

5. sit at table] so L.S.K.; eat with Ar.E.T. (+the faithful Ar.E.S.). Cf. T. ii. 13: If any one be of the household of or related to one who teaches alien things, let him not accord with him and give praise with him, also let him not eat with him for relationship's sake or for friendship lest he deliver ineffable things to a wolf and receive judgement, which seems, from its position, to be derived from 4 and 5.

6. at every act of offering] so Easton renders L., per omnem oblationem. But προσφορά can mean a "meal". Ar.E.S. render, all the time they are eating. | let him who offers] so Easton renders L., offert (= προσφέρει). But Ar.E.S. have let him who eats (= προσφέρεται). It is impossible to say which is right. | they might come] so Ar.E.S., but L., ingrediatur (= ? Gk. middle voice).

Title. So Ar.E.S.; effaced in L. | A. viii. 44 is evidently based on this, but distantly.

7. do it] so L.; eat T.; om. Ar.E.S. | in good order] Cf. A. viii. 44 ...μετὰ εὐταξιας ἑστιᾶσθε. | mock you] so L.T.; you om. Ar.E.S. (perhaps the original was laugh, not mock at). | rather] so Ar.E.S.; om. L.T. | to be made worthy] so L.; om. T.Ar.E.S. | He said] ye have heard T.

8 If you are all assembled ⟨and⟩ offered [*what is called in Greek*] an *apophoretum* [*i.e. something to be taken away*] accept it from him [*i.e. the giver*] ⟨and depart⟩ ⌐and eat thy portion alone⌐.

9 But (δέ) if ⟨*you are invited*⟩ ⌐all⌐ to eat ⟨*together*⟩, eat sufficiently, but so that there may remain something over that your host may send it to whomsoever he wills as (ὡς) the superfluity of the Saints, and he ⟨*to whom it is sent*⟩ may rejoice ⌐with what is left over⌐.

10 And (δέ) let the guests when they eat partake in silence without arguing. But (ἀλλά) ⟨*let them hearken to*⟩ any exhortation (προτρέπειν) the bishop may make, and if any one ask any question, let an answer be given him. And when the bishop has given ⌐the explanation⌐ let every one quietly offering praise [*to him*] be silent until he [? *the bishop*] ⌐be asked⌐ again.

L. 8 Si communiter uero omnibus oblatum fuerit quod dicitur Graece apoforetum, accipite ab eo; 9 si autem, ut omnes gustent, sufficienter gustate, ut et superet, et quibuscumque uoluerit qui uocauit uos mittat tamquam de reliquiis sanctorum et gaudeat in fiducia.

L. 10 Gustantes autem cum silentio percipiant qui uocati sunt, non contendentes uerbis sed qu⟨a⟩e hortatus fuerit episcopus ⟨*audientes*⟩, et si interrogauerit aliquit, respondeatur illi; et cum dixerit episcopus uerbum omnis cum modestia laudans [*eum*] taceat, quandiu iterum interroget.

| T. 10 But if any one desire or the bishop or presbyter ask, let him return answer. But when the bishop says the (or a) word, let every one quietly praising choose silence for himself until he also be asked again. | Ar. 10 But if the bishop ⌐allow any one to ask⌐* about a word, then he may address him. When the bishop speaks let all be silent till he asks them.

[* *Another MS. subst.* ask any one *for* allow any one to ask.] | E. 10 But when the bishop allows, they shall speak, and ask what is suitable; and they shall answer. And when one has finished saying all he wished then again they shall be modestly silent until the bishop again asks them. | S. 10 But when the bishop exhorts (προτρ.) any one to ask for a word, let him answer him. And when the bishop speaks let all hold their peace in modesty until he asks them again. |

8. *om.* T.K. E. *is very confused.* Ar.S. *represent a different text to* L., *having only:* If he gives to you all portions together, thou shalt take thy portion alone Ar. If to all of you should be given portions (μέρις) at once, then thou wilt take up thy portion alone S. *The above, which conflates the two texts of* L. *and* Ar.E.S., *reconstructs the original, I hope, with sufficient fidelity to the sense.* | assembled] *so I translate* communiter *in* L. | what is called in Greek] *an insertion by the translator of* L. | and eat—alone] Ar.E.S. *only.*

9. all] *so* L.; *om.* Ar.E.S. | with what is left over] *so* T. (= ἐν ὑπερουσίᾳ); in confidence L. (in fiducia = ἐν παρρησίᾳ); at your coming Ar.E.S. (= ἐν παρουσίᾳ).

10. *I do not place much confidence in the verbal fidelity of this reconstruction, though again I think it represents the general sense of the original. None of the texts makes sense as it stands.* | The explanation] L.T. word = λόγος. | be asked] *so* T.; asks L.Ar.E.S. | to him] L. *only.*

11 And (δέ) if the faithful (πιστός) should be present at a supper (δεῖπνον) without the bishop, but with a presbyter or deacon present, let them similarly partake ⌜in orderly fashion⌝. But let every one be careful to receive the blessed bread (εὐλογίον) from the hand of the presbyter or deacon. Similarly a catechumen shall receive the ⌜same⌝ ⌜bread⌝, ⟨but⟩ exorcised.

12 If laymen (λαός) ⟨only⟩ are met together ⌜without the clergy (κληρικός)⌝ let them ⌜act⌝ with discipline (ἐπιστήμη). For the layman (λαός) cannot make a blessing [or, make the blessed bread (εὐλογίον)].

L. (p. 114).	Ar.S.
11 Etiamsi absque episcopo in cena adfuerint fideles, praesente presbytero aut diacono similiter honeste percipiant. Festinet autem omnis siue a praesbytero siue a diacone accipere benedictionem de manu. Similiter et catecuminus exorcizatum id ipsut accipiat. 12 Si laici fuerint in unum benedictionem facere non potes⟨t⟩.	11. And if the bishop is not present but the faithful only at the supper, let them take the eulogia from ⌜the hand of⌝ the presbyter if he is present, but if not let them take from ⌜the hand of⌝ the deacon [om. the hand of Ar. bis].

12 Si laici fuerint in unum cum moderatione agant. Laicus enim

⌜Concerning that it is right to eat with thanksgiving⌝

13 ⌜And (δέ) having given thanks⌝ let each one eat in the Name of the Lord. For (γάρ) this is pleasing to God that we should be rivals in zeal even among the heathen (ἔθνος). all of us sober (νήφειν) alike.

L. (p. 114). ⟨Title effaced⟩ Unusquisque in nomine dñi edat. Hoc eñi Dō placet, ut aemulatores etiam aput gentes simus, omnes similes et sobrii.

---

11. om. T. Ar.S. *represent a rather different text to* L.E. (cf. inf.). | in orderly fashion] L. honest⌐t⌐ (? = εὐταξία, cf. xxiii. 7); om. Ar.E.S. | same] so L.; om. Ar.E.S. | bread et..] bread om. L.; bread of exorcism Ar.S.; mystic bread E.

12. act] so L.; eat Ar.E.S. | make] so L.Ar.E.; give S. | blessing] sing. L.; pl. Ar.E.S.

Title. So S. only; om. Ar.E. Title effaced in L.

13. om. Ar. | And—eat] so E.; and—thanks om. L. And let each eat with thanksgiving S.; Let them give and return thanks and not eat... T. | in the Name of the Lord] so L.E.S. (of God S.); om. T. | pleasing to] so L.: due to E.S.; om. T. | that— rivals] so L.E.; that the heathen may envy us S. | sober alike] so L.; alike om. S.; all of us equal and sober and pure and faultless. for God the Father rejoices in us and we indeed ⟨are⟩ his work if we are pure E. | The second half of this sentence appears in T. as...thanks, and not eat with offence and scandal. Let no one taste of that which is strangled or sacrificed to idols.

[*Concerning the gift to the sick*]

E.(T.K.)

E.

14 The deacon in time of need shall be diligent in giving the sealing to the sick.

15 If there be no presbyter to give that which is to be distributed, as much as ought to be received, ⟨? *the deacon*⟩ shall give thanks and shall take note of those who take away ⟨*food to be distributed to the sick*⟩ that they perform this with care and distribute the blessed bread.

T. (ii. 11).

Let the deacon, when the presbyter is not present, of necessity baptise.

E.

16 If there is any one who takes it away, let him bear it to the widows and the sick. And let him who is occupied with the Church take it away.

17 And if he did not take it away, on the morrow having added of that which was with him, he

T. (ii. 11).

If any one receive any service to carry to a widow or poor woman or to any one constantly engaged in a church work, let him give it the same day.

And if not, on the morrow let him add something to it from his own, and so give it. For the

K. (xxxii).

Naught (of the alms) shall be reckoned to him in whose house it is kept.... He has no

---

E.	T. (ii. 11).	K. (xxxii).
shall take it away; for it remained with him as bread of the poor.	bread of the poor hath been kept back in his possession.	share because the sojourn of the bread of the poor was prolonged in his house.

[*Of the bringing-in of lamps at the supper of the congregation*]

18

	[*But in the last week of Pascha on the fifth day of the week, let the bread and cup be offered. And He who suffered for that which He offered, He it is who draweth nigh.*]	[*If a meal or a supper take place which some one gives to the poor and is a Lord's Supper (κυ-ριακόν transliterat-ed).*]

Lucernarium

When the evening is come, the bishop being present, the deacon shall bring in a lamp.	Let the lamp be offered [*in the temple*] by the deacon,	The bishop shall be there at the bringing-in of the lamp. The deacon shall occupy himself with bringing in the lamp,
19 The bishop standing in the midst of the faithful, before he gives thanks shall say: The Lord be with you all.	saying: The grace of the Lord be with you all.	and the bishop shall pray for them, and for those who invited them.
20 And the people also shall say: With thy spirit.	And let all the people say: And with thy spirit.	

---

the whole passage stood in its MS. of Ap. Trad. T. *obviously gives the best text of this verse.*

Title. So E. *only, but something equivalent clearly stood in* K.'s MS.

19. T. *gives the opening salutation to the deacon, not the bishop.*

21 And the bishop shall say: Let us give thanks unto the Lord.

22 And the people shall say: It is meet and right. Greatness and exaltation with glory are due unto Him.

23 And he shall not say: Lift up your hearts, because that shall be said at the oblation.

24 And he prays thus saying:

We give thanks unto Thee, O God, through Thy Son Jesus Christ our Lord, because Thou hast enlightened us by revealing the incorruptible light.

25 We therefore having finished the length of a day and having come to the begin-

A. viii. 37. 3 [ὁ διαγαγὼν ἡμᾶς] τὸ μῆκος τῆς ἡμέρας καὶ ἀγαγὼν ἐπὶ τὰς ἀρχὰς τῆς νυκτός...

ning of the night, and having been satisfied with the light of the day which Thou didst create for our satisfaction, and since we now lack not by Thy grace a light for the evening, we sanctify Thee and we glorify Thee,

26 Through Thine only Son our Lord Jesus Christ, through whom to Thee with Him ⟨be⟩ glory and might and honour with the Holy Ghost now and ever and world without end.

27 And they shall all say: Amen.

E.

28 And having risen after supper, the children and virgins having prayed, they shall sing psalms.

29 And afterwards the deacon holding the mingled cup of the oblation shall say the Psalm from those in which is written "Hallelujah",

T. (ii. 11).

And let the little boys say spiritual psalms and hymns of praise by the light of the lamp.

21-27. E. *only except for one phrase (sup.) preserved by A. in its evening "Thanksgiving"* (εὐμενῶς πρόσδεξαι τὴν εσπερινὴν εὐχαριστίαν ἡμῶν ταύτην) *to be said by the bishop. But this perhaps suffices to show that this passage is not confined to E.*
28. K. xxxii: *Before they go forth they shall sing psalms.*
29. oblation] E. προσφορά *transliterated.*

E.

30 after that the presbyter has commanded: "And likewise from those Psalms." And afterwards the bishop having offered the cup as is proper for the cup, he shall say the Psalm "Hallelujah".

31 And all of them as he recites the Psalms shall say "Hallelujah", which is to say: We praise Him who is God most high: glorified and praised is He who founded all the world with one word.

32 And likewise when the Psalm is completed, he shall give thanks over the cup (sic), and give of the fragments to all the faithful.

T. (ii. 11).

Let all the people answer "Hallelujah" to the Psalm [and to the chant sung together with one accord, with voices in harmony: and let no one kneel till he who speaks ceases].

xxvii. ⌐Of the Supper (δεῖπνον) of the Widows (χ.)⌐

L.Ar.E.S.K.

1 If at any time any one wishes ⌐to invite⌐ those widows who are advanced in years let ⌐him feed them and⌐ send them away before sunset.

L. 1 Uiduas, si quando quis uult, ut aepulentur, iam maturas aetate dimittat

---

32. cup] so all MSS., presumably in error for bread. After 32, E. goes on to reproduce xxvi. 2.

Title. So Ar.E.S.; effaced in L. Hauler conj. ⟨De uiduarum epulo⟩. T. omits this chapter entirely, perhaps because he regards widows, whom he also styles "presbyteresses", as persons of considerable dignity to whom he attributes functions roughly represented by the word (which he does not use) "archdeaconess". He may have felt this obviously "charity" supper was inconsistent with such a view.

1. to invite] so Ar.E.S.; om. L.; to feed K. | those who are advanced in years] om. K. By placing this phrase later L. may mean to imply let him send them away before sunset even though they are advanced in years, but Ar.E.S. certainly take it as above. | let him feed them and] so Ar.E.S.K.; ut aepulentur L.

2 But if he cannot ⟨*entertain them at his house*⟩ because of his clerical office, let him give them food and wine and send them away, and they shall partake ⌐of it⌐ at home as they please.

eas ante uesperam. 2 Si autem nō potest propter clerum quem sortitus est, escas et uinum dans eis dimittat illas et aput semet ipsas, quomodo illis placet, de re sumescant.

[Here E. has ch. 1, then interpolates baptismal prayers.]

xxviii. ⌐Of the fruits (καρπός) which it is right to bring (προσενεγκεῖν) to the bishop⌐

L.Ar.E.S.T.K.Gr.

1 All shall be careful (σπουδάζειν) to bring (προσεν.) to the bishop the first-fruits (ἀπαρχή) of the fruits (καρπός) of the crops (γέννημα).

2 And (δέ) he shall offer them and bless ⟨*God*⟩, naming (ὀνομάζειν) him who brought them, saying:

L. lxxvi. 14 (*p.* 115). 1 Fructus natos primum quam* incipiant eos, omnes festinent offerre episcopo. 2 qui autem offerit benedicat et nominet eum qui optulit, dicens:

---

2. if he cannot] *so* L.; if they cannot come Ar.E.S.; if they be many K. | because of his clerical office] *om.* K.; *lit.* because of the lot which has befallen him L.; because of the lot (κλῆρος)) which they have drawn (κληροῦν) Ar.S.; because of the clergy who have been invited (!) E. | food and wine] *so* L.E.; wine and food Ar.S.; enough to eat and drink K. | and send them away] *so* L.E.; *om.* Ar.S.; and they shall go forth K. | partake] *subst.* do E. | of it] *om.* Ar.E.S.

Title. So S.; Of the first-fruits and fruits wh. they bring to the bp Ar.; Of the fruit wh. it is right to offer E.; Of the first-fruits of the fruits and first produce of the threshing-floor and wine-press K. *Title effaced in* L. *Hauler conj.* ⟨De fructibus episcopo offerendis⟩. *No title* T.

1. All shall] + give and be caref. E. | to the bp] + at all times S.; *subst.* Church for bp K. | first-fruits—crops] *so* Ar.S., *and* L. *also seems to have read this* (? ἀπαρχήν *for* ἀπαρχάς); first-fruits of the crops E.; first-fruits of the crops and first produce etc. *as in title* K. *Cf.* T. *inf.*

2. bless] +them Ar.S. *only* (*cf.* T.) (+with giving of thanks S.); and thank God for them K.

T. *shortens* 1 and 2 *to:* The fruits wh. are brought near to (*or* offered, =προσενεγκεῖν) the bp let him bless thus.

* quam. *Hauler would read* ⟨prius⟩quam, *but* L. *is probably trying to render the text above and* priusquam *would seriously alter the sense.*

3 We give thanks (εὐχαριστεῖν) to Thee, O ⌐Lordꞁ God, and we offer to Thee the first-fruits (ἀπαρχή) of the fruits (καρπός) which Thou hast given us for food, having perfected them by Thy Word, bidding the earth to send forth fruits of all kinds for the joy and nourishment (τροφή) of men and for all beasts.

4 We praise Thee, O God, for all ⌐theseꞁ things, for all [other] things wherein Thou hast been our benefactor (εὐεργετεῖν), adorning (κοσμεῖν) for us all creation with diverse fruits.

5 Through Thy Child Jesus Christ our Lord, through whom [even] to Thee be the glory for ever and ever. Amen.

L. lxxvi. 17 (p. 115). 3 Gratias tibi agimus, Ds̄, et offerimus tibi primitiuas fructuum quos dedisti nobis ad percipiendum, per uerbum tuum enutriens ea, iubens terrae omnes fructus adferre ad laetitiam et nutrimentum hominum et omnibus animalibus. 4 Super his omnibus laudamus te, Ds̄, et in omnibus quibus nos iuuasti, adornans nobis omnem creaturam uariis fructibus 5 per puerum tuum Iēm Chr̄m d̄ōm nostrum, per quem tibi gloria in saecula saeculorum. Amen.

Gr. Goar, *Euchologion to Mega*, p. 522. Εὐχὴ ἐπὶ προσφερόντων καρποὺς νέους. 3 Εὐχαριστοῦμέν σοι κύριε ὁ θεὸς καὶ προσφέρομεν ἀπαρχὴν καρπῶν οὓς ἔδωκας ἡμῖν εἰς μετάληψιν τελεσφορήσας διὰ τοῦ λόγου σου καὶ κελεύσας ⟨τῇ γῇ⟩ καρποὺς παντοδαποὺς εἰς εὐφροσύνην καὶ τροφὴν τοῖς ἀνθρώποις καὶ παντὶ ζώῳ. 4 ἐν (l. ἐπὶ) πᾶσιν ὑμνοῦμέν σε ὁ θεός, ἐπὶ πᾶσιν οἷς εὐηργέτησας ἡμῖν ⟨κοσμήσας ἡμῖν⟩ πᾶσαν κτίσιν πηλίκοις (l. ποικίλοις) καρποῖς, 5 διὰ τοῦ παιδός σου Ἰησοῦ Χριστοῦ τοῦ κυρίου ἡμῶν δι' οὗ [καὶ] σοὶ ἡ δόξα εἰς τοὺς αἰῶνας τῶν αἰώνων. ἀμήν.

⌐Of the blessings (εὐλογία pl.) of fruits (καρπός)ꞁ

6 Fruits (κ.) indeed (μέν) are blessed, that is grapes, the fig, the pomegranate, the olive, the pear (παπίδιον), the apple, the

L. lxxvi. 29 (p. 115). 6 Benedicuntur quidem fructus, id est uua, ficus,

---

3. A. *preserves extensive traces of this prayer, which has also survived into the Great Euchologion of the Byzantine Church* (cited here from Goar's ed., Venice, 1730, p. 522, as Gr.). E. *is very confused at this point and I have omitted its variants as the text seems secure.* | Lord God] so Gr.S.K.(A.); om. Lord caet. | having perfected] L., enutriens, *may represent a different reading.* | Thy Word] the W. T. | bidding] and bidding Gr. | the earth] om. Gr. | of all kinds] so Gr.; diverse T.E.A.; all L.Ar.S. | joy and nourishment] so Gr.L.Ar.A.; joy and delight (? = τρυφήν) T.; profit and j. and n. S. | of men] of the race (γένος) of men S. | for] so Gr.L.; of caet.

4. God] subst. Lord T. | for all] for = ἐν Gr. (error). | these] om. Gr.; hab. caet. | for all other things] so Ar.S.; om. T.; other om. Gr.L. | all creation] the whole world T. | fruits] T.K. *here add independently a prayer for the offerer as directed in* xxviii. 2.

5. *Doxology as in* Gr.L. *The others all vary considerably.*

Title. So Ar.S.; Of the fruits E. *Title effaced in* L. *Hauler conj.* ⟨De fructuum benedictione⟩. *Om.* T.

6. *There are slight differences of content and order in the lists of fruit in this verse.*

mulberry, the peach (περσικόν), the cherry (κεράσιον), the almond (ἀμύγδαλον), the plum; but (δέ) not the pumpkin (πέπων) or the melon (μηλοπέπων), or cucumber or the onion, or garlic, or any other vegetable (λάχανον).

7 But sometimes flowers (ἄνθος) also are offered (προσφέρειν). Let the rose (+ μέν) and the lily (κρίνον) be offered (προσφ.), but (δέ) not others.

8 And (δέ) for all things which are eaten they shall give thanks to [*the Holy*] God, eating them to His glory.

mala grania, oliua, pyrus, malum, sycaminum, Persicum, ceraseum, amygdalum, Damascena, non pepon, non melopepon, non cucumeres, non cepa, non aleus, nec aliut de aliis oleribus. 7 Sed et aliquotiens et flores offeruntur. ⟨*Title effaced*⟩. Offeratur ergo rosa et lilium, et alia uero non. 8 In omnibus autem, quae percipiuntu⟨r⟩, scō Dō gratias agant in gloriam eius percipientes.

Gr. εὐλογοῦνται δὲ καρποὶ τοιοῦτοι· σταφυλίν, σῦκον, ῥόα, ἔλαια, μῆλον, ῥοδακινόν, περσικόν, δαμασκηνά (*et def.*).

xxix. ⟨*The Paschal Fast*⟩

L.T.Ar.E.S.

L.T.	Ar.E.S.
1 No one shall taste any thing at the Pascha before the offering is made, for if any one	Concerning that it is not right for any one to taste anything in the Pascha (πάσχα) before

L. 1 Nemo in Pascha antequam oblatio fiat percipiat. Nam qui ita agit non

---

I follow L., *with wh.* S. *agrees except in omitting the mulberry and plum from the fruits and inserting the leek among the vegetables.* | T. *abbreviates* 6–7 *thus:* Vegetables are not blessed, but fruits of trees, flowers, both the rose and the lily. | Fruits are blessed] *so* L.; These are the fruits wh. are blessed Ar.S.; The priests shall bless these fruits E.

7. sometimes] *lit.* it will be that S. (=ἔσθ᾽ ὅτε?). | also] *so* L.Ar.; *om.* E.S.(T). | rose and lily] *so* L.T.; *pl.* Ar.E.S. (*om.* and the lily Ar.E.). | not others] *so* L.; let them not bring others Ar.E.S. | *After* προσφέρειν L. *has space for a title of which the others have no trace. Hauler suggests* ⟨De floribus⟩.

8. the Holy] *so* L. *only.* T. *paraphrases this verse very strangely thus:* Of all the faithful who receive and eat: Let them give and return thanks and not eat with offence or scandal. Let no one taste that which is strangled or given to idols.

Title. A difference of reading is involved in the title of Ar.E.S. *for which I have subst. the colourless heading above.* Ar.E.S. *fuse the title with the first sentence. Title effaced in* L. *Hauler conj.* ⟨ In Pascha antequam oblatio fiat percipi non debere⟩. *No title* T.K.

1 *a*, L.T. at the Pascha] *om.* T., *thus turning this special Paschal regulation into a*

L.T.

does so the fast is not reckoned to him.

Ar.E.S.

the hour in which it is right to eat. The fast (νηστεία) shall not be reckoned as such if a man was greedy before the hour at which the fast was complete.

2   But (ἀλλά) if any one is pregnant ⌐or⌐ sick and cannot fast the two days, let them fast on the Saturday, taking bread and water if necessary (ἀνάγκη).

3   But if any one be at sea or (ἤ) by reason of any necessity did not know the ⟨right⟩ day, when he has learned it let him fast ⌐in compensation⌐ after Pentecost (πεντηκοστή).

4   It is not the Pascha which he keeps but a likeness (τύπος) of

illi inputatur ieiunium. 2 Si quis autem in utero habet et aegrotat et non potest duas dies ieiunari, in sabbato ieiunet,* propter necessitatem contenens panem et aquam.

L. lxxvii. 11 (*p.* 116). 3 Si quis uero in nauigio uel in aliqua necessitate constitutus ignorauit diem, hic cum didicerit hoc, post quinquagesimam reddat ieiunium. 4 Typus enim transiit, quapropter secundo mense cessauit,

---

general rule about fasting communion. While it is virtually certain that Hippolytus taught fasting communion (cf. xxxii. 1) that is not the purpose of this passage. | before the offering is made] so L.; before the off. is complete T. Both seem to represent πρὶν ἤ προσφέρειν.

1b, Ar.E.S. before the hour in which it is right to eat] so Ar.E.S., apparently reading πρὶν ἤ δεῖν προσφέρεσθαι. Cf. xxvi. 6, where the same difference of reading occurs between the same groups. Connolly (pp. 70 and 190) argues that Ar.E.S. are right in both cases. But the general character of the text in Ar.E.S. and the editing wh. they have undergone elsewhere in this same verse is not such as to inspire confidence against a combination of L.T. | as such—complete] om. E., running this clause into the next: The fast shall not be reckoned to the following, the pregnant or the sick.

2. pregnant or] om. Ar.S. | or] so E.; and L.; om. T. | on the Saturday] on the day of the Sabbath S. | taking] so T.: contenens L. (=συλλαμβάνων); being content with Ar.E.S. | if necessary] lit. on account of necessity L.E.S.; om. T.; because of the necessity and it shall suffice Ar. | bread]+and salt S. | T. reproduces this verse thus: (ii. 20) If a woman be pregnant, sick, and cannot fast these two days, let her fast one, taking on the first bread and water.

3. om. T. | by reason of any necessity] so L.E. (mischance E.); om. Ar.S. | did not know] so L.Ar.S.; mistook E. | in compensation] om. Ar.S.

4. om. T. | There is some confusion in all the texts here. E. is the basis of the above: It is not the P. which he keeps but a type of it after it has passed by. In the second month he shall not omit, and having returned from his journey he shall do it knowing the certainty E.; And it is not a P. wh. he keeps but a type, and the fast is his duty

---

* Hauler punctuates in sabbato ieiunet propter necessitatem, contenens etc., to the detriment of the sense.

it after it has passed by. Wherefore in the second month he shall not fast. ⌜But⌝ (ἀλλά) when he knows the truth every one ought to fast.

et debet quis facere ieiunium cum ueritatem didicerit.

4. *cf.* Num. ix. 10 *sq.*

xxx. ⌜That it is seemly for the deacons and subdeacons to attend upon (προσκαρτερεῖν) the bishop⌝

L.Ar.E.S.T.(K.)

And (δέ) let each of the deacons with the subdeacons attend upon (προσκαρτερεῖν) the bishop; and let it be reported to him who are sick, that if it seem good (δοκεῖν) to the bishop he may visit them; for the sick man is much comforted that the high priest remembered him.

L. (*p.* 116). Diaconus uero unusquisque cum subdiaconibus ad episcopum obseruent; suggeretur etiam illi qui infirmantur ut si placuerit episcopo uisitet eos. Ualde enim oblectatur infirmus cum memor eius fuerit princeps sacerdotum.

T. ii. 21. Of those who are sick. Let them take up [? = ἀναφερεῖν] to the hearing of the bishop, that if it seem good to the bishop he may visit them; for the sick man is much comforted when the high priest remembereth him, and especially when he is faithful.

xxxi. ⌜Of the times at which it is right to pray⌝

L.Ar.E.S.

1 And (δέ) the faithful (πιστός *pl.*), ⌜as soon as⌝ they wake and are risen, before they betake themselves to their work shall

L. lxxvii. 24 (*p.* 116). 1 Fideles uero mox cum expergefacti fuerint et surrexerint, antequam oper⟨a⟩e suae contingant orent D͞m et sic iam ad opus suum

---

by way of compensation Ar.; For it is not a Passover (π.) which we keep, for that which is for a type (π.) is passed by. For this cause we said not in the second month, but that when he knows the truth he ought to fast S. | But] *so* S.; And L.Ar.E.

Title. So Ar.E.S. *Title effaced in* L.; Of those who are sick T.

And] *om.* Ar.E. | rep. to him] + of all who S. | for the sick man *etc.*]*,so* L.T., *but* Ar.E.S. *alter to:* for the sick are consoled when they see the high priest visiting them (+diligently E.) for he remembered them Ar.E. (and that they have been remembered S.). (Ar. *is corrupt in this sentence but at least had the same plural readings as* E.S.) | remembered] *so* L.Ar.E.S.; remembereth T.

xxxi. *This chapter duplicates and condenses* xxxv *and is clearly out of place here, but it is found in this position in* L.Ar.E.S. *On the cause of this apparent dislocation of the text cf. Notes.*

Title. So Ar.E.S. (time E.S.). *Title effaced in* L. *Hauler conj.* ⟨De hora orandi⟩.

1. as soon as] *so* L.; when Ar.E.S. | and are risen] *om.* S. | their work 1°] *so* L.;

[*wash their hands and*] pray to God, and so let them hasten then to their work.

2 But if there should be ⌜any⌝ instruction (καθήγησις) ⌜by⌝ the word, he shall put this first, to go and hear the word of God for the strengthening of his soul. And they shall be zealous (σπουδάζειν) to go to the assembly (ἐκκλησία) where the Spirit (πν.) abounds.

properent. 2 Si qua⟨e⟩ autem per uerbum catecizatio fit praeponat hoc ut pergat et audiat uerbum Dī ad confortationem animae suae; festinet autem et ⟨eat⟩ ad ecclesiam ubi floret sp̄s.

xxxii. ⌜Concerning that it is right to receive of the Eucharist (εὐχαριστία) early [*at the time when it is offered*] before tasting any food⌝

Daily Communion L.Ar.E.S.T.(K.)

1 And (δέ) let every one of the faithful (πιστός) be careful (σπουδάζειν) to partake of the eucharist before he eats any thing else. For if he partakes with faith, even though some deadly ⌜thing⌝ were given him, after this it cannot hurt him.

L. lxxvii. 32 (*p.* 117). 1 Omnis autem fidelis festinet, antequam aliquid aliut gustet, eucharistiam percipere. Si enim ex fide percipit etiamsi mortale quodcumque ⟨d⟩atum illi fuerit, post hoc non potest eum nocere. 2 ⟨*Title effaced*⟩

---

any w. Ar.E.S.(*cf.* A.*ap.* xxxv. 1). | wash their hands and]*so* E.(*cf.* xxxv. 1); *om.* L.Ar.S. | to God] to the Lord E. | so] *om.* Ar.E. | then] *om.* S.

2. any] *so* L. (qua *l.* qua⟨e⟩, *cf.* A. xxxv. 2). | by the word] *so* L.; *om.* S.; any w. of instruction Ar.E. | put this first] *so* L.; they sh. choose Ar.E.S. | and hear] *so* L.S.; *om.* E.; *subst.* there where is the w. of instr. wh. is the w. of God wh. strengthens the soul Ar.E. | zealous to go] *so* Ar.E.S.; *in* L., *l.* autem et ⟨eat⟩. | abounds] *lit.* blossoms (ἐξανθεῖν).

xxxii. *On the question of the authenticity of this chapter cf. Notes.* K. (xxviii) *is evidently based on* xxxii, *though it adds nothing to our knowledge of the text.* T. ii. 25 *reproduces it thus:* But always let the faithful be careful that before he eat he partake of the εὐχαριστία that he may be incapable of receiving injury, *but it places this after cap.* xxxvi. *It is possible that* ii. 10—He who poureth forth of the cup gathereth judgement unto himself. So also be he who sees and is silent and does not reprove him, whoever he may be—*depends on* xxxii. 3 *and* 4, *but it may equally well be* T.'s *own invention.*

Title. So Ar.E.S. *Title effaced in* L. *Hauler conj.* ⟨Eucharistia percipiatur antequam aliud gustetur⟩. at the time *etc. is an interpolation made when private communion from the reserved Sacrament was no longer practised or understood. There would be no room for this in* L.

1. every one] *so* L.Ar.E.S.; always T. | be careful] *so* L.T.S.; make it right conduct Ar.; accept the admonition E. | For if—faith] For if there are believers there S.

THE APOSTOLIC TRADITION

⌜Concerning that it is right to guard the Eucharist carefully⌝

Care for the Reserved Sacrament

2 And (δέ) let all take care that no unbaptised person (ἄπιστος) taste of the eucharist nor (ἤ) a mouse or (ἤ) other animal, and (ἤ) that none of it at all (ὅλως) fall and be lost. For it is the Body (σῶμα) of Christ to be eaten by them that believe and not to be thought lightly of (καταφρονεῖν).

Omnis autem festinet ut non infidelis gustet de eucharistia aut ne sorix aut animal aliud aut ne quid cadeat et pereat de eo. Corpus enim est Chri edendum credentibus et non contemnendum.

⌜Concerning that it is not right to spill any from the cup (ποτήριον)⌝

3 For (γάρ) having blessed the cup (ποτ.) in the Name of God thou didst receive it as (ὡς) the antitype of the Blood of Christ.
4 Wherefore spill not from it, that no alien (ἀλλότριον) spirit (πνεῦμα) lick it up, because (ὡς) thou didst despise (καταφρονεῖν) it, ⌜and become⌝ guilty (αἴτιος) of the Blood ⌜of Christ⌝ as one who despises (καταφρ.) the price with which he has been bought.

L. 3 ⟨Calicem⟩ in nomine enim Di benedicens accepisti quasi antitypum sanguinis Chri. 4 Quapropter nolito effundere ut non sps alienus uelut te contemnente illut delingat: reus eris sanguinis ⟨Chri⟩ tamquam qui spernit prae-[pu]tium, quod conparatus est (*et def.*).*

Title. So Ar.E.S. *Title effaced in* L. *Hauler conj.* ⟨Scrupulose eucharistiam esse custodiendam⟩.
2. take care]+diligently S.; take great care E. | nor a mouse—animal] *om.* E.
Title. So Ar.E.S. *Title effaced in* L. *Hauler conj.* ⟨Nihil effundendum de calice⟩. *From* γάρ *in v. 3 it must be supposed that something equivalent originally stood in the text of the verse.*
3. the cup] *om.* L.; *probably rubricated like the immediately preceding title and effaced with it.* | of God] of our Lord Jesus Xt. E. (Di *in* L. *is certainly* Dei; *so also* Ar.S.) | as the antitype] *so* L.; verily it is the Blood Ar.: because it is the Blood E.; as being the Blood S. *By their protests* Ar.E.S. *witness to the correctness of* L.'s *reading.*
4. Wherefore] *so* L.E.; *om.* Ar.; *subst.* Give heed to thyself S. | lick it up]+and God be angry with thee S. | of the Blood] of the precious Bl. E. | of Christ] *om.* L.; +with which He redeemed thee and became to thee the means of mercy towards thee E. | as one who] *so* L.; because thou hast despised that with which thou wast

* *After* xxxii. 4 L., *for reasons explained, p. 84, has introduced a version of* xxxvii. 1–xxxviii. 2 *which is reproduced on p.* 68 *as the* Lᵃ. *text. Fragment* 78 *of the MS. breaks off at that point. Fragment* 79 *takes up the text at* xxxvi. 5 (*p.* 64) *and gives a second text of* xxxvii. 1–xxxviii. 2 *reproduced on p.* 68 *as the* Lᵇ. *text.*

xxxiii. ⟨Daily Chapter of the Clergy⟩

Ar.E.S.

1 And (δέ) let the deacons and presbyters assemble daily at the place which the bishop shall appoint for them. And let not the deacons especially (μέν) neglect (ἀμελεῖν) to assemble every day unless (εἰ μήτε) sickness prevents (κωλύειν) them.

2 And when all have assembled they shall instruct those who are in the assembly (ἐκκλησία). And having also prayed, let each one go about his own business.

xxxiv. ⌜Of the Cemetery⌝

Ar.E.S.(T.K.)

1 Let there be no heavy charge (βαρεῖν) for burying people in the cemetery (κοιμητήριον) for (γάρ) it is for all the poor; except (πλήν) they shall pay the hire of a workman (ἐργάτης) to him who digs and the price of the tiles (κέραμος pl.).

2 And (δέ) the bishop shall provide for the watchman there

---

redeemed Ar.; mercy towards thee and thou shalt be as having denied Xt. If a little of His Body have fallen or if ⟨any⟩ has dropped from the cup, thou shalt find judgement in that in which He redeemed thee E.; in despising the price with wh. thou hast been bought S. | price] L. praeputium, *error for* praetium.

Title. No fresh section and no title in S. The opening words of 1 are prefixed as a title to Ar.E. T. reproduces nothing from this chapter, but K. (21) is clearly based upon it, though so much is altered that it is of no help for the reconstitution of the text of Ap. Trad.

1. at the place etc.] *so* S.; to the place in which is the bp commanding them to go to it Ar.; daily with the bp in the place where he is that he may command them according to order E. | especially] *so* S.; *om.* Ar.E. *but subst. and* presbyters. | every day] *so* S.; at all times S. | sickness] + of body E.

2. the assembly] *so* S.; *pl.* Ar.E. | also] *lit.* likewise Ar.E.S. | let each one go about his own business] *so* Ar.; they shall turn each to his own work E.; let each go to the work determined for him S.

Title. Of the Cemeteries Ar.S.; Of the grave E.

T. reproduces 2, but omits 1. K. 24 is based upon this chapter, but it has turned the burial regulations into a prohibition of incubation and the κέραμοι into "earthenware pots" to be paid for if they have been broken by the sick.

1. Let there be no heavy charge] *so* S.; No one of the people shall give an unlawful command in the grave of the people in the burial grounds Ar.; No man shall compel by his command to bury a man in a grave E. | it is for all the poor] *lit.* this is made for all the poor Ar.; this work is for all the poor E.; it is the property of all the poor S. | and the price of the tiles] *om.* Ar.E. (*not understanding the allusion?*)

2. Ar.E. *have confused this sentence and omit* so that there be no charge etc. | the watchman] those who are at that place who take care of it S.; *sing.* Ar.E.T. | from

who takes care of it from what they offer ⌐at⌐ the assemblies, so that there be no charge to those who come to the place (τόπος).

XXXV. ⌐Of the times [*proper*] for prayer⌐

Morning Prayers   Ar.E.S.A.T.K.

1 And (δέ) let every faithful man (πιστός) ⌐and⌐ woman (πιστή) when they rise from sleep at dawn before they undertake any work wash their hands and pray to God, and so let them go to their work.

Catechism

2 But (δέ) if there should be an instruction (καθήγησις) in the word let each one prefer to go thither, considering that it is God whom he hears speaking by the mouth of him who instructs (καθηγεῖσθαι). For (γάρ) having prayed with (*lit.* in) the Church (ἐκκλησία) he will be able to avoid (παρελθεῖν) all the evils (κακία) of that day. The God-fearing man should consider it a great loss if he does not go to the place in which they give instruction (καθηγεῖσθαι), and especially (μάλιστα δέ) if he knows ⟨how⟩ to read.

A. viii. 32. 18. Πᾶς πιστὸς ἢ πιστὴ ἔωθεν ἀναστάντες ἐξ ὕπνου πρὸ τοῦ ἔργου ἐπιτελέσαι νιψάμενοι προσευχέσθωσαν· εἰ δέ τις λόγου κατήχησις γένηται, προτιμησάτωσαν τοῦ ἔργου τὸν λόγον τῆς εὐσεβείας.

---

what they offer at the assemblies] *so* Ar.E.; *om.* S.; from the Church T. | T. *reproduces* 2 *thus:* If the Church have a graveyard and there be one who abideth there keeping it, let the bp provide for him from the Church, so that he be no burden to those who come thither.

Title. Of the time proper for prayer S.; Of the times of prayer K. (*wh. is very possibly the original, cf.* xxxi); Of the times proper for prayer and for hearing instruction and signing the head with the cross Ar.E. *There is no division between* 35, 36, 37, 38 *in* Ar.E.S., *and* Ar.E. *therefore adapt this title to cover the remainder of the book. No title* T.

1. man and woman] *so* Ar.E.S.; m. or w. A.; *om.* T.K. *Cf.* xxxi. 1. | from sleep] *so* A.K.S.; *om.* Ar.E.T. | any] *om.* A. | and so—work *om.* A.K. | and so] *so* S.T.; then Ar.E. | let them go] *so* Ar.E.S.; let each go T. | to their work] *so* Ar.E.S.; to the work wh. he wills T.

2. *om.* T. | if—instr. in the word] if—of the word A.S.; if they instruct with the words Ar.; if they sh. tell them where is the place of instr. E.; if there shd. be in a Church an instr. concerning the w. K. | word]+of God S.K. | prefer] *so* A. (*cf.* xxxi. 2); choose (+for himself S.) Ar.E.S.; hasten K. | thither] *so* Ar.S.K.; *om.* E. (Ar.E. *add* to the place of instruction, *and* K. *adds* to share in the instr.) | considering] *lit.* and he shall know in his heart Ar.; and this sh. be fixed in their hearts E.; reckoning this in his heart S. (*Coptic idiom*); and they shall know K. | by the mouth of] Ar.E.; *subst.* in S. | For—day] *so* S.; And it is he who dwells

3   If there is a teacher there, let none of you be late in arriving at the assembly (ἐκκλησία) ⌐at the place⌐ where they give instruction (καθηγεῖσθαι). Then (τότε) ⌐indeed⌐ it shall be given to him who speaks to utter things which are profitable to all, and thou shalt hear things which thou thinkest not ⟨to hear⟩ and thou shalt be profited (ὠφελεῖσθαι) by the things which the Holy Spirit (πνεῦμα) will give to thee by him who instructs (καθηγεῖσθαι) and so thy faith (πίστις) will be established by what thou hearest. And (δέ) further he shall tell thee there what thou oughtest to do in thine own house. And therefore let each one be careful (σπουδάζειν) to go to the assembly (ἐκκλησία) to the place where the Holy Spirit abounds.

xxxvi. ⟨Hours of Prayer⟩

Spiritual Reading   Ar.E.S.(T.K.A.)

1   And if there is a day on which there is no instruction (καθή-γησις) let each one at home take a holy book and read in it sufficiently what seems (δοκεῖν) profitable.

Terce

2   And if indeed (μέν) thou art at home pray at the third hour

A. viii. 34. 1 *and* 3. 2 Εὐχὰς ἐπιτελεῖτε...τρίτῃ ὥρᾳ...ὅτι ἀπόφασιν ἐν αὐτῇ ὑπὸ Πιλάτου ἔλαβεν ὁ κύριος.

T. ii. 24. 2 Let all take care to pray at the third hour with mourning and heaviness either in the Church or in the house because they cannot go. For this is the hour of the fixing (=στηρίζω?, *and so also* Ar.E.S.) on the Cross of the Only-begotten.

---

in the Ch. and he sh. cause to pass away all wickedness in the day Ar.: And he abides in the Ch. and he is able to remove the evil of every day E.

3. If there is a teacher there] *so* E.; If the teacher is present Ar.; Or if the teacher should come S. | let none—arriving] *lit.* he should not put off ⟨coming⟩ Ar.; let him not delay ⟨coming⟩ E.; let none of you be deficient in coming S. (*Perhaps the sense is:* Let none of you stay away.) | at the place] *so* Ar.E.; *om.* S. | indeed] *om.* S. | it shall be given—to all] *so* E.S. (E. +this is profitable for every one what he shall hear); to him who speaks shall be given the word wh. he speaks Ar. | thou shalt] *so* E.S.; he shall Ar. | hear] + there E. | by the things] from the th. S. | and so] and *om.* S. | by what] *so* E.; upon w. Ar.S. | he shall tell thee] *so* Ar.; they sh. tell thee E.; it sh. be told thee S. | And therefore] And *om.* S. | to go to the assembly] to go and to the E. | abounds] *lit.* breaks forth S.; rises Ar.E. (ἐξανθεῖν, *cf.* xxxi. 2).

No title in the versions. T.K.A. *all preserve traces of this chapter.*

1. *om.* T.A. | And] *om.* S. | is 1°] was Ar. | a holy book] *so* Ar.S.K.; the holy Scripture E. (*followed by Easton*). | in it] *so* S.K.; *om.* Ar.E. | sufficiently] as well as he can E. | what—profitable] *so* S.; *om.* K.; what he knows to be good Ar.; for it is good E.

and praise God; but (δέ) if thou art elsewhere and that time (καιρός) comes, pray in thy heart to God.

3 For (γάρ) in this hour Christ was seen nailed upon the tree (*lit.* wood). And therefore in the Old (παλαιά) ⟨Testament⟩ the Law (νόμος) bade the shewbread (bread of πρόθεσις) [*always*] to be offered at the third hour [*as a type* (τύπος) *of the Body* (σῶμα) *and Blood of Christ*]; and the dumb (ἄλογος) lamb was slain which was a type (τύπος) of the perfect (τέλειος) Lamb. For (γάρ) Christ is the Shepherd, and He is [*also*] the Bread which came down from heaven.

Sext

4 Pray also likewise (ὁμοίως) at the sixth hour, for (γάρ) at that hour when Christ had been ⌐hanged⌐ upon the wood ⌐*of the Cross* (σταυρός)⌐ the daylight was divided and it became darkness. And so (ὥστε) let them pray [*at that hour*] a prevailing prayer, likening themselves to the cry of Him who prayed and caused all creation (κτίσις) to be made dark for the unbelieving Jews.

K. (25. ii). They shall pray at the third hour for at this time the Saviour Jesus of His own will was crucified to save and redeem us.

T. ii. 24. 4 But at the sixth hour likewise let there be prayer with sorrow. For then the daylight was divided by the darkness. Let there be then that voice which is like to the prophets and to creation mourning. 5 At the ninth

K. 25. 4 Also at the sixth hour they shall pray, for at this hour the whole creation shuddered because of the evil deed of the Jews. 5 At the ninth hour

A. viii. 34. 4 *and* 5. ἕκτη δέ, ὅτι ἐν αὐτῇ ἐσταυρώθη· ἐνάτη δέ, ὅτι πάντα κεκί-

---

2. if indeed] when E. | indeed] *om.* Ar. | praise] *so* Ar.E.; bless S. | and—comes] *so* Ar.E.; and thou comest by chance to that hour S.

3. Christ was seen] *so* S.; was stripped Ar.; they stripped Jesus Xt. E. | And therefore] And *om.* S. | the tree] + of the Cross Ar.E. (*cf.* T. *inf.*). | always] *lit.* at every hour S.; *om.* Ar.E. | at the third hour] *so* Ar.E.; *om.* S. | as a type—Christ] *so* Ar.S. (holy Xt. Ar.); *om.* E. | dumb] *om.* Ar.E. | was slain] *so* Ar.S.; they sacrificed E. | also] *om.* Ar.E.

4. also likewise] *om.* Ar. | at that hour] *so* E.K.; then Ar.T.; *om.* S. | Christ] *so* Ar.S.; our Lord E. | hanged] *so* Ar.E.; nailed S. | of the Cross] *so* E.S.; *om.* Ar. | it became darkness] *so* Ar. (σκότος ἐγένετο?); the darkness came E.; a great darkness happened S. | cry] *so* Ar.S.; word E. | who prayed] *so* S.; which He prayed Ar.; wh. our Lord J. Xt. prayed E. | and—dark] *so* E.S.; and all the land was darkened Ar. | for the unbelieving Jews] *so* S. (*cf.* K.); for the unbelievers Ar.; *om.* E., *but subst.* and the catechumens shall make a great prayer. ("*The Catechumens*" *may be due to some confusion over* τοὺς ἀπίστους!)

None

5　And at the ninth hour also let prayer be protracted and praise ⌜be sung⌝ ⌜that is⌝ like to the souls (ψυχή) of the righteous (δίκαιος) glorifying God who lieth not, who remembered His saints and sent to them His Word (Λόγος) to enlighten them.

6　*For (γάρ) in that hour Christ ⟨was⟩ pierced in His side [*with a lance* (λόγχη)] ⟨and⟩ shed forth blood and water and brought the rest of the time of ⟨that⟩ day in light to evening. Whereby He made the dawn of another day at the beginning (ἄρχεσθαι) of His sleep, fulfilling the type (τύπος) of His resurrection (ἀνάστασις).

L. lxxix. 1 (*p.* 119). 5 ...D̄m̄, qui non mentitur, qui memor fuit sanctorum suorum et emisit uerbum suum inluminantem eos.

T. hour also let prayer be protracted as with a hymn of praise that is like to the souls of those who give praise to God who lieth not, as one who hath remembered His saints and hath sent His Word and Wisdom to enlighten them.

K. they shall likewise pray, because in this hour Jesus prayed and gave up His Spirit into the hands of His Father.

νητο τοῦ δεσπότου σταυρουμένου, φρίττοντα τὴν τόλμαν τῶν δυσσεβῶν Ἰουδαίων, μὴ φέροντα τοῦ κυρίου τὴν ὕβριν.

L. lxxix. 3 (*p.* 119). 6 Illa ergo hora in latere Chr̄s̄ punctus aquam et sanguem effudit et reliquum temporis diei inluminans ad uesperam deduxit. Unde incipiens dormire pricipium alterius diei faciens imaginem resurrectionis con-

T. ii. 24. 6 For in that hour life was opened to the faithful and blood and water were shed from the side of our Lord. But at evening when it is the

K. 25. Also at the hour of sunset they shall pray because it is the end of the

A. viii. 34. 6. ἑσπέρᾳ δὲ εὐχαριστοῦντες, ὅτι ὑμῖν ἀνάπαυσιν ἔδωκεν τῶν μεθημερινῶν κόπων τὴν νύκτα.

---

5. also] *om.* E. | let prayer be protracted] *so* T.E.; let them pray a great prayer Ar.S. | and praise be sung] *lit.* protracted as with a hymn of praise T.; and a prayer with glorifying E.; prayer and praises Ar.; prayer and a great blessing S. | that—souls] *so* T. (Ar. *is corrupt*); that ye may join in glorifying with the souls E.; that thou mayest know that the souls S. | of the righteous] *om.* T. | God] *so* T.Ar.; the living God E.; the Lord God S. (L. *begins again here*). | who] as one who T. (? ὡς for ὅς). | remembered] remembers E. | and] *om.* Ar.S. | to them] + His Son who is His Word Ar.E.S.; *om.* L.T.

6. For] *so* T.S.; Therefore L.; Because Ar.E. | Christ—water] *so* L.Ar.; the side of Xt. was pierced E.S. | with a lance] S. *only.* | brought—evening] *so* L.; *om.* T. Ar.E.S. *have greatly confused this phrase.* | Whereby—resurrection] *so* L. *This sentence is unintelligible in* Ar.E.S.

* *The copy of the "Epitome of Ap. Const. viii" in MS. Vienna, Hist. Gr. 7, which contains the fragments of the original Greek of* xxv. 1 *sq. given above, reads here* ἔκτῃ δὲ ὅτι ἐν αὐτῇ ἐσταυρώθη ὁ Χριστός, καὶ νυγεὶς τὴν πλευρὰν αἷμα καὶ ὕδωρ ἐξέχεεν, *which Connolly argues convincingly (J.T.S. xix. p. 138) conflates the original Greek of* xxxvi. 6 *with Ap. Const.'s version* xxxvi. 4. *Note the omission of* λόγχῃ *as in L. etc.*

Night Prayers

7 Pray also before thy body rests (ἀναπαύεσθαι) upon thy bed.

Mattins

8 And at midnight rise and wash thy hands with water and pray. And (δέ) ⌐if thou hast a wife⌐, pray ye both together.

9 But (δέ) if she be not yet baptised (πιστή) go apart (ἀναχωρεῖν) into another room and pray and return again to thy bed. ⌐And be not slothful to pray.⌐

Wedlock

10 He who has used marriage (γάμος) is not defiled; for (γάρ) those who are washed have no need (χρεία) to wash again, for they are pure (καθαρός).

10. Cf. Jn. xiii. 10.

pleuit. 7 Ora etiam antequam corpus cubili requiescat.

T. beginning of another day, shewing an image of the resurrection he hath caused us to give praise.

K. day. Also at the lamp-lighting (λυχνικόν *transliterated*) in the evening they shall pray, for David says: In the night I pray.

L. lxxix. 9 (*p.* 119). 8 Circa mediam uero noctem exurgens laua manus aqua et ora. Si autem et coniunx tua praesens est, utrique simul orate; 9 sin uero necdum est fidelis in alio cubiculo secedens ora, et iterum ad cubilem tuum reuertere. Noli autem piger esse ad orandū. 10 Qui in nuptias ligatus est non est inquinatus; qui enim loti sunt, non habent necessitatem lauandi iterum, quia mundi sunt.

T. ii. 24. 8 But at midnight let them arise in a praising manner and in a lauding manner because of the resurrection.... 9 But if any have a consort or wife ⟨not⟩* faithful, let the husband who is faithful go and pray at these times without fail. 10 Let those who are chaste not lessen them.

K. 27. 8–10 A Christian shall always when he prays wash his hands, and also those who have been bound in wedlock. Even when he arises from beside his wife he shall pray, for wedlock is not impure.

---

7. *om.* T. | before thy body rests] *so* L.; before thou restest thy body Ar.E.S. | upon thy bed] + in thy bed-room S.

8, 9, 10. *om.* A.

8. thy hands] *so* L.K.; *sing.* Ar.E.; thyself S. | with water] with pure w. S. | And if thou hast a wife] *so* Ar.E.S., *cf.* T.; If thy wife be present L. (πάρεστι for ἐστι).

9. go—another room] *so* L.; go apart to a place Ar.E.S. | pray] + alone Ar.E.S.

10. has used marriage] *lit.* was bound in marriage (συνάπτεσθαι?) L. | Ar.E.S. *fuse* 9 *and* 10 *thus:* And thou who art bound in marriage be not slothful to pray; for ye are not unclean.

* not *is missing from the Syriac text of* T. *but is found in the Arabic and is clearly required by the sense.*

Purification

L.	Ar.E.S.
11 By ⟨*as it were*⟩ catching thy breath in thine hand and signing thyself with the moisture of thy breath, thy body is purified even unto thy feet. For the gift of the Spirit and the sprinkling of the font, drawn from the heart ⌈*of the believer*⌉ as from a fountain, purifies him who has believed.	But (δέ) when thou breathest into thine hand and signest (σφραγίζειν) thyself with the spittle which thou wilt bring forth from thy mouth thou art purified all over unto thy feet. For (γάρ) this is the gift (δῶρον) of the Holy Spirit and the drop of water are of baptism (βάπτισμα) coming up from a fountain (πηγή), which is the heart of the believer (πιστός) purifying him who has believed (πιστεύειν).

12 [*And* (δέ)] It is necessary (ἀναγκαῖον) for the following reason to pray at this hour and truly (καὶ γάρ) those men of holy memory (*lit.* elders, πρεσβύτερος) who handed on the

11. Cf. Jn. xiii. 10.

L. lxxix. 19 (*p.* 119). 11 Per consignationem cum udo flatu et per manum spm amplectens corpus tuū usque ad pedes sanctificatum est. Donum enim sps et infusio lauacri, sicuti ex fonte corde credente cum offertur sanctificat eum qui credidit.

K. 27. 11 There is no need after regeneration to bathe in water, but only to wash one's hands, because the Holy Ghost fills the body of the believer and purifies him altogether.

L. lxxix. 24 (*p.* 120). 12 Hac igitur hora necessarium est orare; nam et hi qui tradiderunt nobis seniores ita nos docuerunt, quia hac ⟨h⟩ora omnis

---

11. *om.* T.A. | *This verse has caused difficulty to the editors. Ar.E.S. seem here to have departed further from the sense of the original than usual. I have reversed the order of the first two phrases in L. in the translation to make the sense more clear, but there is no reason to doubt its authenticity. Schwartz, followed by Easton, would resolve* L.'s spm *into* sputum, *instead of* spiritum, *to agree with Ar.E.S., but* πνεῦμα *is clearly required here for the analogy with* τὸ δῶρον τοῦ πνεύματος *in the following sentence. The version in Ar.E.S. is obviously badly translated, e.g. in substituting* βάπτισμα *for* λουτροῦ (=L.'s lauacri). | *the heart of the believer]* so Ar.E.S.; *the believing heart* L. (*error for* credentis?).

12. *And]* so Ar.S.; *om.* L.E.K. | *for the following reason]* so L.E.K.; *om.* Ar.S. | those men of holy memory] *our Fathers* K.; *those "presbyters" themselves* S. | who handed on the Tradition to us] *so* L.E.; *were before to us in this* Ar.; *delivered this work unto us* S. |

Tradition to us taught us thus: because in this hour every creature hushes for a brief moment to praise the Lord; stars and plants and waters stand still ⌜in that instant⌝; all the hosts (στρατιά) of the angels minister⌜ing⌝ (λειτουργεῖν) unto Him together with the souls (ψυχή) of the righteous (δίκαιος) praise (ὑμνεύειν) God.

13 Wherefore it is right for all them that believe (πιστεύειν) to be careful to pray at that hour. And (δέ) testifying to this the Lord says thus, Behold a cry was made at midnight of them that said, Behold the Bridegroom has come; arise, [go forth] to meet Him; and He adds, saying, Watch therefore, for ye know not in what hour He comes.

14 And at the hour when the cock (ἀλέκτωρ) crows, likewise (ὁμοίως) rise ⌜and pray⌝, because at the hour of cockcrow the children of Israel denied (ἀρνεῖσθαι) Christ Whom we have known by faith, ⌜daily⌝ awaiting in hope (ἐλπίς) ⌜the appearing⌝ of the eternal light at the resurrection of the dead.

13. Cf. Mt. xxv. 6, 13.

creatura quiescit ad momentum quoddam, ut laude[n]t dōm; stellas et arbusta et aquas stare in ictu et omne agmen angelorum ministrat ei in hac ⟨h⟩ora una cum iustorum animabus laudare Dm̄. 13 Quapropter debent hii qui credunt festinare hac ⟨h⟩ora orare. Testimonium etiam habens huic rei dn̄s ita ait: Ecce clamor factus est circa mediam noctem dicentium: Ecce sponsus uenit, surgite ad occursum eius: et infert dicens: Propterea uigilate; nescitis enim qua hora uenit. T. ii. 25 and K. 27 both preserve these verses in a modified form. A. omits them altogether.

L. lxxx. 4 (p. 120). 14 Et circa galli cantum exurgens similiter ⟨ora⟩; illa enim hora gallo cantante fili Istrahel Chrm̄ negauerunt quem nos per fidem cognouimus, sub spe luminis aeterni in resurrectione mortuorum spectantes

in this hour—instant] om. Ar. | for a brief moment] so L. (in ictu = ? ἐν ἀκμῇ); in that instant E.; om. S. | ministering] so Ar.E.; minister L.S. | God] + the Almighty (παντοκράτωρ) in that hour S.

13. to be careful] so L. (σπουδάζειν?); om. Ar.E.S. | the Lord] + also S. | Behold lᵘ] so all (not in any text of Mt.). | of them that said] so L.; saying E.; om. Ar.S. (not in any text of Mt.). | has come] so Ar.E.S.; uenit L. | arise] so L.E.; om. Ar.S. (not in any text of Mt.). | go forth] so Ar.E.S.; om. L. | He adds] so L. (infert = ἐπιφέρει?); He repeated Ar.E.S. (+ the word Ar.). | in what hour] so L.E.; the day in what hour Ar.; the day nor the hour when S. | He comes] so L.; om. Ar.; your Lord will come E.; the Son of Man cometh S. | S. has been corrected by the T.R. E. agrees with no known version. L.Ar. have approximately the Neutral Text.

14. and pray] om. L. | Christ] our Ld. Jesus Xt. E. | have known] so L.S.; know Ar.E. | Whom—faith] so L.Ar.E.; we who believe in Him S. | daily awaiting—of the dead] There is an early corruption in the text here. L. as it stands is meaningless, Ar.E.S. are defective and confused, T. om. the clause, A. has a much edited version, and

15 These things, therefore, all ye faithful, if ye perform ⟨them⟩ and remember them and instruct one another and encourage the catechumens [to do them] ye will not [be able to] be tempted (πειράζειν) or (οὐδέ) to perish, having Christ always before your minds.

diem in hac itaque omnes fideles agentes et memoriam facientes et inuicem docentes et catecuminos prouocantes neq̄ temptari neq̄ perire poteritis cum semper Chr̄m in memoriam habetis.

T. ii. 25. When ye the faithful accomplish these things, teach and instruct each other, causing the catechumens to make progress, as loving every man; ye do not perish but will be in me and I will be among you.

14. A. viii. 34. 7. (εὐχαριστοῦντες) ἀλεκτρυόνων δὲ κραυγῇ διὰ τὸ τὴν ὥραν εὐαγγελίζεσθαι τὴν παρουσίαν τῆς ἡμέρας εἰς ἐργασίαν τῶν τοῦ φωτὸς ἔργων.

xxxvii. ⟨Of the Sign of the Cross⟩

1 ⌐And⌐ ⌐when tempted⌐ (πειράζειν) always reverently seal (σφραγίζειν) thy forehead ⟨with the sign of the Cross⟩. For (γάρ) this sign of the Passion is displayed and made manifest against

Lᵃ. (Hauler, p. 118). Semper tempta modeste consignare tibi frontem. Hoc enim signum passionis

Lᵇ. (Hauler, p. 121). Semper autem imitare cum honestate consignare tibi frontem. Hoc enim sig-

K. is so much altered as to be useless. For reasons explained in the Notes I believe the original may have run προσδοκῶντες τὸ καθ' ἡμέραν τὴν παρουσίαν τοῦ φωτὸς αἰωνίου .... I should therefore emend the MS. of L. to ... cognouimus, sub spe luminis aeterni ⟨praesentiam⟩ in resurrectione mortuorum ⟨in⟩ diem. [in] Haec itaque etc., praesentiam being supplied from παρουσίαν in A.; cf. Notes.

15. These things] in hac L. Hauler would emend to in ha⟨n⟩c, but this makes no sense. I should om. in as an error from the end of the previous sentence and insert a stop. Ar.E.S. all clearly read ταῦτα as the first word of a new sentence. This, O ye faithful, when ye have done Ar.; All of you faithful doing all this E.; But all of you faithful, if ye do these things S., cf. T. sup. L. should therefore read Haec itaque. ... | therefore] om. S. | all] om. Ar. | and encourage—catechumens] so L., cf. T.; om. Ar.; teach ye this wisdom to the catechumens having first built up ⟨? their faith⟩ E.; and teaching the catechs. to do them S., cf. T. | be able to] so L.; om. Ar.E.S.T. | be tempted] so L.Ar.E.S.; om. T. | or to perish] so L.E., cf. T.; nor shall you ever fall Ar.S.

Title. No title or chapter division in any version.
There is much confusion in the text of this chapter and I do not feel much confidence in any restoration as to the details. T.A. omit it altogether. K. xxix briefly summarises it, but in such a way as to be useless for the text. Owing to the phenomena discussed p. 84 L. is here duplicated. Its first version (Hauler, p. 118) is cited as Lᵃ., its second (ibid. p. 121) as Lᵇ. Ar.E.S. have a third form of text, but in a very confused state.

1. And] so Lᵇ.E.S.; om. Ar.Lᵃ. | when tempted] Lᵃ., tempta, and S. (make proof, πεῖρα translit.) suggest πειράζειν. The rest of the chapter requires that it be in the passive. Imitare, Lᵇ., must be a corruption, possibly representing σημειοῦ (= make the sign ⟨of the Cross⟩), as a restoration of the sense, though this would require the insertion of ⟨et⟩ consignare. More probably it is a simple misreading,

the devil (διάβολος) if thou makest it in faith (πιστίς), not in order that thou mayest be seen of men, but by thy knowledge putting it forward as a shield.

Lᵃ.	Ar.E.S.	Lᵇ.
2 If indeed the adversary seeing the power of the Spirit outwardly displayed in the image of baptism he takes to flight trembling, not at thy striking him but at thy breathing ⟨on him⟩.	For when the ad-versary (ἀντικείμε-νος) sees (θεωρεῖν) [only] the strength of the heart, that the inner man is rational (λογικός), being sealed (σφρα-γίζειν) inwardly and outwardly with the seal (σφραγίς) of the Word (Λόγος), he ⌜trembles and⌝ flees away ⌜in haste⌝ pur-sued by the Holy Spirit who indwells him who makes place for Him within himself.	For the adversary, when he sees the power which comes from the heart as a man displays the outwardly formed image of the Word, takes to flight not at thy spitting ⟨upon him⟩ but at the breath of your mouth.

adversum diabolum ostenditur si ex fide faciat quis, ut non hominibus placens, sed per scientiam sicut loricam offerens.

num passionis aduersum diabolum manifestum et conprobatum est si ex fide itaq̄ facis, non ut hominibus appareas sed per scientiam tamquam scutum offerens.

Lᵃ. lxxviii. 20 (p. 118). 2 siquidem aduersarius uidens uirtutem sp̄s ex corde in similitudine lauacri in mani-festum deformatam tremens effu-gatur, te non illum cedente sed in-spirante.

Lᵇ. lxxx. 20 (p. 121). 2 nam aduersarius cum uidit uirtutem quae ex corde est ut homo similitudinem uerbi in manifesto deformatam osten-dat, infugiatur non sputante sed ⌐ flante [h]ore.*

perhaps παραθείς for πειραθείς. | reverently] om. Ar. | For] om. Ar. | of the Passion] om. Ar.S. | and made manifest] om. Lᵃ. | makest it]+thus Lᵇ.; only if any one makes Lᵃ. | be seen of] so Lᵇ.Ar.E.S. (=ὁρᾶσθαι); please Lᵃ. (?=ἀρέσεσθαι). | shield] so Lᵇ.; breastplate Lᵃ.E. (+of righteousness E.); armour Ar.; ΘΗΡωΝ S. (a vox nihili ? =Gk. θυρεός=large oblong shield, or ? Sah. tharmi=a leather cuirass).

2. Lᵇ. is nearer to Ar.E.S. than is Lᵃ., but there appear to be three separate versions of this verse, none of which is altogether satisfactory.

Variants of Lᵃ. and Lᵇ.: image of baptism and image of the Word represent Greek variants λουτροῦ and Λόγου. Striking him (=cedente=caedente) and spitting at him similarly represent τύπτοντος and πτύοντος.

Variants of Ar.E.S.: adversary]+the devil (διάβολος) S. | only] om. E. | Word]+of God E. | trembles and] om. S. | in has·⌐l om. S. | himself] om. Ar.

[* The Latin here as read by Tidner. H.C.]

Lᵃ.	Ar.E.S.	Lᵇ.
3 This was that which Moses ⟨did⟩ in type by the sheep which was sacrificed by (sic) the Pascha, he sprinkled the blood upon the lintel (lit. threshold) and anointing the two doorposts he signifies that faith in the perfect Sheep which now is in us.	This is that which Moses signified beforehand ⌐by the Pascha and the Lamb which was slain. He commanded to smear the blood on the lintel and the two doorposts, telling us of the faith which was given us in the perfect (τέλειος) Lamb. (=ἀμνός.)	Moses, displaying this by the sheep of the Pascha which was slain, sprinkled the blood on the lintel (lit. threshold) and anointed the doorposts; he signified that faith which now is in us which ⟨trusts⟩ in the perfect Sheep. (=πρόβατον.)

4 ⌐Wherefore⌐ sealing (σφραγίζειν) the forehead ⌐and the eyes⌐ with the hand we ⌐shall⌐ escape him who seeks to destroy us.

Lᵃ. lxxviii. 24 (p. 118). 3 Hoc ipsut erat de quod in typo Moyses in oue quae per Pascha immolabatur sanguem asparsit in limine et duos postes unguens significat eam quae nunc in nobis est fidē in perfecta oue. 4 Frontem et oculos per manum consignantes declinemus ab eo qui exterminare temptat.

Lᵇ. lxxx. 24 (p. 121). 3 Quod deformans Moyses in ouem Paschae quae occidebatur, sanguem asparsit in limine et postes unxit, designabat ea⟨m⟩ q̄ nunc in nobis est fides, quae in perfecta oue est. 4 Frontem uero et oculos per manū consignantes declinemus eum qui exterminare temptat.

---

3. *Easton accidentally omits verses 3 and 4. The variants he sprinkled* Lᵃᵇ. *and* He commanded Ar.E.S. *probably both represent* ἔθηκεν (*cf.* Exod. xii. 7). Lᵃ. *seems the best text. Cf. Notes.*
Variants of Ar.E.S.: This is] + also S. | Moses] + the Prophet S. | beforehand] *om.* E. | by the Pascha and the Lamb] *so* S.; of the L. of the P. Ar.E. | to smear] *so* Ar.E.; that they should sm. S. | the blood] with its bl. Ar. | lintel] + of the door E. | two] *om.* E. | telling us] *so* Ar.S.; and the smearing declared therefore the faith *etc.* E. | which was given us] *so* Ar.S.: wh. He gave us E. | in the] *so* E.; by the Ar.S.
4. *The texts approximate better here, but* Ar.E.S. *still agree against* Lᵃᵇ. *in omitting* and the eyes. | Wherefore] *so* E.; *om.* Lᵃ.; For Ar., *cf.* Lᵇ. (? = δέ); When S. | forehead] *so* Lᵃᵇ.Ar.; *pl.* E.S. | and the eyes] *om.* Ar.E.S. | the hand] our h. S. | we shall escape] *so* Ar.E.S.; let us escape Lᵃᵇ. (declinemus *may, however, be intended for a Fut. Ind.*). | him] those E.

xxxviii. ⟨*Epilogue*⟩

L*.L*.Ar.E.S.(T.)

1 And so if these things are accepted with thankfulness and right faith (πιστίς) they bestow (χαρίζεσθαι) edification on the Church and eternal life on believers.

2 I counsel (συμβουλεύειν) that these things be observed by all who rightly understand. For upon all who hearken to the Apostolic Tradition (παράδοσις) and keep it no heretic (αἱρετικός) will prevail to deceive (πλανᾶν) [nor (οὐδέ) any man at all].

3a ⌜*These are the perverse who went astray and corrupted the teaching of the Apostles. And if men come to them they teach them in this way;*⌝

3b ⌜and⌝ thus [the] many heresies (αἵρεσις) increased (αὐξάνειν) because those who were at the head (προϊστάναι) would not learn the purpose (προαίρεσις) of the Apostles (ἀποστ.) but (ἀλλά)

L*. lxxviii. 30 (*p.* 118). 1 Haec itaque cum gratia et fide recta glorios[a]e cum audiantur, aedificationem praestant ecclesiae et uitam aeternam credentibus. 2 Quae custodiri moneo ab eis qui bene sapiunt. Uniuersis enim audientibus apos-⟨tolicam⟩...(*et defisit*).

L*. lxxx. 30 (*p.* 121). 1 Haec itaq si cum gratia et fide recta praesta⟨n⟩t aedificationem in ecclesia et uitam aeternam credentibus. 2 Custodiri haec consilium do ab omnibus bene sapientibus. Uniuersis enim audientibus apostolicam tra⟨ditionem⟩ ...(*et deficit*).

---

1. And] *om.* Ar. | if] *om.* L*.; when S. | these—accepted] ye accept Ar.E.S. | right] *so* L*.Ar.E.S. (recta gloriose, L*.=ὀρθοδόξη *literally translated.* ὀρθῇ *is the earlier form of text*). | on the Church] *om.* Ar.E.S. | on believers] *om.* Ar.E.S. (*which render the last sentence thus:* ye will be edified and eternal life will be bestowed on you Ar.S.; ye will be ed. and he will best. etern. life E.).

2. T. *reproduces this verse thus:* When ye teach and keep these things ye shall be saved and evil heresy will not prevail against you. | I counsel] *so* L*.*b*.; we counsel Ar.E.S. | these things] *sing.* Ar.E. | all—understand] *lit.* all who have a heart Ar.S. (*Coptic idiom for* "*good sense*"). | For] *so* L*.*b*.S.; *om.* Ar.E. | all who hearken—keep it] *so* S.; If every one who heard kept the teaching of the App. Ar.; He who keeps the teaching of the App. E. | Apostolic] L*. *ends.* | Tradition] L*. *ends.* | keep it] keep them E. | no heretic—at all] *so* S.; nothing of the heresies would be able to lead a man astray from them Ar.; he will not be hindered by any heretic E.

3a. *om.* Ar.S.; *found only in* E., *but the opening of* 3b *in* Ar.E.S.—thus—*indicates that something has fallen out in* Ar.S.

3b. and] *so* E.; *om.* Ar.; for (γάρ) S. | the] *so* S.; *om.* Ar.E. | heresies] heretics E. | those who were at the head] *so* S. (*i.e.* at their head); those who received them Ar. (*mistranslating the Sahidic*); those who listened to them E. | purpose] *so* S.; secret Ar.; command E.

according to (κατά) their own pleasure (ἡδονή) do what they choose and not what is fitting (πρέπειν).

4 ⌜And⌝, beloved, if we have omitted any thing, God will reveal it to those who are worthy, steering (κυβερνᾶν) Holy Church to its mooring in the quiet haven (λιμήν).

---

4. And] *so* Ar.E.; Then S. | beloved] *so* S.; o my brethren most beloved Ar.; brethren E. | omitted] diminished E. | any thing] any doctrine E. | Holy Church] *so* Ar.E., *but* S. *has* the Church which is worthy of mooring. *Schwartz takes this as original but it represents an error of* ἀξίαν *for* ἀγίαν. *Ar.E. are right.*

TEXTUAL NOTES

iv. 10. *Anamnesis*

It has seemed advisable to retain the Greek word here owing to the difficulty of finding an English equivalent which does not misrepresent the real content of the word in Greek. Words like "memorial", "remembrance", etc. have for us a connotation of a purely mental and subjective recollection of something in fact *absent*. ἀνάμνησις has on the contrary the sense of bringing before God something which has happened in the past in such a way that its *consequences take effect in the present*. Thus (i (iii) Kings xvii. 18) the widow of Sarepta complains that Elijah has come "to call my iniquity to (God's) remembrance" (ἀναμνῆσαι ἀδικίας μου) and *therefore* her son has died. So the sacrifice of a wife accused of adultery (Num. v. 15) is "an offering of memorial, bringing iniquity to (God's) remembrance" (θυσία μνημοσύνου ἀναμιμνήσκουσα ἁμαρτίαν). If she has been guilty of the sin, it will now become apparent through the sacrifice. So it is the whole point of Hebrews ix and x that the sacrifices of the Old Dispensation were not an ἀπολύτρωσις for sin which would have removed it, but a yearly ἀνάμνησις of it, which actually "re-called" it. So Philo also declares that the sacrifices of the unrighteous work "not a remission of sins but a reminder of them" (οὐ λύσιν ἁμαρτημάτων, ἀλλ' ὑπόμνησιν ἐργάζονται, *De Vita Moys*. ii. 107).

It is in this active sense of actually *re-calling before God* a fact so that its effects become presently operative that ἀνάμνησις must be understood here. And the fact so "re-called" by the anaphora is not the Last Supper but "His death and resurrection". It may justify this and some other baldly literal renderings adopted in this chapter to point out the character of this prayer and some of its implications.

Whether historically the Last Supper was a *Kiddush* (a solemn but private religious meal) or whether it was the Passover supper proper is a question which has been much discussed of recent years. It does now seem probable that St John is right against the Synoptists, and that the Last Supper was in fact a *Kiddush* and that our Lord died at the moment the Passover lambs were being slain. Such at least was Hippolytus' own belief and that of all the second-century fathers whose opinion on the matter can be discovered. I believe that *Kiddush* formulae have left certain traces on Christian liturgical forms, but that fact is as nothing beside the certainty that the Eucharist was interpreted from the first entirely in terms of the *Passover*. The fact that as early as A.D. 55–56 it represents the "placarding" of a *death* is ample indication of that. *Kiddush* could furnish no such ideas.

We have to remember in this connection the character of the only liturgical commemoration of the primitive Christian year, which goes everywhere by the name of the *Pascha*. It is simply the Jewish Passover feast transcended and Christianised, but the Passover under its Hellenistic Jewish name. We know that this continued to be observed even by so radical a convert as was St Paul, and its observance by all Christian communities in the second century in approximately the same form can be demonstrated. Everywhere it is, like the Jewish Passover, a nocturnal celebration of a single night, preceded by a preparatory fast. In Asia it took place on the actual night of the Jewish Passover (14th–15th Nisan), elsewhere it was transferred to that of the following Saturday-

Sunday. As Dr Brightman once put it,* the *Pascha* "was the commemoration
neither of the Passion nor of the Resurrection, but of both: 'of Christ who died,
yea rather is risen again'; Who 'laid down his life in order that he might take
it again'; 'Who died for our sins and was raised for our justification'". It is
simply the feast of the *Christian redemption*, as the Jewish Passover was the
feast of the Jewish redemption. God by His own initiative had delivered Israel
from bondage and made it His own People in covenant with Himself. God by
His own initiative had delivered the Church from bondage and made that the
new People of God in covenant with Himself (cf. iv. 7 in the anaphora). The
Christian redemption was effected *by the Passion and Resurrection of Christ in
combination*, viewed as a single act. There is no idea anywhere in christendom,
before the fourth century, of a separate commemoration of the Passion on Good
Friday and the Resurrection on Easter Sunday, the one a day of mourning
and the other of joy in our fashion. This idea of a cycle of historical com-
memorations in a Holy *Week* comes from the "ritualistic" fourth-century
Church of Jerusalem, and spread relatively slowly; *e.g.* at Rome it was only
adopted in the later fifth or sixth century. In the *Ap. Trad.* there is no idea of
"Good Friday" as a commemoration of the Passion. It is simply a fast day in
preparation for the *Pascha*, and the fast is not as strict as that of the Saturday.
Baptism, the mystical association of the Neophytes with the effects of the
Lord's death and resurrection, in Pauline fashion, was properly given at the
Paschal Vigil only (except in the gravest emergency), because then they were
annually celebrated in one commemoration.

How completely and explicitly Hippolytus himself shared these ideas will be
clear from the elaborate comparison which he makes between the Jewish and
the Christian *Pascha*.†

Πάσχα μὲν ἑορτάζουσιν Ἰουδαῖοι, τῆς ἐξ Αἰγύπτου σωτηρίας ἀνάμνησιν, θανάτου
πρωτοτόκων ἀποφυγήν. Πάσχα διὰ τοῦτο ὀνομάζονται, ὅτι ἔστιν ὑπέρβασις θανά-
του· τοῦτο γὰρ ἡ λέξις δηλοῖ κατὰ γλῶτταν Ἑβραίων. Πάσχα δὲ ἡμεῖς ἑορτάζομεν
οὐ μερικὴν ἀποφυγὴν θανάτου, καθάπερ ἐκεῖνοι, οὐδὲ προσκαίρου δουλείας ἐλευθέ-
ρωσιν, ἀλλὰ τελείαν μὲν ἐκ θανάτου λύτρωσιν, τελείαν δὲ ἐκ τῆς τοῦ διαβόλου
δουλείας ἀπόλυσιν. Ὁ τῶν πρωτοτόκων θάνατος ἐκείνους ὑπερέβαινε τὸ τυπικὸν
πρόβατον θύσαντας, καὶ τῷ αἵματι τὰ περὶ τὰς θύρας χρίσαντας· ἡμᾶς δὲ ὁ ἐκ τοῦ
πρωτοπλάστου θάνατος ὑπερβαίνει, κατασχεῖν μὴ δυνάμενος τοὺς τὴν θυσίαν τοῦ
θείου προβάτου δεδεγμένους καὶ τῇ πίστει τοῦ σωτηρίου αἵματος περιπεφραγμένους.
Ἐκείνοις ἀπὸ γῆς τὸ πρόβατον· ἡμῖν δὲ ἐξ οὐρανοῦ, κατὰ τὸν Ἀβραὰμ τύπον
γενόμενον, ὅτε πρόβατον ἔσχε θεόπεμπτον ὑπὲρ τοῦ υἱοῦ προσαγαγεῖν· νῦν δὲ ὡς
ἀληθῶς θεόπεμπτον ἐξ οὐρανοῦ τὸ πρόβατον, προσαχθὲν ὑπὲρ ἡμῶν, ἵνα θανάτῳ
κατεχώμεθα, διὰ τὸν ἀκράτητον ὑπὸ θανάτου Χριστόν.... Ἁμαρτίαν γὰρ οὐκ ἀφῄρει
πρόβατον ἄλογον· διὰ τοῦτο οὐδὲ τὸν ἐκ τῆς ἁμαρτίας γενόμενον θάνατον· τὸ δὲ
λογικώτατον πρόβατον ἁμαρτίαν ἔλυσε, θάνατον σὺν αὐτῇ καταλύσας. Ἐξάγει δὲ
ἡμᾶς οὐκ ἐκ τῆς Αἰγυπτιακῆς εἰς τὴν Ἰουδαίαν, ἀλλ' εἰς αἰωνίαν κτῆσιν ἀπὸ κόσμου
φθειρομένου. Πρόβατόν ἐστιν ἅμα, καὶ ποιμὴν τῶν προβάτων καθηγούμενος.
Ἔμπροσθεν γάρ, φησί, πορεύσομαι ἐπὶ τὴν αἰωνίαν ἄγων αὐτὰ ζωήν. Ἀρχὴ μηνῶν
Ἰουδαίοις ἡ τοῦ προβάτου θυσία, καὶ ἡ ἔξοδος ἡ ἐξ Αἰγύπτου· ἡμῖν δὲ ἀρχὴ ζωῆς
τὸ τοῦ Κυρίου πάθος, καὶ ἡ σὺν Χριστῷ μετάστασις ἀπὸ κόσμου.

His Περὶ τοῦ Πάσχα contains much more elsewhere to the same effect. This one
passage may be added here to the foregoing to show how immediately the
thought of the *Pascha* as a feast suggests to Hippolytus the Eucharist.

Τοῦτο ἦν τὸ Πάσχα ὃ ἐπεθύμησεν ὑπὲρ ἡμῶν ὁ Ἰησοῦς παθεῖν. Πάθει πάθους
ἠλευθέρωσε καὶ θανάτῳ θάνατον ἐνίκησε καὶ διὰ τῆς βλεπομένης τροφῆς τὴν

* *J.T.S.* xxv. 268.
† Περὶ τοῦ Πάσχα, iv, ap. S. Chrysostom (*Spuria*), *Opp.* viii. 945.

ἀθάνατον ζωὴν αὐτοῦ ἐχορήγησεν. Αὔτη ἡ σωτήριος ἐπιθυμία τοῦ Ἰησοῦ· οὗτος ὁ ἔρως
ὁ πνευματικώτατος, δεῖξαι μὲν τοὺς τύπους ὡς τύπους, τὸ δὲ ἱερὸν σῶμα τοῖς μαθηταῖς
αὐτοῦ ἀντιδοῦναι. Λάβετε, φάγετε, τοῦτο ἔστι μου τὸ σῶμα· λάβετε, πίετε, τοῦτο
ἔστι μου τὸ αἷμα ἐν καινῇ διαθήκῃ τὸ ὑπὲρ πολλῶν ἐκχυνόμενον εἰς ἄφεσιν ἁμαρτιῶν.
Διὰ τοῦτο οὐκ ἐπιθυμεῖ τοσοῦτον φαγεῖν ὅσον ἐπιθυμεῖ παθεῖν, ἵνα ἡμᾶς τοῦ διὰ
βρώσεως πάθους ἐλευθερώσῃ.*

The significant resemblance of language between clauses in these passages and in the anaphora of Hippolytus only shows how steeped in Paschal ideas Hippolytus' Eucharistic theology really was. The Eucharist is the ἀνάμνησις of the Deliverance from the devil as the Jewish Passover Lamb was the ἀνάμνησις of the Deliverance from Egyptian oppression. Both are in intention sacrifices of the People of God, renewing the communion and the covenant-relation set up by God with His chosen People. Hence the command at the Last Supper to "make the *anamnesis* of Me" with "the bread and cup", is a command "to stand before Thee and minister as priests to Thee" (ἱερατεύειν), and this *sacrificial* character is explicitly brought out in the anaphora. These points need careful consideration in any study of Hippolytus' doctrine of the Eucharist and the Ministry.

iv. 11–12. *The Epiclesis*

The question whether this anaphora as it came from Hippolytus' own pen contained an epiclesis is a difficult one, and depends to some extent on considerations outside the scope of a textual discussion. The textual facts are these: The apparently authentic text in L.E. contains an epiclesis, but it has in this passage undergone some dislocation and without *some* emendation will not make sense or grammar. The interpolated and adapted text found in T. has no trace of an epiclesis, but its reproduction of Hippolytus is in other points an improvement on L.E., and does make sense and grammar where they do not. A. has fused Hippolytus' anaphora with a fourth-century rite in such a way that though A. has an elaborate epiclesis it is impossible to say with any certainty whether its MS. of Hippolytus contained an epiclesis or not. The texts compare thus:

L.	E.	T.
iv. 11. Offerimus tibi panem et calicem gratias tibi agentes	We offer to thee *this* bread and *this* cup giving thanks to thee	We offer to thee bread and the cup giving thanks to thee *who alone art God for ever and our Saviour*
quia nos dignos habuisti	because thou hast made us worthy	because (ἐφ' οἷς, transl.) thou hast made us worthy
adstare coram te et tibi ministrare	to stand before thee and minister as priests to thee.	to stand before thee and to serve thee as priests.
12. (a) et petimus	(a) We pray thee, O Lord, ⌐and we beseech thee¬	(a) om.
(b) ut mittas	(b) to send	(b) om.
(c) sp̄m̄ tuum sc̄m̄	(c) thy Holy Spirit	(c) om.
(d) in oblationem	(d) on this [al. the] oblation	(d) om.

* *ibid.* vi. 961 D.

L.	E.	T.
(e) sanctae ecclesiae	(e) of the Church	(e) om.
(f) in unum congregans	(f) that in joining together	(f) cf. inf.
(g) des	(g) thou mayest grant	(g) grant
(h) omnibus qui percipiunt	(h) to all those who partake of it	(h) that all who partake of
(i) sanctis	(i) that it be to them for holiness	(i) thy holy things
		(f) may be made one with Thee,
(j) in repletionem spē scī	(j) and for filling with the Holy Spirit	(j) that they may be filled with the Holy Spirit
(k) ad confirmationem fidei in veritate	(k) and for strengthening of faith in truth	(k) for the confirmation of the faith in truth
(l) ut te laudemus et glorificemus	(l) that Thee they may glorify and praise	(l) that they may "doxologise" Thee
(m) per puerum tuum.	(m) through thy Son.	(m) and thy Beloved Son J.C. by whom etc.

With these compare A., words underlined being parallel to Hippolytus as found in L.E.:

11. προσφέρομέν σοι, τῷ βασιλεῖ καὶ θεῷ, κατὰ τὴν αὐτοῦ διάταξιν τὸν ἄρτον τοῦτον καὶ τὸ ποτήριον τοῦτο, "εὐχαριστοῦντές σοι δι' αὐτοῦ" ἐφ' οἷς κατηξίωσας ἡμᾶς ἑστάναι ἐνώπιόν σου καὶ ἱερατεύειν σοι·

12 (a). καὶ ἀξιοῦμέν σε ὅπως εὐμενῶς ἐπιβλέψῃς ἐπὶ τὰ προκείμενα δῶρα ταῦτα ἐνώπιόν σου, σὺ ὁ ἀνενδεὴς θεός, καὶ εὐδοκήσῃς ἐπ' αὐτοῖς εἰς τιμὴν τοῦ Χριστοῦ σου,

(b) καὶ καταπέμψῃς

(c) τὸ ἅγιόν σου πνεῦμα

(d) ἐπὶ τὴν θυσίαν ταύτην "τὸν μάρτυρα τῶν παθημάτων τοῦ κυρίου Ἰησοῦ" ὅπως ἀποφήνῃ τὸν ἄρτον τοῦτον σῶμα τοῦ Χριστοῦ σου καὶ τὸ ποτήριον τοῦτο αἷμα τοῦ Χριστοῦ σου.

(e) om.

(f) om.

(g) (h) ἵνα οἱ μεταλαβόντες αὐτοῦ

(i) om.

(k) βεβαιωθῶσιν πρὸς εὐσέβειαν, ἀφέσεως ἁμαρτημάτων τύχωσι τοῦ διαβόλου καὶ τῆς πλάνης αὐτοῦ ῥυσθῶσιν,

(j) πνεύματος ἁγίου πληρωθῶσιν, ἄξιοι τοῦ Χριστοῦ σου γένωνται, ζωῆς αἰωνίου τύχωσιν, σου καταλλαγέντος αὐτοῖς δέσποτα παντοκράτορ.

(l) om.

(m) om.

11. Cf. Col. iii. 17.   12 (d). Cf. i Pet. v. 1.

It is convenient to consider A. first.

In *v.* 11, A. reproduces without exception every word of Hippolytus. In *v.* 12 its certain use of Hippolytus is minimal. After ἀξιοῦμέν σε ὅπως, which is not found in any Syrian source at this point, there is nothing down to (*k*) βεβαιωθῶσιν which offers any unmistakable point of contact with the L.E. text. In (*b*) A. has καταπέμψῃς where L.E. represent πέμψῃς, or possibly ἀποστείλῃς (as in Cyril Hierol. *Cat.* 23. 7). In (*c*) τὸ ἅγιόν σου πνεῦμα is an inevitable point of resemblance between any two epicleseis of the Spirit, and taken alone certainly does not suffice to prove that A. rests on a text of Hippolytus agreeing with L.E. In (*d*) ἐπὶ τὴν θυσίαν ταύτην in A. replaces ἐπὶ τὴν προσφορὰν τῆς ἁγίας σου ἐκκλησίας represented in L.E. θυσία appears to have been the word used at this point in the *Antiochene* epiclesis in the fourth century.* The remainder of (*d*) and much of what follows is clearly Syrian and not based on Hippolytus at all, if we compare it with contemporary Syrian rites: *e.g.* the rite of St James, much of the language of which is actually cited by St Cyril of Jerusalem, word for word, in his *Catecheses* (A.D. 348). (Coincidences with A. underlined.)

τὸ Πνεῦμά σου τὸ πανάγιον κατάπεμψον, δέσποτα, ἐφ᾽ ἡμᾶς καὶ ἐπὶ τὰ προκείμενα ἅγια δῶρα ταῦτα, ἵνα ἐπιφοιτήσαν τῇ ἁγίᾳ καὶ ἀγαθῇ καὶ ἐνδόξῳ αὐτοῦ παρουσίᾳ ἁγιάσῃ καὶ ποιῇ τὸν μὲν ἄρτον τοῦτον σῶμα ἅγιον Χριστοῦ καὶ τὸ ποτήριον τοῦτο αἷμα τίμιον Χριστοῦ ἵνα γένηται πᾶσι τοῖς ἐξ αὐτῶν μεταλαμβάνουσιν εἰς ἄφεσιν ἁμαρτιῶν καὶ εἰς ζωὴν αἰώνιον...εἰς στηριγμὸν τῆς ἁγίας σου...ἐκκλησίας...ῥυόμενος αὐτὴν ἀπὸ πάσης αἱρέσεως κτλ.

Compare A. in 12 (*b*), (*c*), (*d*), also, with the epiclesis as described in the Liturgical *Catecheses* of Theodore of Mopsuestia, an Antiochene (*ob.* A.D. 428). "The priest offers, according to the rules of priesthood, prayer and supplication to God that the Holy Spirit may come down and that grace may come therefrom upon the bread and the wine that are laid (on the altar) so that they may be seen to be truly the Body and the Blood of our Lord, which are the remembrance of immortality...and the priest prays that the grace of the Holy Spirit may come also on all those present in order that as they have been perfected in one body in the likeness of the second birth, so also they may be knit here as if into one body by the communion of the flesh of our Lord, and in order also that they may embrace and follow one purpose with concord, peace and diligence in good works. In this way all of us pray God with a pure mind not to receive the communion of the Holy Spirit for punishment, as if we were divided in our thoughts and bent on disunions."†

Comparing A.'s epiclesis with these Syrian documents it seems certain that A. in 12 (*b*)–(*i*) is based only on Syrian sources and not on Hippolytus at all. Even in (*h*) ἵνα οἱ μεταλαβόντες αὐτοῦ which at first sight offers a point of contact with Hippolytus is closer to "St James" not only in substituting ἵνα (cf. "St James") for L.E.'s διδῷς, but also in omitting ἁγίοις (cf. "St James"). If A.'s text of Hippolytus contained an epiclesis similar to that in L.E. we can no longer trace the fact because *every single word distinctive of* L.E.'s *phraseology is simply not there in* A. We can trace the use of Hippolytus by A. right up to the disputed clause, and in the phrases following it. But for the epiclesis itself A. offers no recognisable evidence. So far as it goes A.'s evidence suggests that it found *no* model for its epiclesis in its text of *Ap. Trad.*

We may next examine E. Apart from the variant in (*i*) "that it be to them

---

* S. Chrysostom, *De Coem. App.* iii (*Opp.* ii. 401 D): ὁ ἱερεὺς τὰς χεῖρας ἀνατείνων εἰς τὸν οὐρανὸν καλῶν τὸ Πνεῦμα τὸ ἅγιον τοῦ παραγενέσθαι καὶ ἅψασθαι τῶν προκειμένων ἵνα ἡ χάρις ἐπιπεσοῦσα τῇ θυσίᾳ τὰς ἁπάντων ἀνάψῃ ψυχάς....

† Theodore of Mopsuestia, *Liber ad Baptizandos*, ed. A. Mingana (*Woodbrooke Studies*, vi), p. 104. Cp. Chrysostom, *De Coem. App.* above.

for holiness" (presumably due to mistranslation), the noticeable point is its incoherence in (*f*) and (*g*), "that in joining together thou mayest grant". Joining what? No MS. of the *Sinodos* (the Ethiopic version of *Ap. Trad.*) offers any suggestion. The text of the Ethiopic "Liturgy of the Apostles", which is based on the *Sinodos*, has patched the passage thus: "We pray Thee, O Lord, and we beseech thee to send Thy Holy Spirit and power on this bread and this cup. Do Thou uniting *them* grant *them* unto all those who receive of *It* and may *It* be to them for holiness and for filling with the Holy Spirit"* where the confusion between "them" and "it" indicates a bungling attempt to restore the passage from an early MS. which contained exactly the same difficulty as the present Ethiopic text of *Ap. Trad.* Some of the other Ethiopic anaphoras also borrow this passage of *Ap. Trad.*, *e.g.* the so-called "Anaphora of St Epiphanius": "May He (*sc.* the Holy Spirit) make this Bread Thy holy Body and this Cup Thy life-giving Blood. Do thou, joining together, grant to those who receive of it that it be unto them etc."† It is clear that MSS. of the Ethiopic *Ap. Trad.* were always incoherent at this point.

The difficulties in E. are precisely those in L.—viz: What is to be "joined together" or "congregated in one" with what? and what is to be "granted" "to all Thy saints who partake"? What is *congregans* doing governing nothing at all, and what is the object of *des*?

It is precisely these questions which are answered by the text of T., which seems on these points greatly preferable on purely textual grounds to that of L.E. If we may reconstruct on the basis of T., we should get something like:

$$\text{ἀξιοῦμέν σε ὅπως (L.E.A.)‡}$$
$$\text{διδῶς (L.E.T.)}$$
$$\text{πᾶσιν τοῖς μεταλαμβάνουσιν ἁγίοις (L.E.T.)§}$$
$$\text{ἑνοῦσθαί [σοι] (T.)}$$
$$\text{εἰς πλήρωσιν πνεύματος ἁγίου κτλ. (L.E.T.).}$$

This last clause does not indicate necessarily that an epiclesis had preceded it. Hippolytus elsewhere explains what he thinks is the effect of Holy Communion.‖

Ἀσεβείας γὰρ ὑπεύθυνοι τῆς εἰς τὸν Κύριον οἱ μὴ παρέχοντες ἐπιτήδειον τὸ σῶμα πρὸς τὴν ἀνάκρισιν τοῦ σώματος αὐτοῦ ὅπερ ἡμῖν ἔδωκεν, ἵνα πρὸς αὐτὸ κιρνάμενοι, πρὸς τὸ Πνεῦμα τὸ ἅγιον ἀνακρινώμεθα· ἐπεὶ καὶ διὰ τοῦτο ὅλως εἰς σῶμα ἔδωκεν ἑαυτὸν ὁ τοῦ θεοῦ Λόγος, καὶ σὰρξ ἐγένετο κατὰ τὴν εὐαγγελικὴν φωνὴν ἵν᾿ ἐπειδὴ μετασχεῖν ὡς Λόγου μὴ οἷοί τε ἦμεν, ὡς σαρκὸς μετάσχωμεν αὐτοῦ, τῇ πνευματικῇ σαρκὶ τὴν ἡμετέραν οἰκειώσαντες καὶ τῷ Πνεύματι τὸ πνεῦμα κατὰ δύναμιν, ὡς ἂν ὁμοιώματα Χριστοῦ κατασταίημεν . . . καὶ διὰ τῆς ἀναμίξεως τῆς πρὸς τὸ Πνεῦμα, τοῦ Χριστοῦ σώματος γίνεται ⟨τὰ μέλη ὑμῶν⟩ καὶ περιέπειν ἐν ἁγιασμῷ, ταῦτα δὲ περιέποντας ὡς μέλη Χριστοῦ.

We have to remember in considering these remarkable statements that Hippolytus is inclined to attribute to the Logos operations which later theology attributed to the third Person of the Trinity. Thus his theory of the Incarnation

---

* Harden, *Anaphoras of the Ethiopic Liturgy*, 1928, p. 36 *sq.*

† Harden, *op. cit.* p. 102.

‡ T.'s omission of this seems to be intended to harmonise the beginning of the resumed text of *Ap. Trad.* with the beginnings of a number of interpolated clauses which T. has just inserted.

§ T. represents ἁγίων for ἁγίοις which is rather better Greek. But cf. Hippolytus, *De Benedictione Jacob* (ed. Diobouniotis and Beis. *T.U.* 38), p. 28, l. 2: . . . τὴν ἁγίαν σάρκα Χριστοῦ, ἐφ᾿ ἣν οἱ ἅγιοι ὡς ἐπὶ κλίνην ἁγίαν ἀναπαυόμενοι σώζονται.

‖ Περὶ τοῦ Πάσχα, iii. *Ap.* S. Chrysostom, *Opp.* (ed. Paris 1836), viii. p. 940 B.

is that the πνεῦμα ἅγιον which came upon our Lady (Lk. i. 35) was *the Logos Himself* acting as the agent of His own Incarnation, a theory which can claim very respectable supporters as late as the fourth century.*

We have still to consider the disconcerting omission of L.E.'s epiclesis in T. As an Eastern (very possibly Syrian) Liturgy of the late fourth or fifth century T. might well be expected to place some emphasis on it. T., moreover, displays a special interest in and emphasis on the Person and Mission of the Holy Ghost in reaction from Macedonian minimising. We have to note also that T. has been following Hippolytus word for word right up to this point, and in the clause which follows is the only version which has preserved a coherent text. It is remarkable that, as in A., the only clause not traceable should be the epiclesis.

To this must be added certain more general considerations. Hippolytus' anaphora reproduces with great fidelity the ancient type of Jewish prayer known as a "Benediction" or *Eucharistia*. In the Jewish conception God is blessed (εὐλογεῖν) or thanked (εὐχαριστεῖν) for or over a thing, and the blessing *of God* blesses the thing. Such a conception leaves no room for a petition for *the thing itself*. It is noticeable that the "Eucharists" over oil, and cheese and olives, and first-fruits in *Ap. Trad.* have nothing comparable to a petition for *blessing the oil* etc. They "thank" God for a mercy and add an appropriate petition for the offerers. In the same way the anaphora without the epiclesis thanks God for His cardinal mercies of Creation and Redemption and the establishing of a means of communion for His Church and adds petitions for the offerers.

I have tried to show elsewhere† that *outside Syria* the use of the Eucharistic epiclesis of the Spirit cannot anywhere be traced back further than c. A.D. 375. In Syria the earliest certain evidence goes back to c. A.D. 330, though there are some traces of the theology it embodies to be found in Syrian documents of the third century. But apart from this no trace of the theology that the Spirit plays some part in the consecration of the Eucharist can be found in the pre-Nicene Church *at all*. Nor do I think fresh evidence to the contrary has yet been brought forward, though I should not now phrase some of the statements made in those papers quite in the same way.

Taking the evidence as a whole, and fairly regarding both the *textual* weakness of the L.E. readings at this point and the excellence of T.'s text we have two alternatives. Either T., an Eastern rite c. A.D. 400, deliberately omitted an epiclesis which stood in a source which it evidently regarded with great respect, and which it reproduces otherwise practically word for word in its anaphora. Or else the excellent MS. of Hippolytus which T. used preserved the authentic text of Hippolytus, which contained no epiclesis. In this case L.E. have interpolated, and in this connection the probably Syrian derivation of the codices from which they were made deserves careful consideration. Syria, so far as the extant evidence carries us, was the home of the epiclesis of the Spirit, and before the middle of the fourth century it was there being treated as the essential of the rite by St Cyril of Jerusalem. Would a Syrian scribe be content with a model anaphora which did not contain one?

For my own part I believe the explanation which best suits *all* the facts is that of interpolation in L.E. I have accordingly bracketed the clause in the text of Hippolytus, though with some hesitation; and I am aware that the whole question needs further discussion than is possible in a textual note.

* Cf. *Theology*, xxviii (1934), 166, p. 189 *sq.*
† *Theology*, March and April, 1934. Cf. also July and November of that year.

vii. *Communion Prayers*

These are accounted spurious by Easton, who does not print them, and by
Jungklaus. They are also rejected, with some hesitation, by Connolly, who
remarks that they contain little which could not have been written in the age of
Hippolytus.

They are certainly spurious. They reproduce with great fidelity the normal
form of the Communion Devotions in all Monophysite Liturgies—a prayer
before and after the *Pater Noster*, followed by a prayer "of the bowing of
heads" (τῆς κεφαλοκλισίας), followed by the *Sancta Sanctis*, Communion, a
prayer of thanksgiving and a prayer of blessing—exactly as here. In the very
numerous Monophysite Liturgies as given by Renaudot the prayers vary
considerably in content, but the structure and general sequence are always the
same.

These prayers are found only in the Ethiopic version of *Ap. Trad.* and in the
Ethiopic "Liturgy of the Apostles". But it is noticeable that while the anaphora of *Ap. Trad.* is very greatly interpolated and expanded in the "Lit. of
the Apostles", these prayers stand in the Ethiopic *Ap. Trad.* word for word as
they are in the current texts of the "Liturgy", even down to the deacon's
proclamations. It is legitimate to suspect that there has been a double process
at work. While the anaphora of the "Liturgy" is undoubtedly based on the
MSS. of the Ethiopic *Ap. Trad.*, the MSS. of the Ethiopic *Ap. Trad.* in their
turn have at some point incorporated these prayers from the developed
"Liturgy of the Apostles".

viii. 2.

The difficulty of the text as it stands is that it contains two contradictory
directions: first, to ordain the presbyter with the same prayer as that used for
the consecration of a bishop, and secondly, to ordain him with an entirely
different prayer. The credit for clearing up this difficulty, which has perplexed
all editors of the *Ap. Trad.* from the author of the *Canons of Hippolytus* to
Prof. Easton, belongs to the late Prof. C. H. Turner, who in a brilliant paper
(*J.T.S.* xvi (1915), 542 *sq.*) has provided a solution convincing by its simplicity.
What may be called "the Preface" of the prayer is to be the same for bishop
and presbyter, but that part of the prayer which specifies the gifts sought for
the ordinand is entirely different for the two orders. The opening words of the
prayer in viii. 2, "O God and Father of our Lord Jesus Christ", are the cue for
the starting point of the common matter, the words which follow "upon this
Thy servant" are the cue for the starting point of the matter proper to the
presbyter. Ep. varies from A. considerably in the prayer for the ordination of
a presbyter, but it also varies from L.E. It seems that Ep., while abandoning A.
at this point, did not, as in the prayer for the consecration of a bishop, revert to
the text of Hippolytus as it stood in *Ap. Trad.* pure and simple, but made its
own adaptation, which is in some points further from the original than A.
Turner, from a most careful comparison of all the sources, restores the Greek
thus:

Ὁ θεὸς καὶ πατὴρ τοῦ κυρίου ἡμῶν Ἰησοῦ Χριστοῦ, ὁ πατὴρ τῶν
οἰκτιρμῶν καὶ θεὸς πάσης παρακλήσεως, ὁ ἐν ὑψηλοῖς κατοικῶν καὶ
τὰ ταπεινὰ ἐφορῶν, ὁ γινώσκων τὰ πάντα πρὶν γενέσεως αὐτῶν·
σύ, ὁ δοὺς ὅρους ἐκκλησίας διὰ Λόγου χάριτός σου, ὁ προορίσας ἀπ'
ἀρχῆς γένος δικαίων ἐξ Ἀβραάμ, ἄρχοντάς τε καὶ ἱερεῖς καταστήσας

τό τε ἁγίασμά σου μὴ καταλιπὼν ἀλειτούργητον, ὁ ἀπὸ καταβολῆς
κόσμου εὐδοκήσας ἐν οἷς ᾑρετίσω δοξασθῆναι· [αὐτὸς καὶ] νῦν ἐπίχεε
τὴν παρά σου δύναμιν τοῦ ἡγεμονικοῦ πνεύματος, ὅπερ ⌈ἔδωκας⌉ τῷ
ἠγαπημένῳ σου παιδὶ Ἰησοῦ Χριστῷ, ὅπερ ἐδωρήσατο τοῖς ἁγίοις
⌈σου⌉ ἀποστόλοις οἳ καθίδρυσαν τὴν ἐκκλησίαν κατὰ τόπον ἁγιάσματός σου εἰς δόξαν καὶ αἶνον ἀδιάλειπτον τοῦ ὀνόματός σου.

Bishop	Presbyter
δός, καρδιογνῶστα ⌈πάτερ⌉ ἐπὶ τὸν δοῦλόν σου τοῦτον ὃν ἐξελέξω εἰς ἐπισκοπήν, ποιμαίνειν τὴν ἁγίαν σου ποίμνην καὶ ἀρχιερατεύειν σοι ἀμέμπτως λειτουργοῦντα νυκτὸς καὶ ἡμέρας, ἀδιαλείπτως τε ἱλάσκεσθαι τὸ πρόσωπόν σου καὶ προσφέρειν σοὶ τὰ δῶρα τῆς ἁγίας σου ἐκκλησίας, καὶ τῷ πνεύματι ἀρχιερατικῷ ἔχειν ἐξουσίαν ἀφιέναι ἁμαρτίας κατὰ τὴν ἐντολήν σου, διδόναι κλήρους κατὰ τὸ πρόσταγμά σου, λύειν τε πάντα σύνδεσμον κατὰ τὴν ἐξουσίαν ἣν ἔδωκας τοῖς ἀποστόλοις, εὐαρεστεῖν τέ σοι ἐν πραΰτητι καὶ καθαρᾷ καρδίᾳ προσφέροντά σοι ὀσμὴν εὐωδίας	ἔπιδε ἐπὶ τὸν δοῦλόν σου τοῦτον καὶ ἔμπλησον αὐτὸν πνεῦμα χάριτος καὶ συμβουλίας ⌈τοῦ πρεσβυτερίου⌉ τοῦ ἀντιλαμβάνεσθαι καὶ κυβερνᾶν τὸν λαόν σου ἐν καθαρᾷ καρδίᾳ· ὃν τρόπον ἐπεῖδες ἐπὶ λαὸν ἐκλογῆς σου καὶ προσέταξας Μωυσεῖ αἱρήσασθαι πρεσβυτέρους, οὓς ἔπλησας πνεύματος ⌈ὅπερ ἐδωρήσω τῷ θεράποντί σου⌉, καὶ νῦν κύριε παράσχου, ἀνεκλιπὲς τηρῶν ἐν ἡμῖν τὸ πνεῦμα τῆς χάριτός σου ⌈καὶ ἀξίωσον ὅπως πιστεύοντές σοι ὑπηρετῶμεν ἐν ἁπλότητι καρδίας, αἰνοῦντές σε

διὰ τοῦ παιδός σου Ἰησοῦ Χριστοῦ, δι' οὗ σοι δόξα καὶ κράτος [καὶ
τιμή] πατρὶ καὶ υἱῷ σὺν ἁγίῳ πνεύματι ⌈ἐν τῇ ἁγίᾳ ἐκκλησίᾳ⌉ καὶ νῦν
καὶ εἰς τοὺς αἰῶνας τῶν αἰώνων. Ἀμήν.

A few small points remain doubtful, especially in the matter peculiar to the
presbyter, but this is likely to be almost verbally correct.

The insertion of καρδιογνῶστα πάτερ before the *bishop's* ordination but not
before that of the presbyter is meant to emphasise the special "Apostolic succession" of the bishop by particularly assimilating his ordination to that of
St Matthias (Acts i. 24). The different functions of the episcopate and the
presbyterate are in all respects noteworthy.

xvi. 1. *At the house*

I suggest that here T. alone has preserved an authentic phrase of the text.
We know from *Acta Justini* and other sources that the Roman διδάσκαλοι
did their teaching as private individuals, not as officials of the Church, on their
own premises, where both baptised and unbaptised resorted to their lectures.
The idea of a congregation assembling in a private house would be strange in
the later fourth century, and all the texts have adapted the original to later
conditions, T. by omitting the mention of the congregation, the others by
omitting the mention of "the house".

A. clearly reflects later practice in bringing would-be catechumens before the
officials of the Church at the outset of their instruction. Originally the hierarchy intervened only at the last stage of their preparation, when they became
competentes, actual candidates for baptism. This was a matter of six or seven
weeks at the most before the Paschal baptisms. Out of the daily instructions
and exorcisms given by the clergy to the *competentes*, as described by Hippolytus (xx. 3), and the fasts and prayers which piety prescribed during this
period for the catechumens, developed the general ecclesiastical institution of

"Lent", which has thus a different origin to "Holy Week", developed out of the universal preparatory fast of two days before the *Pascha*.

At Rome the *competentes* are frequently described as *electi* (cf. **xx.** 1) and the *aperitio aurium*, on the third Wednesday before Easter, at which the *electi* for the first time officially "heard the Gospel" (**xx.** 2), long marked the day at which the hierarchy took over the final preparation of the neophytes (**xx.** 3). Conformably with this the fifth-century Roman Lent only lasted three weeks (Socrates, *É.H.* v. 22). Elsewhere the official instruction lasted six or seven weeks; hence the longer Lent, which Rome eventually took over from other Churches. But for the whole of the preceding three years the catechumens in Hippolytus' time were left to the unofficial διδάσκαλοι.

xxiv. *The Stational Mass*

This chapter is rejected as an interpolation by Easton, chiefly on the ground that it is found only in E. He has not observed the clear traces of it found in T.K. also. It is thus vouched for as an integral part of the text by three separate and independent lines of textual tradition. Its omission by the late Ar.S. recension is of little weight against this, and is probably due to its describing primitive usages long obsolete in eighth- or ninth-century Egypt, where the Ar.S. recension arose.

Hippolytus naturally begins his description of the normal practice of the Christian life after Baptism by a description of the Sunday Eucharist, always the central Christian observance. This chapter is exceedingly important as the earliest witness to certain peculiarly Roman customs (which could only have got into an Ethiopic text from an early Roman source, for which we need not look elsewhere than the *Ap. Trad.*—another indication of the chapter's authenticity). It is therefore regrettable that we are so dependent on the Ethiopic for our knowledge of it.

A single liturgy celebrated by the bishop surrounded by his whole clergy for the whole body of the faithful was the primitive practice. At Rome alone this remained the liturgical ideal, and to some extent the liturgical practice, for many centuries after it had disappeared elsewhere. The solemn "Stational" liturgy celebrated by the Pope at which the whole clergy of the City were present, together with the whole Christian people (or at least their representatives), remained the central liturgical tradition of the City until the Babylonian Captivity, even until the Renaissance, and did not wholly die until the seizure of Rome in 1870.

Section 2 of this chapter appears to have reference to a practice ascribed by the *Liber Pontificalis* (not necessarily rightly) to the institution of Pope Zephyrinus, by which at the Papal liturgy the concelebrating presbyters actually consecrated, not on the altar with the Pope, but on glass patens held before them by the deacons. This was probably a device rendered necessary by the small size of the primitive Christian altar, two or three feet square only. As late as the compilation of the *Ordo Romanus Primus* (eighth century) this usage still persisted on great feasts, though by then corporals had been substituted for the glass patens.

It is to be noted also that in the *Ordo Romanus Primus* these concelebrating presbyters still break the oblations they have themselves co-consecrated and deliver them to the people. But it is *the deacons* who still break the oblations consecrated by the Pope, precisely as in xxiv. 1 and 2.

Section 3 is found only in E., but is not therefore unauthentic, T. and K. giving only extracts from this chapter. Easton notes that it is a sign of a later date,* but in fact the liturgy was celebrated on days other than Sunday very early, on Martyrs' anniversaries (according to the *Martyrium Polycarpi* (c. A.D. 157), though I doubt if this was the Roman practice before the third century) and at funerals, and on the Wednesday and Friday fast days according to Tertullian. There is therefore no need to see in this the mark of an interpolation.

The tenacity with which very primitive liturgical features kept their place in the strictly Papal liturgy is well known. I doubt if any are found more remarkable than those observable in this chapter.

xxvi. 14 *sq.*

Easton regards the whole of xxvi. 14–32 as an interpolation, chiefly on the ground that it is only contained in full in the Ethiopic. But again portions of the text are recognisable in T. and K. and possibly in A. (in one sentence, but of this I am doubtful). Further, Ar.S., whose omission is emphasised by Easton as telling against the authenticity of the passage, do not agree as to the extent of the omission. Ar. having omitted 13 as well as 14 *sq.* and S. having retained it. It is clear that Ar.S. represent a shortened text and E. represents the full text of the archetype from which all three are descended. We have thus again a concurrence of three, if not four, independent lines of textual tradition in favour of the passage.

But against it stand three important considerations. (1) It has no place in L., which goes straight from xxvi. 13 to xxvii. 1. Its Greek original, therefore, presumably did not contain it—at all events in this place. (2) The L. text reads very reasonably, going straight from the private Agape-supper given by one of the faithful to the "Lord's Supper" given to widows by one of the faithful; though it is doubtful whether the description of the public Agape in 14 *sq.* is really out of place. (3) In *v.* 30 *sq.* the directions are the reverse of those given in xxvi. 2 and 3, whose authenticity there is no reason to doubt. (*a*) The cup precedes the distribution of the bread. (*b*) The bishop "offers the cup", whereas at *v.* 3 it is specifically ordered that each person is to bless the cup for himself. (This was the Jewish custom; cf. *Berakoth*, M. 6, and T. iv. 8.)

The blessing of the lamp is also a custom derived from Jewish religious meals. But it is a curious fact that while clear survivals of the practice are known from the Gallican and Eastern churches, in the later Roman church there is no trace at all of the custom. The Holy Saturday blessing of the fire and candle, which offer the closest approach to it, have in fact a wholly different origin, being derived from fourth-century Christian ceremonies connected with the Holy Sepulchre at Jerusalem. These elements only began to find their way into the liturgy of the City in the eleventh century from Gallican sources. There is not, I think, any single piece of evidence to suggest that the Roman Church ever acknowledged the Agape as an official Church observance; though these religious repasts, given by a private host but graced by the presence of the

---

* Easton, p. 58. He has also been led by the blunder of E. in mistranslating "vessel" as "robe" to the flat statement that the deacon's "holding out his robe" whenever he approaches the presbyter is intended as "a gesture of respect" (*ibid.*), and that this also is a sign of a later date (p. 31). This very odd statement is not the only piece of flagrant guessing in his book, and a serious protest is justified against this way of studying Christian antiquity. There is not the slightest evidence anywhere that deacons ever "held out their robe" as a gesture of respect to presbyters; it would be a very curious manner of showing respect if they had.

bishop or some of the clergy, doubtless sometimes came near such a conception. This might account for the absence of all historical trace of the blessing of lamps in the Roman vesper services.

xxxi *and* xxxii

The position of these two chapters is difficult. xxxi is simply a doublet slightly condensing xxxv. 1–3; but it stands in this position in L.Ar.E.S., though A. apparently only had (or has only reproduced) xxxv. i. Dom Wilmart has pointed out the solution from the evidence of L.

The *Ap. Trad.* was apparently in circulation with two different endings, one consisting of xxxi and xxxii followed by xxxvii and xxxviii, the other omitting xxxi and xxxii and containing only xxx followed by xxxiii–xxxviii. L. has reproduced both endings, the one in the Lᵃ. text, and the other in Lᵇ. But Ar.E.S. have made a clumsy attempt at combination by inserting xxxi and xxxii in a text resembling Lᵇ. rather more than Lᵃ., though in fact in xxxvii they represent a third recension.

xxxi is therefore a duplicate of xxxv, and the question arises which of the two endings is original. Here there can be little doubt. xxxiii and xxxiv follow straight on without a break from xxx, whereas xxxii is very awkwardly placed as an instruction to the laity on daily communion from the reserved sacrament coming between two regulations about deacons' duties. xxxiv, also, concerning the cemetery, which was in the charge of the archdeacon, is purely Roman, with its *loculus*-graves closed by tiles. Schwartz, Jungklaus and Easton accordingly reckon xxxii spurious without more ado.

I venture to demur to this excision. (1) xxxii is clearly out of place where it stands in L.Ar.E.S. But it is worth noting that T. cites it after xxxvi (T. ii. 25) where it is exactly *in* place, communion after prayers at dawn. It is also worth noting that besides L.Ar.E.S.T.K., all of which bear traces of the existence of this chapter, St Jerome, *Ep.* 71 (cf. p. xlv), appears to refer to this very passage as being by Hippolytus. (2) The contents of the chapter appear to be as truly and peculiarly Roman as those of xxxiv. There has been some misunderstanding of their meaning. Connolly (p. 79) rightly points out that 1 and 2 must refer to the practice witnessed to by Tertullian, *Ad Uxorem*, ii. 5, of reserving the consecrated species of Bread in the homes of the faithful to ensure their daily Communion on days when there was no public liturgy or they could not reach it. Only so can the precautions against mice, etc. be reasonably interpreted. But Connolly unfortunately goes on to interpret 3 and 4 of the reception of the chalice by the laity at the public Mass, on the ground that reservation of the chalice is unknown in antiquity. The difficulty of this interpretation lies in the language of the passage itself—*calicem benedicens accepisti* (presumably = ποτήριον εὐλογῶν ἔλαβες)—can *only* mean that the person who receives the chalice is also the person who blesses it, which is quite inapplicable to the public Mass. Easton notes this difficulty, but his own suggestions are equally difficult: (i) that this represents a survival of "earlier corporately celebrated eucharists" (a gratuitous invention of his own), or (ii) that the persons addressed in *vv.* 3 and 4 are the clergy (this is impossible if one considers *v.* 3), or (iii) that there is textual corruption.

The matter seems really quite simple. Hippolytus has in mind a single person throughout, in one set of circumstances—the lay communicant at home with his *capsa* containing the consecrated Bread. He himself "blesses" a "cup" with an invocation of "God" and receives it. This is the normal Roman method of Communion from the Reserved Sacrament in early times. It survives to this day in the Roman rite on Good Friday, when in the liturgy of the pre-Sanctified the celebrant takes a consecrated Host and an unconsecrated chalice, says the Lord's Prayer over them, and after intinction consumes both Host and chalice in silence. But it must be emphasised that this is originally a purely *local* Roman custom, unknown in other churches.

It is universally admitted that, whether by Hippolytus or not, this passage is of third-century date. Since it describes a Roman custom, was originally written in Greek, comes from the third century, is found in every extant text of a work written by Hippolytus and seems further to be attested as his by St Jerome, it is reasonable to suppose that this chapter is authentically Hippolytean. The fanciful interpretation of Mark xvi. 18 in *v.* 1 and various points in the language (σπουδάζειν, ἀλλότριον πνεῦμα, etc.) are quite in the manner of Hippolytus.

But allowing its genuineness it seems clearly out of place where it is. Possibly T. is right and it should follow xxxvi. To account for its present position is not very difficult. xxxiii and xxxiv would have little relevance in country churches in Syria and might well be omitted (as T. has omitted all xxxiii and part of xxxiv). The text would then run xxx, xxxv, xxxvi, followed by the present xxxii, xxxvii, xxxviii. The trouble appears to have originated with a clumsy reinsertion of xxxiii, xxxiv. That xxxii originally followed xxxv and xxxvi appears to be indicated by the fact that it is still preceded by a truncated version of xxxv, the remainder of the duplicated matter in xxxv and xxxvi having been omitted. But if xxxii had not originally stood *later than* xxxv, it would hardly have occurred to anyone to insert part of xxxv *before* xxxii as an unnecessary chapter xxxi.

xxxvi. 14. *Daily*

I suspect that what has troubled the versions is the use by Hippolytus of the idiomatic τὸ καθ' ἡμέραν for the more normal καθ' ἡμέραν. (This might account for L.'s *diem in hac* (*l.?* *hoc*, Hauler marks the *a* as doubtful in the palimpsest). The pleonastic article in this phrase is common in some classical writers and I have remarked its use once elsewhere in Hippolytus, *In Dan.* iv. 16, where he says that our Lord concealed the time of His second coming from the Apostles that they might "daily await the heavenly bridegroom":

ποία ἡ ἡμέρα τῆς τοῦ κυρίου ἐπιφανείας; ἐπεζήτησαν ταῦτα μαθεῖν παρὰ τοῦ κυρίου ὁμοίως καὶ οἱ μαθηταί, ἀλλ' ἀπέκρυψεν ἀπ' αὐτῶν τὴν ἡμέραν, ἵνα ἐγρηγόρους αὐτούς τε καὶ πάντας πρὸς τὰ μέλλοντα καταστήσῃ, ἀεὶ μεριμνῶντας καὶ προσδοκῶντας τὸ καθ' ἡμέραν τὸν ἐπουράνιον νυμφίον....

The word ἐπιφάνεια here suggests that it may have been the missing word in *Ap. Trad.* xxxvi. 14, more particularly as it is a favourite with Hippolytus to describe the Second Coming, cf. *e.g. In Dan.* iv. 60: ...εἰς τὴν ἐπιφάνειαν τοῦ ἠγαπημένου παιδὸς αὐτοῦ, etc. It would certainly be appropriate in this *v.* of *Ap. Trad.*, but the occurrence of the equally good παρουσίαν in A. at this point leads me to suggest it as original, despite the somewhat unreliable nature of A.

xxxvii. 3

With the curious statement that Moses *anointed* the doorposts with the Passover blood in Lᵃ., cf. Περὶ τοῦ Πάσχα, i (*ap.* Chrysost. Opp. Paris, 1836, viii. 934 D): διέταττεν τὴν τοῦ πάσχα θυσίαν καὶ τὴν τοῦ αἵματος χρῖσιν ἐπὶ τῶν θυρῶν· καὶ τῇ μὲν τούτου χρίσει σωτηρίαν τῶν πρωτοτόκων ἐπηγγέλλετο. The question is taken up again *ibid.* ii (937 A), where it is explained that the χρῖσις of the "two doorposts (σταθμῶν) and lintel" is the type of the unction of Confirmation, the "doorposts" being the passions, and the "lintel" the reason. The grace of the Holy Spirit is only won for us by the shedding of the blood of the "Perfect Sheep" (τέλειον πρόβατον) as in *Ap. Trad.* **xxxvii.** 3, and a point is made of the fact that the Paschal Lamb was not a lamb (ἀμνός) but a full-grown sheep (πρόβατον). (*Cf.* also the passage on *p.* 74.)

The point to be observed is that the lxx text of Exod. xii. 7 reads καὶ λήψονται ἀπὸ τοῦ αἵματος, καὶ θήσουσιν ἐπὶ τῶν δύο σταθμῶν κτλ. with no suggestion of an "anointing". This appears to be a favourite but private perversion of the text of Hippolytus' own devising. It suggests that Lᵃ. is here original and Lᵇ. has corrected to the biblical text.

I should add that Origen *Selecta in Exodum* on Exod. xii. 7 has the interpretation of θήσουσι as a χρῖσις, but on Exod. xii. 22, *ibid.*, he distinctly states that he is quoting ὡς ἀποδέδωκέ τις πρὸ ἡμῶν and, from the passage he goes on to quote, it is clear that he is citing the περὶ τοῦ πάσχα, ii, of Hippolytus. From Origen various fathers, notably St Gregory Nazianzen, carry on the analogy of the Passover blood with the unction of Confirmation. But Hippolytus appears to have been its real inventor.

ADDITIONAL NOTE ON iii. 3

"Thy holy Apostles who established the Church which hallows Thee."

E. (with minor variants among the MSS.) reads for this: "Thy holy Apostles of the Church ⟨? working⟩ *with the plough of Thy Cross* and in the place of Thy holiness." ['working' is not represented in any MS, but suggested by Horner.] I had omitted to note all E.'s variants here as being corruptions with no bearing on the Greek text of Hippolytus. But after this book was in print I observed that Dom Connolly (p. 24) has suggested that the phrase italicised above represents an authentic fragment of Hippolytus' text preserved by E. alone. His chief argument is that the plough is found several times in the earlier Christian literature as a symbol of the Cross. Without denying this, I doubt the authenticity of the phrase here. (1) The ungrammatical state of E.'s text in all MSS. in itself points to interpolation. (2) No trace of the phrase occurs in any one of the other texts, which are here exceptionally abundant and faithful. (3) I have several times come across the phrase "Thy Apostles who (ploughed, or some similar word), with the plough of Thy Cross" in other Ethiopic prayers, where it has something of the nature of a set liturgical 'tag'. The following example from the Intercession of the Ethiopic 'Anaphora of St John the Evangelist', which happens to be in print, will illustrate this, I hope, sufficiently: "Thy Flesh and Thy Blood we offer to Thee... for all Thy Apostles who ploughed the land of the nations with the ploughshare of Thy Cross" (*ap.* Harden, *Anaphoras of the Eth. Liturgy*, 1928, p. 78). Despite its primitive sound the textual evidence strongly suggests that this phrase is just one of those little late interpolations with which the various MSS. of E. abound, and which I have generally not recorded to avoid further complication of the apparatus.

GENERAL INDEX

[*passim* implies frequent mention in the *apparatus criticus*]

SCRIPTURAL REFERENCES IN *AP. TRAD.*